Although it is often said that social workers are not counsellors, as this wonderful book shows social work uses counselling skills all the time. The book is an absolute goldmine of theoretical and practical insights into how to work with service users in skillful and humane ways that can reduce suffering and help them to change. It is essential reading for all social work students and experienced practitioners who wish to keep up with new knowledge and approaches to good practice.

– **Harry Ferguson**, Professor of Social Work, University of Birmingham, UK

Counselling skills are rarely given the proper attention in social work education and practice. This much needed text addresses this gap by covering the three key social work counselling skills. Bridging day to day communication skills with counselling skills through case examples and reflective exercises, the reader is able to assess their level of skill and practice building effective therapeutic relationships with service users in their social work practice.

– **Barbra Teater**, PhD, Professor of Social Work, College of Staten Island, City University of New York, USA

Here is an extensive, detailed, in-depth exploration of core counselling skills for social workers that also considers complexities set in wide ranging social and professional contexts, discussed in a thoughtful, thought provoking way and accompanied by illustrative examples and exercises. There are also useful chapters on the application of social work counselling skills to solution focused, motivational interviewing and group work approaches.

– **Stewart Collins**, Honorary Research Fellow at the University of Wales, Bangor, UK, Associate Lecturer for the Open University

Counselling Skills for Social Workers

Counselling skills are very powerful. Really listening and providing compassionate empathy without judging is a core part of social work practice with service users.

This book provides a theoretically informed understanding of the core skills required to provide counselling interventions that work. It provides detailed discussion of three core skills which are identified as: talking and responding, listening and observing and thinking. Over 11 chapters these core skills are described in terms of what they mean, how they can be learned and developed, how they can be used and misused and, most importantly, how specific skills can be employed in a coherent and evidence-informed counselling approach. Loughran also looks in detail at the skills required to deliver interventions consistent with three approaches: Motivational Interviewing, Solution-Focused Work and Group work.

Illustrative case examples and exercises offer further opportunities for reflection and exploration of self-awareness as well as for practising and enhancing skills development, thus making the book required reading for all social work students, professionals looking to develop their counselling skills and those working in the helping professions more generally.

Hilda Loughran is an Associate Professor in Social Work/Social Policy at University College Dublin. Before becoming a full-time academic she worked as a social worker in housing, a social work addiction counsellor and a relationship counsellor. During her career she has maintained her counselling social work practice through voluntary work, mostly working with service users in the substance use field. She teaches Motivational Interviewing, Solution-Focused Work and Group work to Masters in Social Work students and is involved in participatory research with service users enhancing social work education.

Student Social Work

www.routledge.com/Student-Social-Work/book-series/SSW

This exciting new textbook series is ideal for all students studying to be qualified social workers, whether at undergraduate or masters level. Covering key elements of the social work curriculum, the books are accessible, interactive and thought-provoking.

New titles

Becoming a Social Worker, 2nd ed.
Global Narratives
Viviene E. Cree

Social Work and Social Policy, 2nd ed.
An introduction
Jonathan Dickens

Mental Health Social Work in Context 2nd ed.
Nick Gould

Social Work in a Changing Scotland
Edited by Viviene E. Cree and Mark Smith

Social Theory for Social Work
Ideas and Applications
Christopher Thorpe

Human Growth and Development
An Introduction for Social Workers
2nd Edition
John Sudbery and Andrew Whittaker

Counselling Skills for Social Workers
Hilda Loughran

Counselling Skills for Social Workers

Hilda Loughran

LONDON AND NEW YORK

First published 2019
by Routledge
2 Park Square, Milton Park, Abingdon, Oxon OX14 4RN

and by Routledge
52 Vanderbilt Avenue, New York, NY 10017

Routledge is an imprint of the Taylor & Francis Group, an informa business

British Library Cataloguing-in-Publication Data
A catalogue record for this book is available from the British Library

Library of Congress Cataloging-in-Publication Data
Names: Loughran, Hilda, author.
Title: Couselling skills for social workers / Hilda Loughran.
Description: Abingdon, Oxon ; New York, NY : Routledge, 2019. |
Series: Student social work | Includes bibliographical references and index.
Identifiers: LCCN 2018036709 | ISBN 9781138504158 (hardback) |
ISBN 9781138504202 (pbk.) | ISBN 9781315145853 (ebook)
Subjects: LCSH: Social service–Practice. | Counseling. |
Counselor and client. | Social workers.
Classification: LCC HV10.5 .L67 2019 | DDC 361/.06–dc23
LC record available at https://lccn.loc.gov/2018036709

ISBN: 978-1-138-50415-8 (hbk)
ISBN: 978-1-138-50420-2 (pbk)
ISBN: 978-1-315-14585-3 (ebk)

Typeset in Helvetica
by Out of House Publishing

Printed and bound in Great Britain by
TJ International Ltd, Padstow, Cornwall

To the colleagues, students and service users who over my career have laughed and listened and learnt with me.

Contents

Figures

Tables

Exercises

Acknowledgements

A special word of thanks to my family and friends who are always there for me and in particular my sister Gwen who was so supportive through this process.

I want to mention some of the amazing people who have taught me so much about teaching and practising counselling skills: Jill Stevens, Anhtony Donoghue, Sheila Lyons, Paula Rock, Trish Walsh, Melinda Hohman, Bill Miller, Terry Moyers, Steve de Shazer, Imelda McCarthy, Chris Iverson, Maryellen McCann, Bernie Price Gabriel Kiely, Valerie Richardson, Maryellen Lee, Pearse Barnett.

Thanks to Georgia and all the staff at Routledge for encouraging and supporting me.

When something is worth doing it's worth doing together!

PART I

Counselling skills for social work

1 Social work

Conversations, counselling and therapeutic interventions

- Present a discussion of issues in adopting a professional approach to counselling including boundaries around befriending, helping and caring for those with whom we work.
- Consider the place of theory, methods and research in the development and application of counselling skills.
- Exploration of what these three terms mean.
- Consideration of these as a continuum of communication-based contexts which share some similarities but which demand different levels of communication skills, theoretical understanding and ethical base.

Introduction

Social work has its roots in holistic vision of helping people across three domains; one-to-one casework, group work and community work. It's probably fair to say that these three aspects of social work have not retained equal parity in terms of the identity and activities of social workers. There is, it seems, a tension between the social work mission to engage in advocacy and promoting social justice on the one hand and an increasing emphasis on responsibilities of social workers in terms of assessing and responding to cases of child protection. Perhaps part of the difficulty is the long-standing problem of finding an evidence base to prove the value of preventative and early intervention measures. The challenge of finding evidence to support activities such as group work will be discussed in a later chapter. Over time, interventions focusing on one-to-one type interventions seem to have established a stronger base in evidence. Counselling, psychotherapy and psychology have contributed to a strong evidence base that working with people and building on the therapeutic relationship is helpful (Bland et al. 2006, Cooper 2011, Miller & Rollnick 2013). Ironically, the place of social work and what was originally historically called casework has not been strongly associated with this growing body of evidence, but has resulted in a debate in social work as to the place of evidence-informed practice and the identification of an urgent need for social work to develop its own evidence base. This text will look at the correlation between the activities of social work and the established evidence of the importance of the counselling/therapeutic relationship with service users. Reflecting this emphasis on one-to-one interventions, each chapter will focus on the connections between what have been identified as counselling skills and the skills employed in social work.

The fundamental social commitment of social work is clearly defined in the global definition of social work approved by the IFSW General Meeting and the IASSW General Assembly in July 2014:

> *Social work is a practice-based profession and an academic discipline that promotes social change and development, social cohesion, and the empowerment and liberation of people. Principles of social justice, human rights, collective responsibility and respect for diversities are central to social work. Underpinned by theories of social work, social sciences, humanities and indigenous knowledge, social work engages people and structures to address life challenges and enhance wellbeing.*
>
> (http://ifsw.org/get-involved/global-definition-of-social-work/employed by social workers)

Mission and practice

Unfortunately, social work appears to be struggling with the continued tension between its value base and ethical position promoting social justice, advocacy and equality and the social control connotations that are now so strongly associated with social work in child protection. Keen et al. (2009, p. 144) emphasise 'the recognition and management of risk is a fundamental part of being a social worker whatever specialism you choose. For child protection social workers it has to be at the forefront of your decision-making processes. The recognition of risk is often drawn out to the assessment process and the enquiring nature of the social worker. Making decisions regarding child protection issues is not the responsibility of anyone social worker, newly qualified or not. Child protection is a joint responsibility both within your organisation and on a multi-professional basis.' It has been all too easy to both associate sole responsibility for decision-making and child protection issues with social workers and also to mistakenly assume that child protection is the only activity engaged in by social workers. In essence, Keen et al. (2009, p. 144) remind us that the process of assessment has been developed to respond to needs early and thereby to work proactively to prevent crisis happenings. In a climate of limited resources, the ecological and more holistic aspirations of the Common Assessment Framework (Children's Workforce Development Council 2009) may be undermined by a lack of recognition of the counselling skills required to conduct such assessments effectively.

This identification of social work with the task of assessment in relationship to child protection may in part be responsible for undermining the counselling aspect of social work intervention and practice. And yet conducting assessments in this context requires a very skilled and high level of competence in terms of interpersonal communications, which this text will argue are fundamentally counselling skills.

While developing criteria to regulate the use of the term counsellor/therapist are to be welcomed, it is unfortunate that these steps appear to be at the expense of recognising the employment of counselling skills as part of competent professional practice in other disciplines. In this text the essential interpersonal communication which social workers employ to conduct competent social work practice will be referred to as counselling skills. In addition, it will be argued that the purpose of social work practice is to be helpful, healing and rehabilitative. All these factors are compatible with the goals and purposes of therapeutic interventions. However, these findings do support the view that once the relationship is prioritised then social work interventions are indeed therapeutic interventions.

It is worth asking if the distinction between professional conversations, interviewing assessment, counselling and therapy are helpful in relation to social work practice or do they in fact simply reflect **context rather than content, process or purpose**. Communication will be considered along a continuum recognising that communication is an important component of social life in general ... particularly important in such professions as social work and social care (Thompson 2011, p. 1). There is a risk that because we might take communication for granted that we may not take time to consider what it actually involves (Thompson 2011, p. 11). Therefore, while it is important that social workers have 'good listening skills' and are interested in 'helping people' these and many more elements of communication must be developed from a social conversational level to a more advanced level of professional competence. This advanced level will be referred to as counselling skills, but will include the concept of therapeutic intervention skills.

Thompson (2011, p. 9) points out that because 'they often have to deal with conflict and sensitive issues while building a positive relationship, social workers require high levels of communication skills ... this involves building up a more sophisticated understanding of the intricacies of how people interact. [He clarifies that] we must take account of the social context and the importance of meaning in communication' (2011, p. 16). Having shared meaning or shared assumptions would no doubt make communication easier. It is, however, very difficult to assess if such shared assumptions exist in communication between social workers and service users. Perceptions of each party on issues such as the purpose of the interaction, roles, responsibilities, authority and power may differ significantly, adding to the complexity of building a collaborative relationship.

Communication: a culturally informed activity

Communication also has a cultural dimension. This can be seen, for example, in the use of language to communicate. Not only may there be a difference in the language requiring a translator, but indeed even when speaking the 'same' language meaning may be attributed differently to both verbal and non-verbal communication.

Good examples of this might be the traditional importance given to greeting by shaking hands and making direct eye contact. Different cultures interpret these activates very differently; instead of being a sign of engagement, they may be considered as disrespectful or challenging. Being culturally aware is an essential component in positive communication. Other factors relating to social context include the issue of power differentials between those communicating. Thompson (2011, pp. 31–34) reminds us that social status, self-esteem and discrimination can also impact on communication.

Taking these factors into account, it is evident that social workers need to have a very high level of communication skill. They are often attempting to build relationships and engage service users in situations that are emotionally charged and open to misunderstandings, involving the attribution of different meanings and assumptions and also where there may be perceived and real discrepancies in power, status and autonomy. Add to this the fact that sometimes there is an immediacy about decision-making and that a social worker may be under time constraints due to resource limitations, the need for sophisticated counselling skills and ongoing support and supervision to provide reflective space for social workers is clearly a prerequisite for practice.

Collaboration with service users though relationship building

Social workers employ counselling skills for therapeutic purposes and all activities should have a therapeutic purpose. The importance of the relationship built between social worker and service user is central to successfully working together to achieve positive (therapeutic) outcomes (Bland et al. 2006). Lambert and Barley (2002) reported that this therapeutic relationship consistently correlates more highly with client outcome than specialised therapy techniques and that the connections between the therapeutic relationship and client outcome are strongest when measured by client ratings. Norcross (2010) and Wampold (2010) support this view. It is useful therefore to consider what it is that service users say about social workers. This research (Lambert & Byerley 2002, p. 26) explains that what clients identify as helpful is 'more understanding and accepting, empathic, warm and supportive and engaging in fewer negative behaviours such as blaming, ignoring and rejecting'. These findings help to clarify the challenge for social workers. They are attempting to build a relationship with service users, often nonvoluntary service users to convey the characteristics of support, warmth, understanding and empathy while essentially working towards a change that the service user may strongly oppose. Instead of undermining and marginalising the counselling skills required in social work, it is critical to become more conscious and fluent in the use of these skills.

We should consider the implications of the evidence which supports the importance of building a therapeutic relationship and of spending time working towards collaboration with service users and then look at the increasing pressure of caseloads and waiting lists to deal with urgent cases with the potential difficulty of trying to do too much in too short a time. The essence of social work has always been the importance of this collaborative partnership with service users, yet we must question whether social work has developed to a point where policies and structures are actually actively undermining the very basis of social work by requiring that social workers attempt to do their work in a context where there is little time to build the basic foundation for that work. Service users have noted the study and palliative social work the importance of continuity and building a relationship over time (Beresford et al. have noted in a study of palliative social work 2008). In contexts where neither continuity nor sufficient time are prioritised in working with service users, it is not surprising that social workers are viewed negatively by the service users. For the most part, practice which does not allow time to build a relationship, to develop understanding to express empathy and to demonstrate caring for service users is not consistent with the very basis of the value system of social work, nor is it in line with the evidence of what is likely to make a difference (Cooper 2011). Social work is therefore at serious risk of being undermined by pressures which do not acknowledge the important elements of the value base and skills required to do the job properly. This is further complicated by experienced social workers taking for granted the very skills that are core to their work and therefore not being in a strong position to advocate for the importance of having time to develop and engage those skills. In the light of this, it is perhaps not surprising that some service users have begun to develop a negative attitude to social work. Managing high caseloads with insufficient time is a very short-sighted approach, as ultimately building a negative cultural perspective of social work only serves to make the job more difficult and to create an environment in which service users talk about dreading interaction with social workers rather than appreciating the opportunity to work with somebody towards resolving their difficulties.

Social work counselling skills invisibility issues: just friends

One of the many challenges for social work is what will be referred to as the invisibility of their skills. It is difficult to assess social work counselling skills when research suggests that service users view that successful professional relationship with social workers is like a friendship. In their research on service users' perspective, Beresford et al. (2008) stated that service users, who reported on positive experiences, said things like not seeing them as a social worker or thinking of social worker as a friend. This makes it easy to assume that social workers are therefore only using social conversational skills and not employing more complex counselling skills. When a social worker employs a high level of professional skill they can create a trusting environment in which the service user can talk more freely and be open to accepting support. Professional ethical standards preclude social workers from 'befriending' service users in that the social worker must maintain professional boundaries both for their own and for the service users' well-being. Hence, they are not a friend in the social sense, but have employed their competence in counselling skills to put the service users at ease. It is possible, then, that good social work can be seen and described as not being social work at all.

Social work counselling skills invisibility issues: divorce from theory

To complicate matters further, social workers, ironically, when they have more experience may begin to divorce themselves from a conscious engagement with thinking about and applying theory. Healy (2014, p. 22) states that we may even encounter social workers who profess to have abandoned theory once they finish their formal education. Yet it is essentially their skill in critical and informed thinking that provides social workers with the foundation for their professional practice. Munro (1998, p. 102) in a discussion of social work knowledge base suggested that social workers experienced difficulties in 'articulating their reasoning or in specifying which theories , if any , they were using'.

Our theoretical framework guides us in deciding who or what should be the focus of assessment or intervention. This will be explored in more depth in a later chapter. For now it is sufficient to highlight the dilemma for social work. Good social work may be experienced as 'friendship not social work', making social work skills 'invisible' to the service user. Social work can be almost unnoticeable as a professional interaction by service users and therefore the skill involved in social work is invisible. The challenge that this lack of visibility presents is complicated by the fact that many social workers also believe that they have left theory behind them and therefore may be unconsciously competent, thus contributing to limitations in being able to articulate and validate their own skills. Losing sight of the connections to their fundamental theoretical foundations, the rationale for social work, contributes to making that 'invisible' too. All in all, it is a recipe for making social work and the skills they use 'invisible' to all, including social work professionals themselves. If you lose sight of the foundation it becomes more difficult to stand up to scrutiny and demonstrate that you not only know what you are doing but also can provide a legitimate, theoretically and evidence-informed rationale for doing it. This dilemma may at least in part provide some insight into why social workers have become estranged from their counselling skills. Social workers function not at a social conversational level of communication but at a more developed and purposeful level best equated with counselling skills.

In researching what works to establish a sense of role adequacy and role legitimacy for social workers in relation to working with substance use, Skinner et al. (2005) found that role support was a key factor. For social work such role support can be provided through accessible and timely supervision. Support is, then, not just about accountability, but should encompass validating/legitimising the employment of the counselling skills that social workers require to build relationships with service users, perhaps even more so in the context of scarce resources and nonvoluntary engagement which often impact social work practice. This legitimacy will be discussed further, but the main focus of this book will be to provide a basis to inform and support role adequacy for social workers in identifying, thinking about and employing their counselling skills.

Counselling skills for social work

The aim of this book is to provide a theoretically informed understanding of the core skills required to provide counselling interventions that work. It revisits well-established core skills including listening, responding, building empathy, questioning, assessing and supporting change. Over 12 chapters, these core counselling skills will be described in terms of what they mean, how they can be learned and developed and how they can be used and misused. In exploring these skills, a case will be made for looking at these skills along a continuum of proficiency from ability to practising them in day-to-day social interactions to employing them as part of strategic counselling interventions. The challenge for the reader will be in identifying where they sit on that continuum and what they need to do to develop those skills to a professionally proficient standard.

To facilitate this process, examples will be presented to illustrate the skills and the dilemmas as discussed in each chapter. In addition, a second part of the text will demonstrate how specific skills can be employed in a coherent and evidence-informed counselling approach. Three intervention methods will be explored in order to provide clear examples of the application of the skills to practice. The final three chapters will therefore look in detail at the skills required to deliver interventions consistent with three approaches: motivational interviewing, solution-focused therapy and group work.

The objective is to provide the reader with a well-informed, insightful yet challenging account of the traditionally established core counselling skills. It will present counselling skills with a twist. The twist involves directly encountering the interface between day-to-day communications skills and what are called counselling skills. The book will help the reader to understand what is required to develop and fine-tune these skills to harnesses them for the purposes of professional helping. The provision of illustrative examples will facilitate applying the ideas to real situations. Some exercises will support reflection and exploration of self-awareness and provide the bases for practising and enhancing skills development.

The goal will be to look at micro skills so that readers can be clear about how they develop those skills, but also to set the application of and acquisition of the skills in the broader context of a continuum from everyday life to professional practice settings. This involves an appreciation of how personal experience and perspectives and theoretical knowledge and understanding can shape where you go with those skills. Without that broader picture the micro skills alone do not convey the importance of ethical and practice standards that are a necessary part of good counselling. This is so critical in social work.

Exploring not just the 'how' of using specific skills but just as importantly in taking cognisance of 'why' and in what context you engage certain skills. The idea of starting with how people use 'counselling skills' in their personal conversational interaction is premised on the view that in that context you can often 'get away' with not considering: emotion, self-awareness, culture, life course and theories of human behaviour and social interactions. Moving on to develop from simple social skills to more sophisticated professional interventions skills (counselling skills) involves paying attention to what we think about what we are doing (as influenced by theory/culture/personal experience/emotion/personal life stage), why we are doing it and how we are doing it. In the book this emphasis on informed and critical thinking will be a recurring consideration associated with many of the micro skills. In fact, the overall premise is that without the framework and insight provided by theories, ethics, social work values and personal and profession reflection, a social worker may be dependent on what are essentially basic interpersonal communications skills that are suitable for social conversations but not for the complex and often highly charged communication involved in counselling and therapeutic intervention, which are fundamental to the social work professional conversation.

This book is written from the perspective that social work is a professional interaction between social worker and service users. This relationship is based on building engagement which is founded on collaboration, respect and genuineness; it is nonetheless one boundaried by professional expectations and responsibilities and is conducted in the context of broader societal responsibilities. In reviewing research on what worked in counselling, Cooper (2011) confirms the importance and centrality of building the relationship with service users. Social workers therefore need to be equipped to work at a high level of skill in terms of communicating these complex parameters with service users, often at times when service users are under pressure or even in crisis. The debate about counselling, therapy and social work is not one that draws fruitful results. The reality is that social workers, in managing the complex relationships and responsibilities, must deliver therapeutic interventions (helpful interventions) drawing on high levels of communication skills. These skills go well beyond a good conversational style and enter the realm of highly developed, theoretically informed, ethically boundaried and professionally delivered interpersonal communications.

While this could be said of other professionals and even volunteer counsellors, there is an additional element for social work. The clue is in the title: Social Work. For the professional social worker, whatever the situation, they must also take cognisance of the social dimensions to service users' experiences. This means that while engaging in building a strong therapeutic alliance with an individual or family they must also be aware of and consider the social context within which the communication is taking place. This requires that social work be a more holistic form of communication, as it must consider the social context of the individual/family and how that context may contribute to the development of the issues or problems and also how it may impede finding solutions or supporting change. The social worker must also take account of such factors as power and role authority, which creates the framework within which the interaction with service users is transacted. Hence, for social work, a focus on individual psychology, motivation and change is inadequate to meet the needs of service users. The social worker must also bring an understanding and appreciation of the social factors that may contribute to or impede service users' attempts to improve their lives and the lives of those they care for.

Nelson-Jones (2011, p. 7), in attempting to distinguish between counselling and psychotherapy, social work and what he refers to as helpers, suggests that 'counsellors are primarily trained to counsel, whereas helpers may be primarily trained to be social workers, nurses, probation officers, priests, welfare workers, managers and a host of other occupations'. He then defines counselling's primary purpose as being to help clients address psychological issues in their lives while the 'helpers use counselling skills to assist people to deal with goals where the overt psychological dimension appear secondary if not irrelevant … receiving pregnancy advice and probation and parole support'.

The goals of helping can overlap, yet differ from those of counselling. According to Shebib (2003, p. 4), 'one special feature that distinguishes social work counseling from that performed by other professionals is its dual focus on working with individual as well as the environment. Social workers assume that the individual can only be understood in the context of their environment'. He goes on to emphasise that point about the social in social work. 'For him this means that social work has a responsibility to look beyond the individual, which might be the focus of other counselling and work towards promoting change or adaptation in social and political systems so that they can respond more effectively to the needs of clients' (Shebib 2003, p. 4).

Conversation

A brief discussion about conversation is as good a place to start as any in this consideration of counselling skills for social work. Taking this as a starting position allows us to consider the place of conversations skills that we all typically develop quite early on in life. These skills start out at a very basic level when we begin to identify our needs and communicate that to others, initially only employing non-verbal and then more basic verbal signals, but later for most adding communication through conversation. Maybe it is because there is a sense of achieving in learning to communicate through talk that leads us to privilege this form of communication. Unfortunately, those who, for whatever reason, do not develop this skills set are at risk of being marginalised and/or even isolated. But it does seem that talking/the ability to converse takes precedence over the communication skills that we relied on prior to that phase of development such as the non-verbals of demonstrating emotion through facial expressions and movement. Over time, then, it seems that we rely more heavily on language, words and conversation. So it is not surprising that conversation should become the cornerstone of helping. After all, conversation might be considered to be the key element of 'talk therapies'. This point is being highlighted for a number of reasons:

1. First, it helps to identify conversational skills as part of a developmental progression. There are of course specific areas of research that can help us to understand this development, such as neurolinguistics and sociolinguistic studies.
2. The second reason is to draw attention to the limitations of a dependence on conversational skills in facilitating communication. Conversation is one small element of communication skills. This reminds us to be more inclusive and creative when

we think about how to communicate with those who may have limited conversation but rely on alternative skills and also to take account of the level of skill attained developmentally.

3. Finally, given the importance placed on our conversational/talk skills in the counselling and therapy context, it is essential to look at moving these skills to a level beyond general interpersonal conversation. If these skills are to serve as the core tools in any 'helping' relationship then we must accept the need to reach a level of competence well beyond a socially developed interpersonal style.

It might be true to say that a natural fluency in conversation which takes cognisance of social and cultural conventions is a good starting place. But when conversation becomes one of your main tools in helping, it is important to break down the elements of good conversational skills and to consider these as a little more than the foundation stone rather than the cornerstone of professional helping.

Conversation, then, can be defined as 'a collaborative process in which meaning and organization are jointly created. Conversational participants interact through linguistic exchange improvised in real time' (Jordan et al. 2009, p. 2). Social conversation is informed by social conventions, can be spontaneous, informal, but it is still context-based and has a purpose in itself. The purpose and process of the conversation is informed and shaped by interpersonal knowledge and each participants' understanding and enactment of their part in that social interaction. In general, it is a face-to-face talk-based interaction, although Jordan et al. (2009, p. 2) do comment that with developing new technologies some online communication could be included in a wider definition of conversation. Therefore, conversation may be a good starting place to build interpersonal communication skills. While conversational ability is an important element of good communication skills, the level and depth of skill required to apply these skills in a professional social work counselling situation demands additional development and focus. In fact, the 'talk' in social work and talk-based therapeutic intervention is of a different dimension than social conversational talk. It must be embedded in a context of ethical and value-based professional standards, be informed by relevant theoretical frameworks and conducted with high levels of competence that are for the most part set by professional bodies or state regulation requirements.

Many writers (Koprowska 2010, Woodcock-Ross 2011) agree communication skills come naturally. In fact, communication is happening all the time when people are together; even when they are trying to avoid communication that, too is communicating something (Koprowska 2010, p. 6). However, when you are in a profession where communication is a critical tool of your work then you have to build more advanced levels of skills. This entails not only being able to demonstrate these skills as and when required, but also being able to work from a knowledge base so that you can make decisions about what skill is required or is most appropriate in any particular interaction with a service user. This will be explored later in this chapter.

Exercise 1 Observing conversational communication

Probably one of the most helpful things to do in beginning to become more aware of counselling skills is to start by paying close attention to the communication skills you employ in your conversations. I am not suggesting that you become only an outside observer in your life, but rather that you take some time to sit back and listen to what's going on around you in everyday life. For example, next time you're in a group with your friends, take some time out of the conversation and listen to how the conversation moves along. Pay attention to who brings up topics, how they're handled, who does most of the talking, how difficult situations are managed. Other examples of what might be useful to observe is how information is exchanged. You will notice that information among friends is often freely exchanged. You barely have to ask one question and you will get most of the information about an issue or something that's going on in the person's life pretty quickly. Think about the skills you and your friends use to communicate with one another. Look at how the context of having a trusting relationship changes how you talk to one another. Perhaps take the time to compare how conversations flow in a setting with your very good friends, people you are really close to, and then look at the formal situation perhaps at work. So, for example, pay attention at a meeting and look at how people communicate there, how different that is from a social situation. Then consider which of these situations fits more with your professional social work interactions. Social work interactions, counselling situations, are more formal, often with somebody with whom you have not yet built a relationship and very often about highly charged emotional issues. Think again about your friends. Remember how conflict is contained and managed in a situation where there is a lot of support and closeness. Look again at how these conflicts even emerge in the first place. It is valuable to learn about and be more aware of your own discomfort or comfort with conflict situations and how you tend to manage it.

The notion of 'informal' counselling

It is probably true that most informal counselling is done by parents, family, spouse, friends and of course by oneself (self-talk). It is really only when these sources of support, guidance and counselling are not available or feel that they are not able to deal with the issue(s) that professional help is brought into the picture. Depending on the circumstance this 'outside' help may be sought by the individual or by one of the 'informal counsellors'. It may also be sent in (mandated) because of the individual's reluctance to seek help or because the seriousness of the issues and the potential risk to self or others has been recognised by someone aware of the circumstances.

Because we all have played this role of informal counsellor to family or friends at some point, and maybe you were drawn to social work because of these experiences of helping, it might seem that counselling is second nature to you. People comment that they have always been a good listener and that people confide in them easily. It is important to make a distinction between this informal counselling and the subject matter of this book, which is professional counselling skills for social workers.

As the informal counsellor I describe above you have a number of important advantages: you probably know the person very well or at least know quite a lot about their circumstances, relationships and life in general; you may have even been around to help out in previous situations and been experienced as really helpful and supportive, hence one of the reason you are back in that role again; even if you are not 'close' to the person you may be connected through someone else they trust and have confided in so you have an advantage of having a second perspective on what's happened from your mutual acquaintance and also because of the connections you are more likely to be seen as trustworthy. Because developing a connection and fostering trust are core components of a successful counselling relationship you are already doing well. Add to this that someone, either the person themselves or your mutual connection, probably sees you as a good listener and someone who usually gives good advice, then the opening is there to influence what's going to happen next.

The other side of the story is that there are additional but less helpful possibilities which should be considered. It is probable that you are aware of the limitations of what you know and what you can contribute unless it is something you have manged yourself before or that you have a level of confidence in your own ability in these circumstances. If you don't know your limitation, it might be called unconscious incompetence, as opposed to the conscious incompetence of someone who appreciates their limited skills in this area.

The professional counsellor has to work on the things that the informal helper may take for granted: building a connection, trust and understanding what's going on for the person. However, it is also possible that the informal helper's very connection makes it difficult to talk to them about what's really going on. Some problems and concerns are too personal, too intimate to share with those we know. Maybe it would be embarrassing or exposing to have someone in your circle knowing these things about you even if you do trust them. Individuals need to have a sense of self-protection when it comes to sharing personal and difficult information. Sometimes this is underdeveloped and they share too easily, even with a professional counsellor, and then withdraw as they feel overexposed and vulnerable.

Therefore, an informal counsellor might be in a strong position to get a sense of what's going on. We know that many, maybe even most, problems are resolved through these informal/friendship and support networks. In the addiction field it is known that about one-third of people with addiction issues probably resolve these without formal help or treatment. So the question is, will your natural informal helping skills be sufficient to work with someone you don't know and whose own informal network has not succeeded in helping? I suggest not. You need to build on whatever interpersonal communication skills you bring to social work, and to be honest, you may also have to question some of these and their appropriateness in a professional counselling context.

Boundaries

An issue to consider in relation to this level of what I'm calling informal counselling is that of boundaries. When you begin to feel overwhelmed by the nature or persistence of the problem brought to you by an acquaintance or friend, it may be that you are just not equipped to deal with that problem. It may also be that you are experiencing a breach of those boundaries that define our appropriate level of contact and communication with others. Boundaries differ depending on the relationship you share with a person. What would be comfortable and acceptable with one person may be completely unacceptable with another. When someone has 'crossed the line' we know it and can often manage that situation. However, when someone who is asking for your help/advice has put you in a counselling role that you have accepted, then this shift in terms of keeping your distance becomes problematic.

The same can happen with professional counsellors, but because the potential for this is recognised, training and education prepares professional helpers to watch out for it and to divert the shift, if possible before it becomes damaging. With the informal counselling relationship it may be that you will develop a closer relationship with the person than before and this may even develop into a more intimate relationship. Sometimes living through adverse situations can draw people together. This is a major transgression in professional work. Given the vulnerability of the person seeking help and the known danger of them seeking to feel safe with the person they have confided in, this shift to a more personal or intimate contact is completely unacceptable. In professional counselling it is an ethical requirement to maintain appropriate boundaries. The corollary of this is that as an informal counsellor you take on too much responsibility.

Knowledge

Just not knowing what to do or how to handle the situation you find yourself in can also be an issue for the informal counsellor. This can, of course, happen to a professional as well. That is why through training and education a person using professional counselling skills is expected to work within a set of ethics and values to guide their work. The professional will also have access to a more experienced supervisor who can work with them on both the knowledge required to respond effectively but also to help them to process the emotional and personal impact of the work. The availability of a reflective space and the preparation of being able to use reflection to safeguard not only the service user but yourself is one of the marks of the professional nature of counselling. There is a level of accountability and support for the professional counsellor that is not there for someone who is just helping out. Along with this is a responsibility to have the knowledge base and skills to deliver a professional service.

Counselling

Counselling and therapy skills will continue to reflect some of the basic elements of good conversations. In fact, someone not trained in professional level of counselling skills might not see much more than a regular interpersonal conversation. However, 'helping' conversations, whether you call them counselling or therapy, are more sophisticated and complex. This involves understanding not only the skills but the theory informing the application of those skills and also the way in which specific skills are utilised to deliver particular methods of intervention. Luckily, we have some clear information about what works in communication, so it is possible to build on these identified skills. Koprowska (2010, p. 7) makes a helpful distinction between first-order and second order-skills. In first-order skills she includes those that require direct communication, and in second-order those employed in planning, thinking, observing and feedback, reviewing and modifying the next communication informed by these. A range of different terms can be applied to describe this professional employment of communication skills for the purpose of building a relationship with service users. Terms used include: social work interventions, counselling, assessment, interviewing, social work practice, therapeutic conversations. These terms have somewhat different nuances, but essentially all required the sophisticated application of high-level communication skills. In the current context some of these terms will be used interchangeably. It will also consider listening, in its broadest sense, and responding as first-order skills, while second-order skills are encompassed in the concept of processing.

So, definitely not just a chat!

Conversation is a widely employed approach to communication. Of course, it is not the only method of communication as non-verbal, visual and other ways of communication are also among other available options. This may well be one of the most distinguishing differences or perhaps limitations of conversation and definitely one not shared with what is more broadly considered when discussing counselling and therapy. There are multiple forms of counselling and therapeutic interventions that draw on a much broader range of interpersonal communication skills than conversation alone.

In discussing counselling and interviewing, Ivey (1994) clarified that these terms would be used interchangeably. He suggested that 'interviewing may be considered the most basic process used for information gathering, problem solving, information and advice giving ... Counselling is a more intensive and personal process ... Both interviewing and counselling may be distinguished from psychotherapy, which is a more intense process, focusing deep-seated personality behavioural difficulties' (1994, p. 10). So counselling and interviewing are being distinguished from psychotherapy. Social work is often associated with interviewing and perhaps assessment interviewing in particular. Ivey's sense that counselling and interviewing are interchangeable activities supports the position in this text that social workers, whether you define their activities as counselling or not, are fundamentally using counselling skills to conduct their professional practice. This argument will be further explored throughout the chapters. Given that one aim of the book is to remind social workers of their counselling skills, the term counselling will be used rather than interviewing. However, when addressing interviewing, specifically assessment interviewing, the position that social work interviewing can only be usefully conducted through the employment of counselling skills will be discussed more explicitly.

Counselling skills are organised into three core activities: talking, listening and thinking. Each of these can be subdivided into more specific skills as in Figure 1.1 breakdown of social work counselling skills.The skills interact with each other even if one seems at times to be more obvious or relevant (see Figure 1.2).

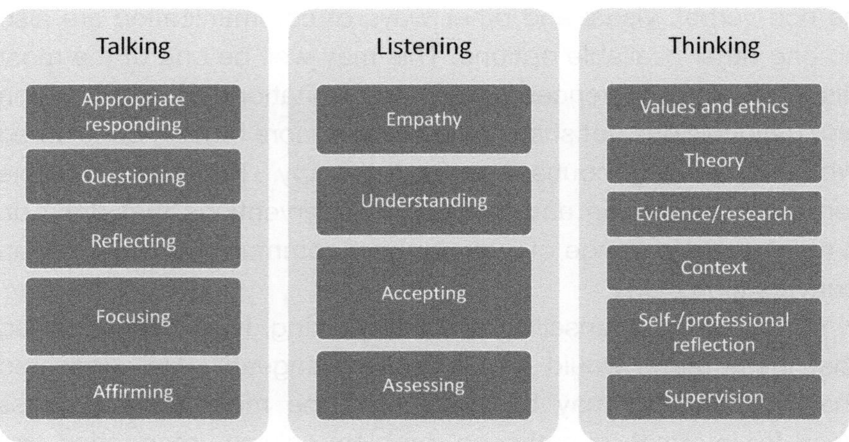

Figure 1.1 Breakdown of social work counselling skills

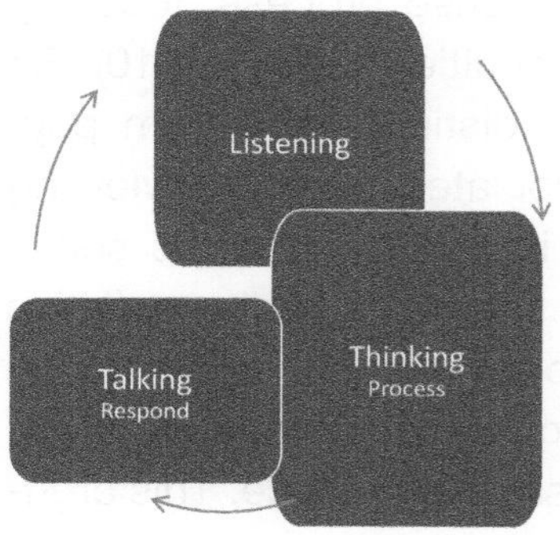

Figure 1.2 Interaction of social work counselling skills

Exercise 2 Observing and noticing differences in focused use of communication skills

The next aspect of this that is worth considering is to look more closely and pay more attention to settings where interviews are happening. For example, if you have some programme like a detective show that you are interested in looking at or a movie where people are being interviewed, for example in a legal setting or in relationship to detectives investigating a crime. Just listen to how questions are formed and compare them to what you do in your social life and then what you might do in a social work setting. I am often amazed to see how skilled even in an acting scenario people are in terms of avoiding asking too many questions, something that we as social workers really need to pay attention to. In order to do this observation, it's useful to just set yourself a small task of observation. I would suggest that in each of these scenarios you decide to look at just two things.

The use of closed questions.
The use of open questions.

Later on, you might want to review these things again and add a few additional skills or techniques to observe; for example, use of reflections or self-disclosure. You might also look out for ways in which communication is affirming to somebody and whether people are actually speaking only about a problem or actually thinking about and asking about solutions.

Therapeutic intervention

Sharry (2004), reflecting on Rogers as qualities required for a therapeutic relationship, emphasises that these active listening skills would not work unless the core attitudes of empathy, acceptance and genuineness are communicated to the service user. Sharry (2004, p. 24) suggests then that the important issue is not whether we are being non-judgemental, accepting and empathetic, but rather whether our service users actually feel supported, not blamed accepted and understood. There is a broad acceptance that the therapeutic relationship is an important part of counselling. However, the issue in relationship to social work would appear to be whether social workers are counsellors/therapists. For the purposes of this text, the distinction between social workers, social care workers, counsellors and therapists as distinct professional identities will be acknowledged. The discussion will focus not on the debate about whether social workers are counsellors, which is typically not their professional attributed title; however, the emphasis will be on counselling skills and therapeutic interventions as skills required by a range of 'helping professionals' and which are part of professionally competent social work activity. The term therapeutic incorporates ideas such as: healing, beneficial, helpful, curative, remedial, restorative and corrective (Word thesaurus). The *Oxford English Dictionary*, in addition, adds having a good effect and being rehabilitative. With these terms in mind and given the mission statement, values and ethics of social work, there can be little doubt that social work by its nature is meant to be a therapeutic, interventive interpersonal activity.

Social workers are employing their professional competence among other purposes in order to help, heal and assist rehabilitation, and as such are engaged in therapeutic interventions. Perhaps some confusion about this lies in the strong associations between therapy and counselling and psychologically informed one-to-one or family interventions. Social work, influenced by its origins, continues to hold a position which is informed both by psychological and sociological influences. This adds a layer of complexity to the task of social work, which is further exacerbated by the role of social work as part of what might be seen as agents of social control, such as child welfare and protection and probation. Nonetheless, in whatever capacity social workers engage with service users, their value system and role must be consistent with promoting the well-being and care of service users. This means that social workers engage in therapeutic interaction with service users. Maintaining professional boundaries to distinguish between a level of social interpersonal communication and the demands of professional competence in communication can present a challenge to social work. Therefore, each chapter will consider the differences between social and professional levels of communication skills and make the case that social workers engaged in professionally competent communication are in fact employing counselling skills for therapeutic purposes in their work.

Exercise 3 Editing in retelling

One person tells a somewhat detailed story to one person while a number of others (3–7) wait outside the room and don't hear the original story. Then the listener calls in someone from outside and retells the story ... repeat this a few times to see if the story changes, what, if any, aspects of the story are emphasised or left out, etc.

Exercise 4 Listening for content and feelings

One person tells a story with content and feelings to a few people (at least three but preferably six). The speaker should be given preparation so that they know to select a story that they are comfortable to share. Remember to respect confidentiality issues. They should be asked for a story that does not have deep issues that are not yet resolved, but rather a story that describes an event that did raise some emotional responses from them, positive and/or negative. The story should last for 5 minutes. The listeners are not told until the story is finished what they have to do.

Task 1: Half the group should be asked to take it in turns to say one thing of content that they heard, e.g. you did a lot of work on that project; you sound like you learned from this. Each person names one item of content in turn and continues this until the group feel they have covered all the content involved. The speaker can then give feedback about how accurately the group heard what (s)he said. The speaker may also comment on the order in which the content was given back: did the first responder start at the beginning or end of the story, for example. The responders should also reflect on how that went for them, did they find it easy to remember content aspects of the story, did they hear more feeling than content or did that stick with them more or not, did not knowing what they were going to be asked put them under pressure, did they have something in mind to say and then someone else said it first, etc. The half of the group observing can then add in anything they think was missed.

Task 2: The other half of the group do the same task, but this time they identify and name the feelings they picked up on. The speaker can give them feedback when they have run out of feelings, but it might be OK to confirm or reject each one as it is identified. The same reflection/feedback process as task 1 should assist in the group learning about content versus feelings and their own skills at listening under pressure and the place of interpretation and self-awareness in the task of listening.

Wind down: Finally, ask the person who told the story for a response. How did it feel, did the groups get the main points, was the story the same or distorted, different emphasis than they would have thought, etc. Ensure that all participants have had the chance to reflect and are OK before finishing.

2 Talking and responding

- Looking at talking as an informed activity connected to and dependent on listening and thinking. Considering what it is we say and why. Talking as a counselling skill is an informed, directed activity; it is part of a response repertoire which should be congruent with the non-verbal responses we make.
- Address the limitations of talk therapy and look at the place of self-disclosure in building a relationship between a service user and social worker.
- Consider the challenges of avoiding 'social chat' and developing the skill of considered reflective talking and responding.

Introduction

Counselling, as we have mentioned, can go beyond what are sometimes seen as talk therapies. However, in the context of this book the focus is on the skills required to deliver counselling that relies on talking as a core method of communication. It is important to state that this is a deliberate and acknowledged limitation, but not intended to be an exclusive endorsement of talk therapy as a method. Most counselling methods do employ talk as part of the skilled activity. Often talk is used in conjunction with music, art, play, drama or other activities. Delivering talk counselling with these other communication and interactive styles may be particularly relevant where there are developmental issues that further limit the effectiveness of talk only. These may relate what is most appropriate given age, capacity, culture and language, the topic of concern or evidence of effectiveness.

The focus of this chapter is not on the micro skills that are delivered through talk as applied in a social work setting such as open question and reflections; these will be discussed in later chapters. The purpose of this chapter is to draw attention to the place of talk in the cycle of counselling and in particular to highlight the concern that talk may overshadow listening and thinking to the detriment of building collaborative relationships.

Talking as a social skill

It may be useful to consider language and speech as the vehicles for conducting conversations. Thompson (2011, p. 89) suggests that 'becoming competent in the art of using speech in conversation ... involves learning the rules of these language games and being able to determine which words or forms of language are appropriate in particular sets of circumstances'. He adds that there is also the aspect of cultural literacy to take into account and that 'the skilled conversationalist needs to be able to understand not only which words are appropriate but also which meaning systems and cultures apply' (2011, p. 89). Talking is, then, a complex communication interaction which happens in a social context and reflects such factors as language, meaning, culture and power. Social conversation requires a level of understanding and skill so that we know how to talk in an appropriate way in different settings. Some of our talking is conducted through socially defined scripts. In general, there are 'routine' conversations that happen, for example, in work or social settings. Participants in these conversations usually know what topics are appropriate and also what language is acceptable and even what aspects of a topic are suitable.

When you are in conversation with others you can use listening skills as mentioned before, including non-verbal skills, and through these you can read people's reactions to what you say. These two sides of the conversation, talking and listening, can then produce a form of feedback. You can tell if you are talking in an acceptable way by the response of those involved in the conversation. If you do not pick up on the response then you may get into difficulties with social conversations and participants may have to engage in more direct feedback to indicate they are not happy with your talk/conversation; for example, leave the company or challenge what you are saying. The interplay is complex, and yet because these talking skills are used routinely, we may be unaware of just how skilful we are when we engage with others. We have to be versatile in matching our conversation or talk with others across a range of social situations or contexts from personal friendships to informal social or family setting and then more formal situations with more prescribed rules of engagement. The service user may experience the interaction with a social worker as a conversation rather than a meeting, interview or even assessment. However, it should be noted that in all interactions the social worker is engaging counselling skills and not a social conversational level of communication.

Talking as a counselling skill

Counselling is then a more formalised and prescribed type of conversation or talking. Perhaps one of the most challenging skills for the social worker is to convey to a service user that despite the formality of the context the service user can utilise the same talk skills that they employ in more familiar settings. This means that the social worker as the professional needs to create a comfortable space for the service user to engage in the conversation. We will explore in later chapters some specific counselling techniques/skills that assist in mirroring the service users' talk style and aims to encourage and support service users' engagement in the counselling process.

So let's think of counselling as a talking and listening interaction which differs from the typical social format. The counselling context creates a setting whereby one participant, the service user, is attempting to engage with a somewhat unfamiliar formulation for talking and listening. Not only that, but they are probably trying to engage in this more formal conversation at a time when they are under stress. In addition, it is often the case where social work is involved that the service user feels they are in a vulnerable position and that the power differential is felt but may not be recognised or acknowledged. On the other hand, the other participant, the social worker, should be engaging in this conversation with a set of more advanced talking and listening skills, i.e. counselling skills. It is therefore part of the role of the social worker to help the service user negotiate this formal conversation by paying attention to developing a therapeutic collaborative relationship and by applying the skills of talking and listening at a level of professional competence rather than at the level of other forms of social interaction. This therapeutic relationship is acknowledged as being the most important factor in working collaboratively (Norcross 2010, Wampold 2010). As we will see, talking and listening are only two aspects of the skills employed by social workers. In fact, it will be argued that a third set of skills required, which we will refer to as thinking and processing, should impact both talking and listening. Thinking shapes both what we say and what we hear. You might say that this skill of thinking and processing (what we hear and say) is the hallmark of counselling. Figure 2.1 shows the flow of these skills. They operate in a cyclical movement through thinking, talking, listening then thinking and back to talking, listening and so on. Listening and thinking are explored in Chapters 3 and 4 in more detail. Thinking informs talking and listening and then listening informs and shapes thinking. Thinking is the conduit from listening to talking, and if the social worker is not aware of making sense/thinking about what they hear, then it is unlikely that they will make full use of the information they get from talking to service users and then listening to the responses. See Appendix 2.1. *The counselling cycle can be illustrated as a flow of communication which occurs in a typical counselling session* (see Figure 2.1).

Obviously some talking input will take place at the introductory stage of any meeting; however, it should be emphasised that thinking should be the first skill the social worker engages in in any situation, so that once you start talking, it is an informed and considered 'talk'. We are characterising this as starting the conversation with introductory clarification. This may include sharing information about a referral or a request for information about why the service user has come to be meeting the social worker. Shebib (2003, p. 11) suggests that a prerequisite to the counselling relationship is clarity about what is expected on all sides of the relationship. This involves talking through a clear introduction which covers the expectations of both parties in the counselling interaction. This 'starting talk' is very important because it literally sets the tone for

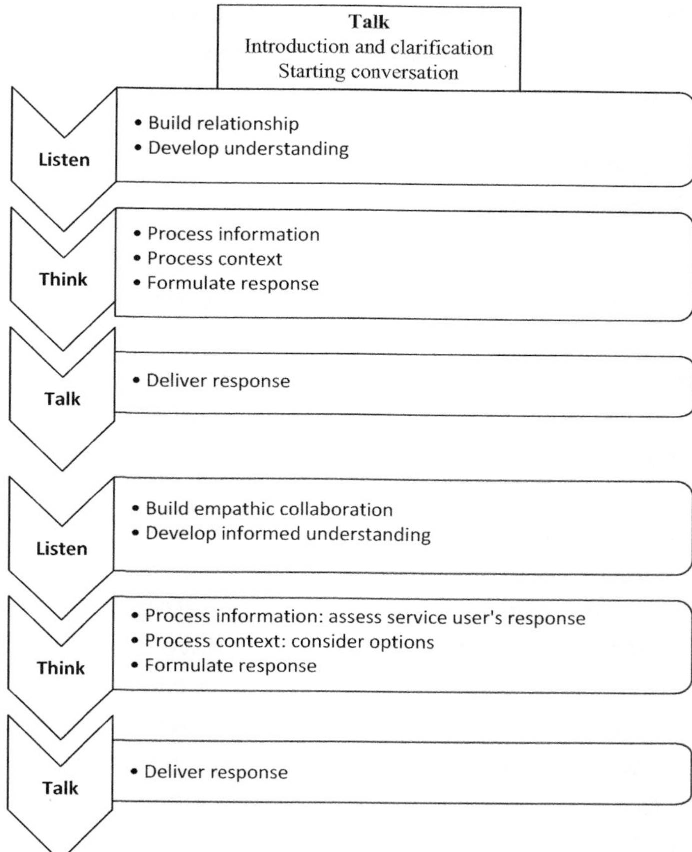

Figure 2.1 Flow of counselling process

the rest of the interaction. It sets the tone in the talking sense; what tone of voice is used, is it a friendly, soft and warm tone or is it rushed, sharp and intimidating. What is the tone of the content is it delivered in a way that will be perceived as supportive or challenging, is it clear or confusing, is it inviting or directive?

Talking is not listening

Talking is perhaps overemphasised, overvalued and possibly overused as an aspect of counselling. In the chapter on listening we discuss the suggestion that when you are talking you are not learning or listening. It may be all too easy to prioritise talking above the more critical skills of listening and thinking. This is a very difficult balance to master.

Advantages to talking

There are many advantages to talking.

- It gives the talker a sense of control
- You can deliver information and advice and give direction and focus
- You might feel that you are 'getting your point across'
- You believe you are fulfilling your responsibilities in giving necessary information

Delivering or receiving

These are, of course, outcomes of talking, but these are not sufficient outcomes when it comes to talking in counselling. In counselling talk the desired output is not that you have spoken or delivered the information, but that it has been received. This is where listening comes in. You can get a sense of whether the talk is being received when you listen for a service user's response. So talking must be guided by the feedback from the receiver and this is an important consideration in guiding the social worker in how to measure the amount of talk they engage in at any one time in the interaction.

A good basic formula is to remember that the more you talk the less time there is for the service user to talk. Your skill in helping the service user to express themselves is perhaps one of the most important parts of counselling. You will see the connections with active listening and with empathic responding as discussed in that chapter.

Getting the balance right between talking and listening is an ongoing process for any social worker/counsellor. It will become very tempting to talk more when:

- You are working with a less talkative service user
- You are more anxious to give information
- When the concern is particularly serious

- When there is limited time and or resources (just remember: doing more talking isn't necessarily getting the job done faster)

Sometimes there is external pressure to give factual information and this may need to be done, for example to fit with agency or statutory protocol. While it is essential that you meet with such regulatory requirements, it is also useful to recognise the limitations of information overload. There is a risk that the service user will not be in a position to take in or listen to what you are saying. In some cases the service user may hear what is said, but not be ready or able to respond. The outcome may be counterproductive in that the service user will withdraw from the communication.

How much do you talk?

The only really accurate way to find out who is doing the talking is to record yourself in conversation. This is possible in professional contexts as audio and video recording of interviews/counselling is now more commonplace. I have at times been disappointed myself when reviewing recordings as I realise I was talking more than I thought or planned. Co-working can also help you to identify if you are talking too much once there is constructive feedback between colleagues.

The task of monitoring your talk time is something that needs ongoing feedback, self-awareness and reflection. We will talk about self-reflection and feedback later. There are some helpful hints that can help with this.

Watch out for:

- When you are working harder than the service user
- Talking more and trying to ask more question to keep the conversation going
- Notice when you are working hard to generate possible answers or solutions

Then in all likelihood your intervention/counselling is not working. You are working, but the interaction isn't working. Working through what's happening and what needs to happen requires support from social worker, but also requires some level of engagement and contemplation by the service user. If the service user doesn't have the opportunity to talk, listen and think for themselves then change will be difficult. The social worker should be prioritising thinking and listening so that they give every chance to the service users to talk. Facilitating the service user in thinking through the situation(s) and listening can be built from this. Social work counselling is the opportunity for the service user to work on what is worrying them, or on the issue that has brought social work into their lives. Ideally the service user discovers that talking, disclosing, contemplating and reflecting will help them towards change and a sense of self-efficacy. They can't do this if you are doing all the talking!

Talking is, of course, a key part of the communication that takes place in counselling. From the service user's perspective their commitment to talking and disclosing information about themselves will be influenced by the skill with which the social worker facilitates the conversation. Many other factors will also play a part. These may include: stage of development, the personal and social context, the focus of the meeting, etc. The social worker needs to understand the other elements that will impact the service user's engagement in the interaction. However, the onus is on the social worker to operate at a level of competence in terms of their knowledge and skills and within the value base and professional context to optimise that engagement. Getting the balance right between talking themselves and creating a safe and supportive space for the service user to talk is critical. Interestingly, there is little evidence that any one particular model of counselling or intervention is more successful (Cooper 2011). The core element of success is the establishing of a collaborative relationship.

Skills in talking

Beyond the global concerns discussed above, it is useful to consider some of the specific skills that can be applied in how you talk and also how you can encourage and support the service user to talk. Some of these will be discussed in more detail in Chapters 4,

5, 7 and 8, such as asking questions, reflecting, affirming and empathy. These are all interconnected skills in the production of a talking and listening balance and also connected are the thinking or processing skills.

For the rest of this chapter we will look at two related aspects of talking skills: self-disclosure and silence.

Self-disclosure

Self-disclosure involves talking about your personal experiences with the service user in the work setting. Rogers (1965) was a proponent of self-disclosure and associated it with the genuineness and congruence which he saw as preconditions for change. There is a high level of skill required in using self-disclosure appropriately. The aim of self-disclosure is to both humanise the worker and also to facilitate the service user's identification and disclosure of thoughts and feelings (Woodcock Ross 2011, p. 35). However, it is a contentious issue in social work and counselling. Self-disclosure can be seen as of great importance in developing a therapeutic relationship or as potentially unhelpful. This is what Cooper (2011, p. 114) refers to as 'the polarisation of views on self-disclosure'. Miller and Rollnick (2013, p. 150) provide this helpful distinction 'in close friendships, self-disclosure is routine and mutual. In professional helping relationship, however, we believe there should be a specific reason for self-disclosure'. Perhaps the familiarity with self-disclosure as a way of deepening friendship relationships accounts for some of the importance placed on it in counselling. However, there are, as mentioned, divergent views. Woodcock Ross (2011, p. 35) makes the point that 'self-disclosure may raise issues about professional boundaries'. She references Shulman (2009), who emphasised that social workers need to be clear about the purpose of their work and that self-disclosure is appropriate to the function and task; this offers direction and protection when considering the use of self-disclosure. There is a need to be very purposeful and considered in the application of self-disclosure. This may risk undermining the intent of creating a sense of genuineness as the application of this skill in the professional context is not the same as the spontaneous self-disclosure seen in building friendships. Caution is recommended in the use of self-disclosure. Nelson-Jones (2011) identifies seven guidelines for appropriate application of this skill. These include:

- Having sufficient emotional distance from the experience
- That the disclosure follows the service users disclosures
- To be aware of service user reaction as the disclosure may not be experienced as helpful
- Share personal experiences sparingly
- Be sensitive to cultural, social class, race and gender differences
- Beware of using self-disclosure ethically and not to connect with service user to meet your need for approval or to deal with your own unresolved issues

Both Nelson-Jones (2011) and Miller and Rollnick (2013) caution about self-disclosure taking attention away from the service user/client focus. These are very serious points and indicate that self-disclosure needs to be managed very skilfully if it to be used at all.

Perhaps some of the challenge in understanding the appropriate use of self-disclosure comes from the fact that different approaches to counselling place different emphasis on its place in developing the therapeutic relationship. Humanistic informed methods such as client centred place a strong emphasis of self-disclosure connecting it directly to core conditions for positive alliances. Methods informed by psychoanalytic theory do not encourage self-disclosure on the part of the counsellor. Postmodern theoretical frameworks address self-disclosure in terms of the need for a counsellor or social worker to be aware of and take account of their own positioning in society in general and in the counselling relationship specifically.

Self-disclosure and self-involving statements

The debate about whether self-disclosure is helpful or harmful is certainly contentious and complex. Another layer of this complexity can be seen in the different views about what self-disclosure actually means. One way of trying to make sense of this would be to look at what we know from the research on self-disclosure and, if it works, how it works. In an analysis of the effectiveness of self-disclosure in counselling, Cooper (2011) makes the helpful distinction between different types of self-disclosure. He distinguishes between *self-disclosure*, which refers to a 'therapist's statements that reveal something personal about the therapist' and *self-involving statements*, which are 'a form of self-disclosure, in which the therapist expresses a personal response to the client in the here and now' (Cooper 2011, p. 114). So now we have two different type self-disclosures: one which draws in the personal experience of the social worker or counsellor and another which focuses on giving a real-time response to the service user. This distinction is also discussed by Nelson-Jones (2011, pp. 87–90) when he supports the distinction between disclosures showing involvement and disclosures sharing personal experiences. This may appear to address some of the perceived problems with self-disclosure, as it recognises that openness sharing some information may be helpful in building trust but then differentiates this from crossing a boundary into more personal information. Both Cooper (2011) and Nelson-Jones (2011) seem to support the use of self-involving disclosures, which can serve to humanise the social worker.

Professional transparency

Some disclosure of information, for example regarding professional qualifications, can be considered to be the right of the service user. It might be helpful for social workers to consider what types of information they are comfortable sharing and clarifying with supervisors or their agency what information they are required to share. Because building the relationship is acknowledged as a core activity, it is important to think through what sorts of questions a service user might have and be prepared to deal with them in a responsive way. Sometimes we are talking about self-disclosure (specifically as defined by the concept of self-involvement) as being more transparent with the service user rather than necessarily disclosing personal experiences that relate to life outside of the counselling relationship. In her study of social workers and self-disclosure, Knight (2012) found that participants in the study made limited use of self-disclosure but were more willing to be transparent with clients. She also found that 'disclosures about the clinician's life beyond the session – self-involving disclosures – are generally less helpful than those that reveal her or his reactions to and thoughts about the client in the here-and-now (transparency) ... The exception to this is the worker's disclosures about her or his professional background' (p. 299).

These findings make a case for social workers being more transparent in their relationship with service users as a way to build and support a collaborative relationship. However, the findings discussed do highlight a further difficulty in reaching convincing conclusions about the place of self-disclosure in social work counselling. As you might have noticed, Cooper (2011) and Knight (2012) appear to use almost completely contradictory definitions of self-involving type of self-disclosure. For Cooper (2011), these are personal responses in the here and now and not personal life experiences, while Knight (2012) citing Knox and Hill (2003) defines these here-and-now disclosures as transparency while referring to the more personal as self-involving. Such contradictions in terms of agreed understanding of what elements of communication are perceived as self-disclosure may be a contributory factor in the ongoing disagreement about whether self-disclosure is helpful.

It seems that a level of self-disclosure which promotes openness in relation to the here and now and professional background is supported as being helpful while the place of other aspects of self-disclosure is less certain.

One central goal of self-disclosure is to demonstrate the involvement and humanity of the social worker. Although we continue to struggle with lack of clarity about whether this refers to the more limited levels of disclosure implied in transparency or a more personal definition of self-disclosure, the evidence does suggest that a perceived openness on the part of the social work has a positive impact on the relationship with service users. Yet we are discussing self-disclosure not as the spontaneous talk between friends but as a skill to be developed. This may seem to be an inherent contradiction in self-disclosure. However, Neukrug (2010, p. 186) explains this apparent contradiction by clarifying that 'it is when the therapist is natural and spontaneous that he seems to be most effective. Probably this is a "trained humanness" ... but in the moment it is the natural reaction of the person'. This suggests that self-disclosure that is actually genuine and real can also be learned. The key is in being prepared and really understanding the boundaries regarding the type of self-disclosure that is therapeutic and helpful and when self-disclosure is a mistake.

Service user perception of self-disclosure

There is a growing interest in researching the service users' perception of self-disclosure by the social worker or counsellor. Cooper (2011) cites Hanson's (2005) findings that self-disclosures were twice as likely to be rated as helpful by clients. He goes on to explore other studies and notes that Orlinsky et al. (2004) found in their work that studies which directly correlate the amount of self-disclosure with outcomes generally fail to find a positive relationship. Perhaps these ambiguities around what we mean by self-disclosure are also contributing to a degree of ambivalence in their application in the social work setting. However, there does seem to be sufficient evidence to support at least some use of self-disclosure, or more accurately what we have defined as transparency as being connected to building a positive relationship with service users. Because of this it is important that social workers pay attention to developing their competence in the appropriate use of self-disclosure, avoiding potential problems while harnessing the positive relationship benefits to be gained from demonstrations of their active involvement and engagement in service users' experiences. It should be noted that self-disclosure is not a substitute for knowledge and skill.

Exercise 5 Be prepared

Remember that there are different types of self-disclosure. While the terminology in the literature is confusing, there is basic separation between disclosure that is about your personal life outside of work and that which is clearly work-related, including what's happening while you are engaging with the service user. Knox and Hill (2003, p. 530) provided a useful categorisation of seven different types of disclosure. These involved disclosure of: facts, feelings, insight, strategy, reassurance/support, challenge and disclosure of immediacy. They summarise their findings (2003, p. 538) by saying that 'When used sparingly, when containing nonthreatening and moderately intimate content, and when done in the service of the client, therapist self-disclosure can help establish and enhance a therapeutic relationship, model appropriate disclosure, reassure and support clients, and facilitate gains in insight and action'.

Think about the particular setting you are working in. What issues might emerge among the service users that would resonate with your own experiences? Do you feel ready to manage your reactions to working in a setting where personal memories, problems you have dealt with or problems that remain unresolved for you might arise? If you continue to have unresolved issues pertinent to the setting, is that an appropriate setting for you to work in at this time? Do you have access to supervision that will provide a suitable place to differentiate between your own experiences and that of the service users you will meet? Is self-disclosure likely to create an unsafe situation for you or the service user? What impact, if any, might self-disclosure have on your ability to carry out the responsibilities of your role?

Skills

Develop an understanding of the goals of self-disclosure and in particular the distinction between being transparent and disclosing more personal information. In your setting, take the opportunity to discuss what levels or aspects of your professional or personal experiences are appropriate to disclose. Familiarise yourself with what the literature identified as helpful and potentially harmful aspects of self-disclosure (see summary in Table 2.1). Develop other skills that can complement or substitute for self-disclosure.

Reflect on power issues

Take some time to reflect on your reactions to the service user asking questions about your experiences, professional or personal. Consider the power relationship between you and the service user. In particular, reflect on the level of disclosure that you are expecting/

TABLE 2.1 Points to consider about self-disclosure, self-involvement and transparency

Use therapist self-disclosure because it is a helpful intervention, but use it infrequently and judiciously	Return the focus to the client after therapist self-disclosure
Use appropriate content in therapist self-disclosures	Consider using disclosures of immediacy
Use appropriate levels of intimacy in therapist self-disclosures	Consider using disclosures to facilitate termination
Fit the disclosure to the particular client's needs and preferences	Ask clients about their responses to therapist self-disclosure
Have appropriate reasons for self-disclosing	Return the focus to the client after therapist self-disclosure

Adapted from Knox and Hill (2003).

requiring of the service user and identify appropriate opportunities where you can model an open response to the service user's questions. Many of the questions can be answered without creating the problems discussed with regard to self-disclosure and may serve to prevent creating barriers in communication that can grow when a service user experiences you as distant, disinterested, aloof or controlling.

Social work and self-disclosure

Much of the discussion about self-disclosure emanates from counselling settings other than social work. Despite this, the literature does make a case for social work to consider the potential use of self-disclosure in the social work repertoire (Woodcock Ross 2011; Knight 2012). The cautionary and controversial nature of the support for self-disclosure should be taken seriously. Social workers are working towards evidence-informed practice which embodies the values of respect and genuineness in their relationship with service users. They are also committed to hearing the voice of service users. With these goals in mind it might be useful to reconsider the place of self-disclosure in the social work repertoire of skills. In particular, to evaluate the broader definitions discussed in this chapter which emphasise not the disclosure of more personal or intimate information, but rather a responsiveness to service user vulnerability when they are attempting to engage with social worker services.

It should be acknowledged that the context within which the relationship with service users is developed should also be taken into account. There are differences to consider between a counselling setting where a service user requests help and may actually attend for counselling at a formal venue as distinct from many social work contexts. Social workers may be attempting to develop a relationship with a service user in a situation where they have been imposed on the service user. This may give rise to a service user having the perception that this is an adversarial rather than a therapeutic conversation. In some situations the social worker too may see these conversations as more challenging and adversarial, depending on the reason for being involved and the seriousness of the issues being addressed. These circumstances may certainly make building any type of alliance with the service user more difficult. In this context any decision about applying self-disclosure needs to take account of worker and service user safety and where indicated maintenance of more formal boundaries may be more appropriate.

Finally, remember that self-disclosure is only one skill that can be applied in building trust and empathy. The research suggests that judicious and moderate self-disclosure may suffice (Cooper 2011). In fact, Knox and Hill (2003, p. 262) go further and advise that self-disclosure should be infrequent. Self-disclosure is not enough in itself and may not necessarily be required if other relationship-building skills are used, for example reflection, expressing empathy, checking accuracy of empathic responses, etc. Cooper (2011) discusses evidence that self-disclosure is a 'promising and probably effective' element of the therapeutic relationship. This guarded endorsement of self-disclosure may contribute to social workers cautious approach to its use.

The skill of silence

While consider the place of talking in counselling it seems appropriate to look at the place of silence. This does not imply that these two skills are opposites. Rather, they are two aspects of the same communication movement within counselling. The flow from talk to silence and back to talk creates what might be called a rhythm between the social worker and the service user. So far we have discussed the importance of not allowing talking by the social worker to take over and overshadow the more important elements of listening and thinking. Talking should always be accompanied by thinking, as should listening. Silence shares that trait. It is best when it is a purposeful silence.

In the most simplistic terms there are three formats for silence:

- Silence on the part of the social worker as they listen to the service user speak
- Silence on the part of the service user as they allow the social work to speak
- A silence shared by the two people in the conversation. These shared silences can be either productive or counterproductive and may shift from one to the other depending on the duration

Let's look at this a bit more. When asked a question that needs some thought, the social worker or the service user might take a few minutes to think of a response; this is viewed as a productive silence. It is about taking the time to think. In Chapter 10 on motivation we will look at this notion of contemplation as a precursor to change. Contemplation often involves a productive silence. Another example of a productive silence might be when a very emotional conversation has occurred and both parties feel that respectful moment (or more) of silence is actually a positive way to share the experience. Such a silence could be considered as an opportunity to process your response to the emotion. Silence is an opportunity to give space to the service user to compose their thoughts and consider what and how they want to express themselves. These silences are respectful, relationship-enhancing and productive.

On the other hand, there are silences that can be counterproductive. This is a very different interpretation of silence, which considers silence as disruptive, uncooperative or even aggressive. Silence may be misunderstood by either the social worker or the service user. This difference in understanding or reading of silence can make it counterproductive. A negative interpretation of silence can emerge where the social worker is uncomfortable with silence. Silence may be viewed as resistance or a form of conflict. It may also be seen as a breakdown in communication. This breakdown may create a sense of frustration. Sometimes the social worker's response to silence on the part of the service user is to talk more. Talking more, as we have discussed, is not always helpful. Here the skill of thinking is important.

Exercise 6 Some things to think about

What is the silence about; is there likely to be any productive outcome of this silence; is the silence difficult because of my own response to silence or is it difficult for the service user and should I intervene to take the pressure off; would some discomfort be a good thing in terms of sticking with uncomfortable feelings associated with the topic we are discussing; what do I know about this service user's ability to cope with silences; are they using it to think things through, or is it more likely to be a form of defiance, or a way of protecting themselves against being vulnerable; if it is about being defiant, have I contributed to this need to be defiant; or is use of silence a position that is contributing to the difficulties being experienced by the service user?

These are just some examples of what you need to think about. You can see that your theoretical knowledge informs your view of what silence is about and will also provide direction about how best to use silence. For example, some theoretical views would see silences as resistance, while others see the same silences as the service user's way of cooperating. When working with a social construction lens, for example, I think about silence on the part of the service user as perhaps their opportunity to feel some sense of control when they are feeling particularly vulnerable.

You need to think through what is the best response: start talking or allow the silence, or use a prompt to dissipate the tension but then allow the silence to continue for a while. Combining the skills of using talk and silence, informed by knowledge based on theory and method, helps you to make good decisions about silence. As a social worker you need to read the silence, what it might mean for the service user, what it means to you and what the most productive way of moving forward is. Retaining the silence as a means of putting pressure on the service user is most likely going to be counterproductive. It may increase tension and work against enhancing engagement and facilitating disclosure. However, interrupting the silence where it is actually being productive is also going to disrupt the development of engagement and disclosure.

Develop the skill of using silence

Exercise 7 Balancing talk and silence

To develop your skill in manging talk and silence you need to work on your self-awareness. Ask yourself:

How do you respond to silence?
Do you respond to silence differently in different situations?
In what situations are you aware that you enjoy silence?
Have you ever used silence to give yourself a sense of control?
Do you break silence to regain a sense of control?
Do you think you feel more secure when you are talking or being silent?

If you haven't had the opportunity to give some thought to these points in your training as a social worker, you will need to create opportunities to do this. Different things work for different people, as we know so well in social work, so you need to find a way that suits you. Some things that might help would be peer discussion or supervision. An opportunity to work on your general skills development would also work: just make sure that you get a chance to think and talk about silence and what it means for you, particularly in your professional life.

Final comments

This chapter has explored talking as one of three overarching skills in social work. Whether you want to think about it as a counselling skill or not really does not detract from the importance of understanding the place of talking in our interaction with service users. This chapter has considered talking and silence as interconnected activities whose impact can be optimised when we are informed by the critical skill of thinking or processing. We have also explored the controversial debate about self-disclosure as part of social work 'talking'. We will now look more closely at some of the micro skills employed in social work counselling that are delivered through the medium of talk.

3 Listening

- Looking at listening as a familiar social skill and considering how that differs from employing it in a counselling social work context. Connecting active/informed listening to actually listening to the information.
- Exploring how the information we receive is categorised and stored and what happens to it before we act on it, which we will call processing.
- Setting tasks to assist in making connections between the readers' ability regarding listening skills and the challenge of developing these to a level of professional proficiently.
- Reflect on emotions and how they impact on the counselling process both for social worker and service user and specifically what that might look like in developing the specific skills in this chapter.

Introduction

We've established that communication is something that we all develop to some extent. Physical or cognitive factors may require that communication with and between some people takes on a level of skill beyond the basic talking and listening that is the focus of most of the communication literature. So too the stage of development: the ages of the communicators indicate what skills are necessary to understand and be understood. Key social work counselling skills have been identified in the introductory chapter as listening, thinking and talking. This simplification can help to organise how we can explore the skills, but it is useful to note here that there is a complex interactivity between the skills.

Talking, listening and thinking: interconnected

It could be argued that talking can happen with little attention to listening or thinking; for example, the old adage recommending us to engage brain before speaking probably arose as a warning for those who talk without thinking. It's possible that thinking can happen independently of talking and probably can happen without listening; however, thinking would be limited by lack of inflow of new information that can be gained through verbal and non-verbal listening. It's difficult to envisage any form of real listening that does not involve thinking. Opinions may differ on this point, but in my experience it is helpful to use thinking skills in conjunction with listening to assist in interpreting and organising what is said so that I have a better chance of remembering. It would be worth considering not just listening and hearing but also remembering as associated skills. Have you really listened to a service user if you can't remember what they have said? It is not possible for most of us to remember all that is said, so thinking does play a part in distinguishing information to be or not to be retained or responded to. Experience and working with service users are key to ensuring that you don't assign important information to the non-retained category. A non-retained point may be remembered or triggered by new information and may then get swapped into a 'retain that' category. For the purposes of social work counselling, listening and thinking are co-dependent activities and unlike social talking the skill of talking in social work should always be associated with both listening and thinking.

While we have different levels of innate communication skills, we can acquire additional skills and proficiency through training and practice. As you might expect, to some extent the same is true of listening. Speaking and making yourself understood are connected to developmental and cultural factors. Even where physical factors create perceived barriers to hearing, or auditory faculties, or to picking up visual cues as with some visual impairment and other perceptual issues, a person is still communicating. For more discussion on special communication needs you can check out

Koprowska (2010, pp. 126–139). While acknowledging these particular needs, the focus of this book is on counselling that is based on communicating that draws on listening skills as a core component of the activity. However, it will consider a much more complex appreciation of listening as a skill and in particular explore how that skill is applied in a professional 'helping' or counselling context. To learn about and understand listening as a skill, we need to unravel multiple layers of what is involved in the business of listening and consider what the connection is between listening and hearing. To do this we will start with the familiar, our own everyday listening skills.

Social listening

In a social context we have lots of ways of describing not listening; for example, listening with half an ear, I switched off, you never hear what I'm saying, you just don't listen, you were miles away, you were daydreaming, etc. The opposite would be something like: I'm all ears. We seem to have less about listening other than the global comment I am/you are a good listener. What does that really mean? Before we can really appreciate the professional level of skill required for listening in counselling and social work, it is useful to explore what we think listening is in our everyday life.

Exercise 8 Feeling heard and understood

Feeling heard is one result of good listening skills. This leads to building the therapeutic relationship. Think about times when you did feel heard/listened to:

What was happening?
Who did you talk to?
Was it easy or difficult to express yourself?
What was the listener doing?

What signs did you pick up on that told you that you were being heard?
How did the listener respond non-verbally then verbally?
How did the listener encourage and support you?
What was the impact of felling that someone was listening to you?

Listening and processing: how they work together even in social listening

Example: *Listening*

You are out with your friends on a night out. You may be in a noisy pub or at a party. You are part of the chat, communicating with your friends. What's going on? How important is the content of the conversations. Given the context, both social and environmental, it is hard to pay attention to content. Socially the purpose is enjoyment, fun and building a sense of being part of a group. The environment is consistent with these goals: lots of people all talking at the same time, loud music, probably alcohol being consumed depending on the cultural setting. How much of that communication will you remember the next day, and is that even important?

Processing: factors to think about

Situation: What if a friend because of the casual setting talks about something they have been finding hard to discuss, will it be heard, and if it is heard will it be possible to pay attention, i.e. to attend to the disclosure in this setting, or will it get lost in the noise? Perhaps the choice to talk about it in this setting is influenced by the context; it can be said and lost; having consumed alcohol (s)he is less inhibited/ guarded; perhaps it is said inadvertently and (s)he will regret it in the morning if they remember they said it; perhaps it is said hoping that someone will pick it up.

Context: The social or physical context is obviously important and we have identified some points about the context that might make a difference to whether the disclosure is heard, listened to and/or responded to. There are other contextual factors that might make a difference: how well do you know the person; what level of shared information is typical in your relationship, is this something very different; what is your disposition at the time, are you interested in something else that's going on rather than talking to this friend?

Concern: Is this friend someone you have been concerned about. In the context of a pre-existing concern, despite the social/physical context, you may be more alert to the disclosure. It may be that you have been more or less waiting for an opportunity to find out what's going on. In those circumstances you may well switch gear and take the opportunity to pay attention to the disclosure.

Content: The actual information itself might make a difference. If the disclosure is that they have broken up from a relationship you may: be relieved/you thought it was not a good relationship anyway; you may be shocked and even more concerned because you know that it was very serious relationship that was working well for your friend; is your friend sounding really distressed/possibly depressed/angry and is that more or less worrying? What if the disclosure is that there has been some physical violence in a relationship? Or that (s)he has gotten into trouble using drugs?

Response: There are so many things that your friend might say and of course you will have a different response depending on the content, what it means to you, what you think it might mean to your friend, what knowledge you have about the issue, what your understanding is about how serious that issue might be and ultimately whether you are prepared to attend to the issue your friend has raised. If you are prepared to pay attention then you will probably have to do something to find out more about what is happening and what your friend needs. If you decide it's not appropriate, not your business, it is just your friend being drunk, (s)he is not a close friend so you don't want to get involved then you can: not listen to what was said; dismiss it; minimise it; put it off until another time. We have lots of skills to help us ignore paying attention to what we hear.

Give some further consideration to this or another situation that fits in with your life. Generate ideas context, content and concern in relation to what your friend might say and then consider how each of these elements would impact on your response. You might find it helpful to make a list of possibilities under each of the three headings that will help you to see how they interact with each other to influence your response.

This is a very simplified exercise to help you consider the factors that impact our listening skills. The point of the exercise is to begin the process of finding out about the layers of skills you have already developed to manage listening in your everyday life. As mentioned, you hear much more than you listen to. Listening involves paying attention to what you hear and actively engaging with what the other person is talking about. As you can see, it's not hearing that counts, it's listening, but active listening which is really paying attention. What happens next is shaped by our thinking; decisions can happen often in less than a few seconds and these dictate what we do next. This thinking can go unnoticed in our social world because we are so accustomed to the process, but in our professional world we need to become more conscious about how the skill of listening works and what factors in our thinking process impact what we decide to do next. For this reason this chapter will look at listening and the thinking process to help us track how the interaction between these skills shapes our responses.

Tuning out

Think about how and when you find it more difficult to listen. This can happen even when you have initiated the conversation. You can ‘tune out’ either consciously or unconsciously, hence the need to be really paying attention to this skill. Even when you are more aware of this risk of tuning out/not listening well it is going to happen; it’s more important that you know yourself well enough to recognise the signs and address them. Once you notice you can rectify and pay attention, re-engage with listening actively. There are so many reasons why you might drop your attention when trying to listen; for example, listening is tiring so you might just drop your attention temporarily, the speaker might raise a difficult topic, you may be feeling overwhelmed, you may be in a hurry, you’ve heard it before, you are impatient to get on to some other point; you may be reacting to the speaker, finding their tone of voice difficult to listen to, be reacting to the speaker being angry and so feel defensive, feeling upset by the topic, annoyed by the speaker, frustrated, getting distracted, getting caught up in something that was said earlier and not following what’s being said now. It is useful to think about a variety of situations and discover more about the sorts of situations where you might not be listening as well as you can. Gordon (1970) wrote about how we can block ourselves from listening; these activities can be use instead of listening. However, noticing if you are using any of the techniques can help you to address why you need to use them and then of course help you be more aware of what might be going on such that you find it hard to listen.

When you begin to notice where you use these blocks then also reflect on how they might have an impact on the speaker, a good place to start is to think about when someone has used one of the blocks on you: what was that like? When you are doing any of these you are not listening. See more about these blocks later in this chapter. In the traditional psychoanalytic framework these might be seen as defence mechanisms whereby we use ‘blocks’ or defences to protect us from painful experiences. This highlights that there may be personal reasons why we use these blocks need to be addressed, particularly where they interfere with developing the skills of listening as required for professional practice. Supervision and reflective practice are important here and will be considered in Chapter 7.

Listening and thinking

Exercise 9 Hold that thought

You are with a group of friends and there is a lively conversation going on. You start to contribute with a story about a recent experience you had that relates to the topic of the conversation; let's say the discussion is people at work who try to take all the credit for ideas. You start with an example of someone at a meeting who was doing this with one of your ideas and before you get to the end of the story one of the group says, Oh I know exactly what you mean, the same thing happened to me ... and goes on with their story.

Do you?

(1) Wait for the opportunity to jump back in to finish, e.g. well with me it was more like ... continue your story {this involves you not really listening to the other story because you are thinking of your own story and waiting to finish it}
OR
(2) Stop thinking about your story and move on to your friend's version {this involves focusing on the new story and listening to that}

Another example of hold that thought

You are involved in a discussion about booking holidays. One of the group mentions a website that offers great deals, but before you can follow up on it the conversation moves on to something else.

Do you?

(1) Move on with the chat and forget about the question you wanted to ask (listen to what's being said now)
(2) Hold that thought, make an opportunity to bring the conversation back to the website and ask about it (keep some of your attention on the question so you don't forget it and not fully listen until you get the answer you want)

The social worker's context

Professional listening happens between the social worker and the service user who come to the interaction with preconceived ideas, expectations and goals. The understanding and information that comes from listening must then be added and will influence those ideas, expectations and goals. In order to explain this we will consider it as a way of processing the information gathered through listening and Figure 3.1 maps out some of the filters that may be important to take into account in reaching the outcome of this processing skill. The map illustrates three phases in counselling.

Phase one: Building the relationship and developing an understanding of the issues.

Phase two: Processing that understanding though a range of filters. This involves being aware of a range of factors that influence what the social worker listens to and for and then how the social worker will interpret information they have gathered from listening. Processing is a key element in developing an understanding of the situation and ultimately will impact the next phase.

Phase three: Formulating a response and working towards an action plan.

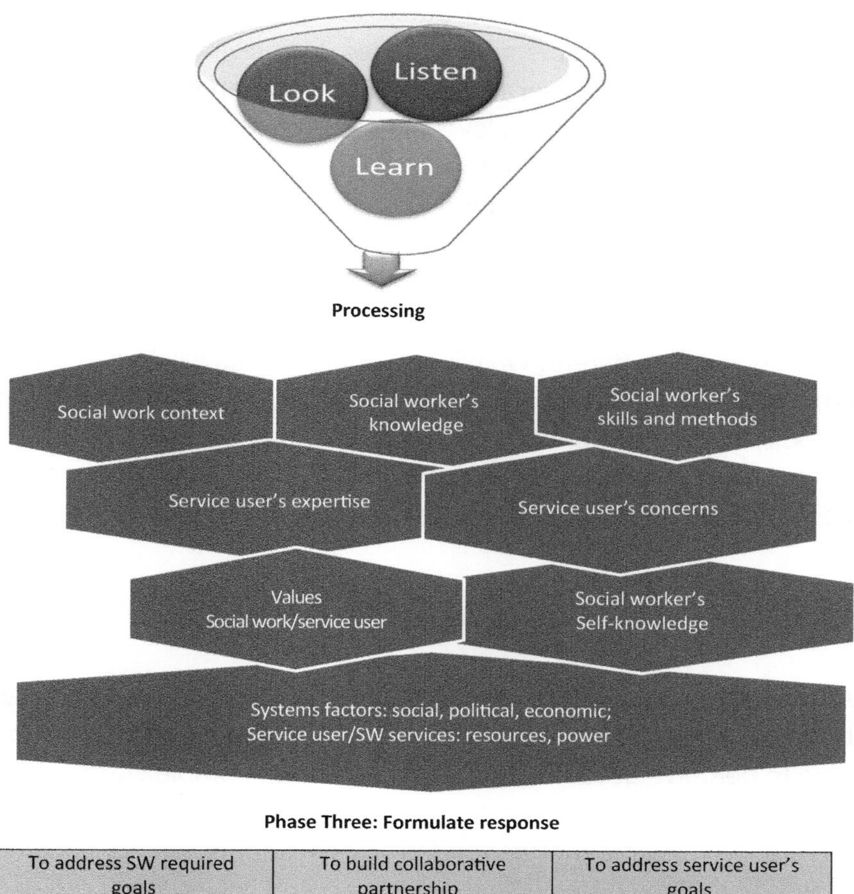

Figure 3.1 Map of three phases in the counselling process

Look, listen and learn

Listening is part of a repertoire of skills that combined provide us with the basis for developing the type of relationship with service users that is required if we are to work collaboratively with them around concerns and problems they encounter. It is important to remember that the skills are like notes in music; it's only when you play them together in a harmonious sequence that they work.

Listening and processing are skills that work almost simultaneously. Yet the skill of processing is one factor that differentiates listening as a profession from the listening as a skill we utilise in everyday life. By understanding these two skills and how they interact it becomes easier to distinguish between the listening we use in everyday life and the level of listening skill required in a professional counselling context.

We will look firstly at listening and processing as separate skills and then consider how processing adds to but also has the potential to limit listening. Both these skills are part of basic communication; it is the application of the skills in a professional 'helping' capacity that is different. We will look then at what will be familiar in terms of the use of these skills in your everyday life before beginning to explore how the professional listening and processing may differ not in its fundamental elements, but in the more advanced recognition and understanding of the purpose and more skilful application.

The concept of listening

According to Shebib (2003, p. 97) 'effective listeners need to hear, but simply hearing words is insufficient ... skilled listeners must be able to perceive associated relevant and often complex non-verbal information, such as voice tone or gesture, ... listening involves separating relevant information from irrelevant, assigning meaning to words and experiences, remembering and linking related data'. He goes on to remind us that 'for social workers listening is an act of acceptance and caring ... It is not passive but involves the task of trying to comprehend what is happening for the client' (Shebib 2003, p. 98). This definition of listening actually incorporates both listening and processing. The aspects of manging the information we learn about from listening fits more accurately with the skill of thinking which we will refer to processing (your cognitive skills processing information is a way of understanding part of the thinking activity) and we will explore this later in the chapter. Suffice to say that we are separating these two skills for consideration so that we can begin to understand how they interact. In practice, the listening and processing actually work so closely together that even experienced practitioners lose sight of the fact that they are two separate activities. In fact, one of the main challenges in learning how to use listening as a social work or counsellor is being able to recognise how processing impacts on listening and vice versa. As processing is actually part of thinking we will look at this in more detail in Chapter 4, which explores thinking as the third key social work counselling skill.

Listening in a professional context

The skill of good listening is connected to empathy because empathy is one way of expressing or demonstrating good listening. With social listening, for example between friends, there is typically an expectation of reciprocity: you were there for me so I'm here for you. Professional boundaries are different than friendship boundaries: with friendship there is reciprocity, a pre-existing trust, a mutual engagement outside of the problem. In a professional situation the social worker or counsellor has to develop a level of trust that supports the helping process without the pre-existing relationship or the expectation of mutuality. This may be a reason why it is important to redress this imbalance in the relationship. With friends you may be in the advisor role sometimes and the receiver at other times. If it seems you are always getting help then it may be undermining. It certainly risks creating a power imbalance or perhaps more accurately reinforcing a power differential that is already there. In particular with social work where there is already an authority aspect to the engagement then valuing the service user's input though good listening can demonstrate that you are trying to learn from the service user, that you acknowledge their expertise in their own lives and have respect for them even if you do not agree with what they are doing.

Listening: a core skill

Listening is the foundation of the counselling and social work relationship with service users. It is arguably the most critical aspect of building the relationship. Without that relationship there will be little opportunity to build trust, agree goals or work towards change. We have already acknowledged that we probably all have some listening skills, and perhaps because of this it is an underrated skill. Many of us think we do a pretty good job of listening. The focus of this chapter will be on the first aspect of this, exploring the concept of listening and what that means in counselling and social work. There will be some mention of how good listening is delivered, but this brings us into a whole range of additional skills which will be explored in more detail in the following chapters. Listening is a critical part of building the working relationship with service users, but is not in reality the starting place. Research supports the importance of listening. Cooper (2011, p. 44) states that 'correlational research suggests that listening – in the sense of providing clients with the space to talk, and actively attending to their verbal and non-verbal expressions – is experienced by many clients as one of the most facilitative aspects of therapy'. He later (2011, p. 45) comments that 'listening alone is not always enough, as people may appreciate a more balanced talking and listening relationship, in particular, one where some explanation of the helping process is provided'.

Different types of listening

Listening, then, as counselling skill is a complex mix of paying attention to information from the service user and adding that to your knowledge and value base and making sense of what you are listening to. I refer to this as *informed listening*. Listening to service users also involves 'as much as possible, accurately understanding their meaning' (Nelson-Jones 2011, p. 81). This may be viewed as *accurate listening*. However, you also want your listening to be effective. *Effective listening* is not just about gathering information and making sense of it, but is also about using listening to build a relationship with the service user. There are relationship and information dimensions to the application by the counsellor of the skill of listening. Wilkins and Whittaker (2017), in discussion on the findings in their study on social workers' use of participatory skills in child protection, make the point that demonstrating an understanding of the parent's perspective (showing empathy) was usually made easier if the worker could listen reflectively.

Reflective listening acknowledges the importance of being informed, i.e. taking account of your knowledge, values and professional reactions to the interaction with the service user. Reflective listening emphasises the importance of understanding the more personal and emotional responses to the interaction for both the social worker and service user. While the social worker is making sense of what's happening in the interaction, so too is the service user. This generates reactions, emotional, behavioural, cognitive and relational between both parties. Reflective listening allows the social worker to take these into account as they process what is happening for them during the interaction. Often reflective listening is enhanced after the actual interaction by accessing supervision where reflective practice can be supported and developed. Sometimes the combination of these aspects of listening are referred collectively as *active listening*. Active listening describes a cluster of skills that are used to increase the accuracy of understanding. 'Attending, being silent, summarising, paraphrasing, questioning and empathising are all essential skills of active listening … it becomes a continuous process of attending, hearing, exploring and deepening' (Shebib 2003, p. 103). As a skill, active listening is then a core requirement of good social work practice as it 'builds rapport because it shows that the listener is non-judgemental and is interested in understanding' (Shebib 2003, p. 104).

Checklist of types of listening

- Active listening
- Accurate listening
- Informed listening

- Effective listening
- Reflective listening

A good listener

Good listeners are curious, they want to understand and they know that they don't know, they know how and when to wait, they show they are interested without interrupting, they don't have another question or an answer ready, they don't finish your sentence or respond by saying 'I know'. They want to listen to others more than to themselves, they know how to signal (verbal and non-verbal invitations to talk/keep talking). As Dalai Lama XIV said, 'When you talk, you are only repeating what you already know. But if you listen, you may learn something new'. You risk hearing what you listen for, hearing what fits with your expectations, listening for what you expect: preconceived ideas based on prejudice, preferred knowledge base, or experience.

Good listening, then, is not about solving but searching, it's not judging but respecting, not hearing what you expect but being open to the unexpected, not hearing what you were listening for or listening to only what you want to hear. In a study on developing an analysis of listening, Witkin and Trochim (1997) proposed that based on their findings there were a number of important clusters that formed different types of listening.

1. **Critical listening:** concentration, conscious, critical listening, discrimination, evaluation, gathering information, meaning and organisation
2. **Sensory impression:** attention, auditory processing, images, patterns, perception, receiving, sensory impressions

tied with

3. **Active listening:** active, affective processes, alertness, appreciation, conclusions, effort, motivation, purposeful

activity, responding, sustaining, voluntary, echoic memory (minus echoic memory)

4. **Context:** constructs, context, experiences (previous), feedback, filters
5. **Composite processes:** association, composite processing, decoding, mental activity, recall, retrieving information, storing information.

Adapted from: Witkin and Trochim (1997).

The interaction between listening and processing is clear in these identified aspects of listening. Good listening involves not just being alert and active but includes thinking or processing what you listen to; developing impressions, generating associations, decoding, applying critical thinking and taking cognisance of the context. All of these then assist in creating a suitable response/ follow on from the listening activity.

Barriers to listening

Earlier we mentioned that in social listening you may consciously or unconsciously 'tune out' from listening. This can happen for many reasons and it is worth paying attention to when this happens to you. What situations does it happen in, and is it the topic, the people, or something going on with you that contributes to the not listening? The point is that it can and does happen. Not listening may not be a very popular trait in a friend, but it can be a serious problem in a professional context. That is not to say that your attention may drift or that you may, as we have already explored, get caught up in something that was already said and not move on with the conversation. It is different with listening as a skill in the professional context. In social work counselling it is widely recognised that listening is a pivotal skill that we must develop and nurture.

Exercise 10 Barriers to listening

Think about these as possible barriers to listening professionally. Go through each of the blocks listed and try to think of at least one example of when you used it or could see why you might use it:

1. Ordering, directing or commanding
2. Mourning, cautioning or threatening
3. Giving advice, making suggestions, providing solutions
4. Persuading with logic, arguing, lecturing
5. Telling people what they should do; moralising
6. Disagreeing, judging, criticising or blaming
7. Agreeing, approving, operating
8. Shaming, ridiculing or labelling
9. Interrupting or analysing
10. Reassuring, sympathising or consoling
11. Questioning or probing
12. Withdrawing, distracting, humouring, changing the subject

(Gordon, 1970)

Not listening has been described by Gordon's 12 roadblocks (Gordon, 1970). It is useful to consider which of these you are most skilled at using when you don't want to listen to someone. We use these skills sometimes consciously but also unconsciously. The purpose of the chapter is to make you more conscious of the blocks to listening you may employ and to understand when they are helpful and when they are disruptive and destructive.

The result of using these barriers is that you cannot listen effectively. Goh (2012, pp. 595–597) identified what he referred to as bad habits that impact on our ability to listen actively. He suggested three main categories. 'Firstly, mind wandering, multi-tasking, thinking ahead; secondly, external distractions such as noisy environment, interruptions and time pressure; and finally filters that prevented active listening. Filters might include factors such as a preconceived idea about the situation or prioritising a particular theoretical interpretation such that the service user's perception is not listened to/heard'.

As professionals we must have a level of self-awareness that can assist us in recognising when/if we are engaging in these 'bad habits' or barriers. They may be used when the professional listener is under pressure for time, has some unacknowledged reaction to the speaker or the topic or just does not want to engage in a conversation at that time. It can also be a reaction to a perception of how the speaker sees them. Even as a professional listener you can dislike dealing with conflict or find listening to anger more challenging and attempt to avoid it. Self-awareness is facilitated through the skills associated with self-reflection and these will be considered in more detail later. We cannot rely on always tuning into our reactions and so when building your skill in listening it is really useful to get feedback from others. It is particularly useful to get that feedback from the service users themselves. Feedback may not necessarily be a formal evaluation of your listening skill, but it will almost certainly be evident when you attempt to use reflecting, summarising in conjunction with checking in with the service user if you have understood what they are communicating to you.

'Hold that thought' in social work practice

You can apply this same exercise to your work. When a service user raises a point that catches your attention and you want to find out more about it, do you keep that in your mind until you get a chance to follow up on it and as a result risk missing some of the detail of what is being said while you 'hold the question'?

On the other hand, how do you 'hold that thought' when you are hearing a lot of information and you are trying to listen to it all?

Listening is closely associated with reflection and empathy. These two aspects of skills help you to take time to check that you are listening to and hearing the service user's points/information and also to check that you understand their story. We will look at these in more detail later; however, for example: using reflective summaries intermittently though a conversation/interview facilitates working with the service user to keep you on track. It is also an opportunity for you to check out points you want to follow in a respectful way, acknowledging that you have heard what was said and that this has raised a different point/question so that the service user and you can follow the train of thought. This makes it easier to listen, hear, interpret and store the information.

In some situations it may be necessary to take notes or fill up a form with key information. It is important to develop a skill in doing this that allows you to take time out to write but which does not interfere with your active listening. Writing and listening are difficult to do at the same time.

Listening to yourself

One of the most fundamental challenges in effective listening for counselling and social work is negotiating the balance between listening to yourself and listening to another. The difficulty is that you have to be able to do both but in a very different way than you have been used to doing in your social/pre-professional life.

Let's look at listening to yourself in a personal or social context. You will probably know the saying that you should listen to your 'gut', or sometimes if you are having an argument the other person might say 'just listen to yourself' or 'can you hear what you're saying?'. This might be said in a defensive way to deflect the argument or even in an angry way, but it can be used to signal that for them at that moment you are not making sense or that you are making the situation worse or perhaps that you are contradicting your own arguments. Whatever the intent the message is that you need to listen to what you are saying. So listening to yourself can serve to provide you with a level of self-protection, can be a method for checking if you are making sense, or if you are being rational and consistent in your thinking. All of these can come out in what you say. So that's a very simplified version of listening to yourself in everyday life. Consider how important this ability to listen to yourself is in terms of keeping a check on how you are thinking, how you are expressing yourself and also listening for signs of risk or potential problems.

Challenge for the social worker: valuing listening above talking

The skill of listening to yourself may be one that the service user has not developed or has lost confidence in. It may also be that the messages they are giving themselves have become unhelpful. Examples of listening to yourself in an unhelpful way might be: where you prioritise problem behaviour over helpful behaviours – I need alcohol to cope with stress. Or you might convince yourself that a problematic behaviour is not a problem or that it is only a problem for the social worker/counsellor/someone else – why is everyone on your back about this, you just don't understand. Another example might be listening to the message that you are not good enough, that you can't change or that nobody cares about what happened to you. Some of these messages may unfortunately be a reflection of the situation the service user finds themselves in where they may be estranged from family and friends, but sometimes this is about listening to the negative and losing the positives. Exploration of cognitive theory will provide more information on how this notion of listening to yourself may be unhelpful (see Loughran 2010, pp. 77–82). Part of listening as a skill in counselling and social work is engaging the service user in conversation so that they can listen to themselves, but importantly that they listen to the more positive messages. This means switching that balance in your professional role from listening to yourself to facilitating the service user to listen to themselves. In counselling and social work, listening is learning. By the social worker listening they are learning about what's really going on. The service user gets the chance to listen to themselves and begin to notice inconsistencies and negative self-talk. Listening to the service user is one way to facilitate building trust and encouraging disclosure.

I mentioned earlier that you need to negotiate the balance between listening to yourself and listening to another. While building a collaborative relationship with a service user requires you stepping back from listening to yourself talk, it does require that you listen to yourself in a different way. You need to be tuned in to factors other than speech that impact on you as you are listening. While the service user is talking and you are listening, you are also listening to your knowledge, values and experiences which help you to listen more effectively and start to organise the information you are getting from listening and even help you to formulate a response (processing). You also listen to that voice which helps you to discern the tone or direction of the conversation. You can pick up if the conversation is building a relationship or creating barriers, whether your listening is eliciting appropriate information or not. Fundamentally, there is a difference in the application of listening in counselling and social work from a social type of listening in that social listening presumes some level of reciprocity, while professional listening predominantly focuses on the needs of the service user. Nelson-Jones (2011, p. 82) offered this distinction between listening in a social and professional context: 'Social conversations are geared towards meeting the needs of both participants ... counselling conversations primarily emphasize meeting client's needs: they place a high premium on rewarding clients' by listening and showing understanding of them'.

It might be helpful to look at listening as a skill that builds on or relies on the application of other skills over the period of a conversation. Good listening means that the social worker must recognise that listening is a skill that works as part of a more elaborate suite of skills. As mentioned earlier, what we are referring to listening is actually demonstrated through the application of a range of interactions or communication skills. Unless we have conveyed to the service user that we are listening then the interaction will not be constructive. Performing listening is not a passive receptive action but rather needs to let the speaker know that the listener is actually paying attention, being respectful, committed to learning from them and most importantly trying to make sense of what they are hearing so that they can better understand and empathise with the service user's situation.

Exercise 11 Context, concern and content

With an appreciation of the component parts of listening, let's try another exercise. Using a list of all the parts of listening we have considered, pick one of your favourite television or online interviewers. This time I want you to rate the interviewer on the basis of the aspects of listening in the chapter so far. Sometimes just thinking about what you like and what you don't like about the way the interview is conducted is enough to help with unravelling skills and the application of the theory of engagement. We can use the same considerations to guide us that we used in the example of social listening.

Context: So you are listening to an interview which is then technically a public conversation. That already shapes the context. Whatever is said will be heard by people and there is little control over who will hear it. You don't know if people will be listening attentively or whether they will pick one point made and repeat this out of the context in which it was raised. In some interviews the content is agreed beforehand and if that is the case the person will be able to decide beforehand what they intend to reveal and what will remain private. But there is already a difference between, for example, a pop culture-type interview and a political interview. Typically, an interview will specialise in one or the other, mostly because of this context issue. If you are interviewing about music or movies then you need to demonstrate some familiarity with these in the same way that if it's political you need to be familiar with the issues involved. These 'specialist' aspects of the conversation are often couched in some of the social interaction/conversation so that the basic listening skills are still required. However, now there is a preparatory aspect to the listening. You are utilising the social, asking questions, eliciting information and listening to responses to set the scene a different focus of the conversation later.

Watch how this is done. Things to look for when it's a group of people are if they already connected by an interest or some other angle. If not, which, if any, skills does the interviewer draw on to engage the different people in the conversation? If it's a single person, how does the interviewer start the conversation, at what point and in what way is the focus of the interview introduced and then watch out for the style in terms of asking unprepared challenging questions and working through a prepared set of topics where the interviewee can use the conversation to get their own point across unchallenged. For example, you will notice the prepared topics when the interviewer asks a direct question and frames it in a story that has not yet been raised in the conversation. Another pointer in what I will call commercial interviews is sometimes how little the interviewer is actually listening. You might notice this by spotting a change in topic which is not connected to the previous response. Sometimes this is facilitated by having a note card or sheet that the interviewer draws attention to in order to indicate they are moving on to a specific question. See what skills you can spot and make note of them so you can compare them with another interview style.

Concern: Are they listening? What are the signs you notice that tells you they are interested, following the conversation. Are there verbal and visual clues that they are taking in the responses to their question and connecting with the interviewee or are they preoccupied with getting through a set agenda? Listen out for interest or concern on the part of the interviewer. Some interviewers can present this genuineness through connecting with the person and giving them time to talk about the topic. This usually happens in one-to-one interviews rather than group interviews because it requires time and has a different pace than other 'commercial' interviews. You can begin to hear that giving people time to give a considered answer might involve silence; this does not often fit with the aims of such public interviews. In particular, if the conversation moves onto something more personal, it requires some connection and trust between interviewer and interviewee and yet this is a conversation that will be publically available. Sometimes you can pick up a better sense of this listening when you are listening to a documentary-style programme, where there is time to allow the interviewee to explain and explore the topic under consideration.

Example: I remember listening to an interviewer ask a member of the public about a very sensitive issue. The person revealed very personal information. The interviewer was skilled at making a connection with the person, they gave all the signals that they were interested and concerned and offered no more than prompts to keep the person talking. Such was that connection that they seemed to get engaged with the interviewer and forget the context, that it was a live broadcast. Would you consider this to be great listening? Probably it was very skilled use of listening skills to draw out a person; however, as a counsellor what I heard was overexposure of a vulnerable person. They got caught up in the conversation and forgot it was not just between the interviewer and themselves. This might seem like a great skill to have, but it must be used in conjunction with the guidance of a value base. For social work the corollary would be a service user telling you too much before they have a relationship with you and then withdrawing because they feel overexposed.

Content: Often in these 'commercial' interviews that content is already in the public domain or the point of the interview is to bring the information to the public's attention. In these situations the content is then known beforehand. There may be some unexpected points that emerge as the conversation progresses, but by and large there is a focus on a previously known content. The interviewer knows what they are looking for and so listening is less significant than directing the interview towards a specific outcome.

Response: In listening to a commercial interview it is useful to consider to what extent the interviewer actually employs listening skills. Is this context more given to the exploration of asking questions than listening to answers? Can this medium cope with silence? Listen out for the interviewer drawing out a topic by keeping the focus on that topic, asking follow-on questions, giving signs of empathic responses. Use your understanding of good listening and communication skills to notice what is happening.

Comment: Interviewing is another term for communication or conversation. Thompson (2011, p. 88) clarifies that there are many different types of interviews. For a police officer it may refer to an interrogation, for a recruitment consultant it could be a job interview and for a social worker the term can refer to either a formal or informal meeting with a client. As discussed in the first chapter the variability in terminology about this interaction between social worker and service user can pose a problem when certain aspects of the social work interview are dismissed. When the concept of an interview excludes acknowledgement of the therapeutic context of the interaction, it is misleading for both social workers and service users. All social worker interaction with service users, whether they are called interview, conversation or assessments, should have at their core the therapeutic relationship and a therapeutic agenda. The social worker's role and professional responsibility presupposes that the interaction and communication is shaped by the rationale of being a helping process.

Processing as a counselling skill

The concept of processing will be included as an element of the broader definition of the skill of thinking, which will be explored in Chapter 4. However, it is important to note the relationship between thinking/processing and active listening – you will see that it is difficult to identify where its influence begins and ends. For the sake of simplifying what is involved, we will mention here how processing is associated with listening. Processing influences what information we actually listen to, receive and remember. It then shapes how we interpret and respond to situations as we understand them. In the context of social work and counselling it is this processing of information that leads us to the decision about what if any action we will take.

As we have already discussed, listening does not take place in a vacuum. Processing is part of all communication. In the context of counselling and social work, however, it takes on a different significance. Processing in social conversation, if it is even recognised at all, might be regarded as just an instinctive reaction to information. We may pass off our responses to what we hear and see as nothing more than a natural reaction, but processing in social work and counselling is recognised as an important skill that we need to understand and develop. It is associated not only with listening but with all aspects of counselling.

There are many factors that are taken into account in the thinking/processing skill and because it has been identified as a key social work counselling skill we will discuss 'thinking' further in Chapter 4. The easiest way to outline the connection between listening and processing is to think about it as a set of filters that listening passes through on the way to being registered as 'heard' or taken on board as information.

Filters through which listening is processed include, to name a few, preconceived ideas, previous experiences personal and professional, theoretical preferences, methodological preferences, research informed ideas, interpretation of what is said, context and purpose of the 'conversation', political ideology, religious and cultural influences, power differences, social, economic and even educational disadvantages, attitude to and response to the service users. Because these filters are also associated with the broader skill of thinking, we will explore these in more detail in the next chapter.

Final comments

Social workers might find it helpful to think about the need to be ALERT. We may be familiar with ideas of being culturally alert. In other words, making sure that we are aware of our own cultural and social formation and the need to be competent to recognise and respect cultural and social norms that differ from our own. The suggestion of being ALERT as described here goes beyond cultural alertness to encompass a way of interaction with service users that can act as a guide to social workers in counselling and therapeutic interactions.

A: ask affirming questions
L: listen constructively
E: engage empathically
R: reflect in service users' language and reflect on your own thoughts, feelings and actions
T: thoughtfulness; here this refers not only to being thoughtful of service users in a supportive and concerned way, but also to be cognisant of the professional boundaries of the interaction and being aware of the filters through which you process your listening prior to responding to service users' disclosure and communication

The reality is a service user is talking to you in your professional capacity. They deserve that you employ the range of knowledge, skills and values that have been core aspects of your professional formation. This means drawing on theoretical knowledge that may pertain to the service user's experiences, challenges and hopes, to think through the options that such frameworks might generate, to process these in the context of a value base that privileges respect for service users and commitment to the care and protection of those for whom you have responsibility.

4 Thinking, processing and reflective practice

- Consider the place of thinking in social communication.
- Discuss the use of the terms, thinking, processing and reflective practice as the differences in thinking skills required for professionally competent social work practice.
- Explore informed and critical thinking as a pivotal social work counselling skill.
- Consider challenges for counselling in social work attributable to lack of acknowledgement of thinking and processing skill: when theory and thinking skills are invisible.

Introduction

As you have hopefully picked up by now, this text promotes thinking as one of the most important skills for counselling social work. Thinking is, of course, an activity that forms part of our everyday life, but the level of competence and proficiency required in applying thinking as a skill in a professional setting is often difficult to appreciate and to practice. We will consider, firstly, where thinking fits in with our social skills before we explore what is involved in developing your thinking skills to the professional level of competence required for social work practice. To assist in distinguishing the different aspects of thinking in social work, thinking will be presented as comprising three stages: thinking, processing and reflecting. These aspects will be explored and set in the social work context. We will also consider thinking for professional practice and explore ways to help us think about thinking by discussing the ideas of informed, critical and reflective thinking. The various factors that need to be thought will be identified and conceptualised as sets of thinking filters.

Thinking as part of social communication skills

The skill of thinking is related to the thinking that happens for all of us as part of our social interactions. However, the level of thinking and the content of this thinking is substantially different in the context of professionally qualified competence.

Thinking is a cognitive activity and of course there are biopsychosocial theories that offer interpretations on the nature of that activity. However, for the purposes of this chapter we will take a more focused view by exploring some ideas to help us to think about thinking as a skill in social work counselling.

Considering the skills of talking and listening in relation to their everyday or social use is probably easy to follow. However, considering the skill associated with processing is less obvious in our normal social conversation. We probably do not pay much attention to how we process the information we gather around us and may indeed spend very little time thinking about or processing the information. One explanation for this might be that social conversation happens in a very spontaneous and natural manner and to some extent at a progressive and a very unconscious level. In familiar and well-established relationships we probably do not spend much time giving consideration to our responses. Such consideration may be more associated with communication where some difficulties have emerged and some thought needs to go into how the issues or misunderstandings can be resolved. Not so in counselling social work situations. Indeed, professional communications, especially ones in which the social worker has undertaken responsibilities at some level for leading the conversation in a therapeutic direction, must be firmly based in theoretically informed knowledge and professional values.

A good starting place is to try to take account of how conscious we are about thinking. There are aspects of our lives that are critically important that we don't even think about. Involuntary biological action such as breathing is a good example. Breathing is literally giving us life; it might be classified as involuntary because we breathe without having to think about breathing. Yet, if you are engaging in something like meditation or mindfulness, one of the first things you'll probably be taught to do is to become more conscious of your breath and to think about your breathing. This process of becoming more conscious of every breath often involves both appreciating each breath and taking more control of your breathing. The purpose of this is usually to help you to use your breathing to relax, slow down your thinking and become conscious of something that you are taking for granted.

There are times when thinking becomes a much more conscious and deliberate activity. For example, the engagement with thinking that is involved when you are attempting to learn new skills.

An example of thinking and the experience of learning to drive a car

For those of you who have not had this experience yet, I apologise. This example speaks to my own experience of learning in a more social context and the impact it has had on my appreciation of social work thinking.

When you start to learn to drive the car you need to have a clear and comprehensive understanding of the rules the road. You discover that there are many skills of driving a car, which include: hand–eye coordination and, for that matter, hand–feet coordination. You have to understand the relationship between the clutch and the brakes, you have to be conscious of steering the car, looking in mirrors; you have to keep an eye on speed limits, watch out for other drivers, pedestrians, bike riders; and all of this is going on at the same time and you make decisions in milliseconds. I remember when I started driving wondering how I would ever manage to get the car up to 30 miles an hour and still manage to steer, look in mirrors, observe other drivers, use the clutch, get up through the gears and be ready to break if necessary. It all seemed a bit overwhelming. I was really conscious of every single aspect of what was involved. Roll on years of experience and of course I now take some of these very much for granted. Shifting gears and steering simultaneously is a skill that I don't even think about any more. I automatically check mirrors regularly and am really only conscious of doing it when I see something of concern or when I'm reversing. So at some level I have gained a level of unconscious competence and do some of the tasks of driving with what might appear to be very little thought. Perhaps more accurately, it is that I am thinking more quickly and in that process I am less conscious of what I'm doing or of the fact that I have developed a proficiency in the skill of driving.

In Chapter 1 we talked about the four levels of learning that Robinson (1974) described: unconscious incompetence, conscious incompetence, conscious competence and unconscious competence. As I said, I am not a fan of unconscious competence, although I appreciate that we do have to make decisions quickly, on the spot, if you like. However, our thinking skill is critical in making sure that we are aware of what we are doing and why we are doing it, even if some of that awareness is after the fact.

From social to professional thinking

The skill of thinking in social work counselling operates at a level of conscious competence. Processing is a thinking/cognitive and thoughtful skill applied in all cases to ensure that the service given to the service user is the most appropriate for their needs at that time. This means that the social worker should be filtering the information they gather through their professional knowledge base as well as through a reflective practice process in order to evaluate and make decisions about the appropriate next steps. Social workers, in their professional practice, need to know what they are doing and why they are doing it and should be able to relay the rationale for their actions to others. The challenge, as we have mentioned already, is that sometimes social workers rely too heavily on their practice experience and lose sight themselves of the professional knowledge base that is informed practice. This knowledge base is only helpful when it is actually employed and where knowledge and research are critically and reflexively considered by social workers.

So let's apply this to learning in social work. In the beginning, students in particular are really conscious of all the parts they have to keep track of: research evidence, diverse theoretical frameworks, their own personal experiences, the experiences of the service user, the social worker's emotions and the service user's emotions, the social context, agency requirements, the legal and statutory regulations, resources, professional values and ethics. It's a lot to keep track of, but this is what the skill of thinking involves, because it is only by taking all of these into account that you can develop an informed response to any particular situation or case. It's only later, with experience, that social workers become less conscious of thinking and some of the risk identified earlier, including the invisibility of these skills, becomes a factor.

Social work education and training that point to the importance of this thinking skill

Woodcock Ross (2011, p. 16) reminds us that 'we cannot rely on the fact that skills will be learnt in the same naturally acquired matter within the social work situation. Rather, an active thinking process is required'. She refers to this as 'reflective consideration'. While we are looking at talking, listening and thinking as interconnected communication skills activities, it is perhaps the skill of thinking and processing that is pivotal for the professional competence required in social work.

Firstly, the commitment to integrating theory and practice. In the earlier days of social work, psychoanalytic theory prevailed. In many ways, this made the integration of theory and practice more straightforward. It is conceivable that given the dependence on one particular interpretation of human behaviour workers became very fluent in that theoretical perspective and therefore it was possible for them to internalise the basic premises of this theory and see the world through that framework. This may account, at least in part, for a period where this integration of theory and practice became less critical in social work. However, social workers are required not only to have an in-depth understanding and ability to apply one theoretical framework, but also must have a working knowledge of a number of other possible interpretations (HCPC 2017). This means that the skill of thinking is all the more relevant. In order to apply different theoretical ideas to the events and experiences of service users, the social worker must have a familiarity with multiple ways of understanding the service user's life. The multiplicity of options then requires the social workers engage with service users to begin to unravel the most helpful and meaningful interpretation in order to move forward and work towards change. This requires decision-making based on knowledge and values and the service user's needs, which are at the core of the skill of thinking. The skill of thinking seeks to enhance social workers' awareness of all the factors that impinge on that decision-making; in essence, it is the opposite of the unconscious competence referred to earlier. Making decisions and engaging with service users does, of course, involve a level of spontaneous relationship interaction; however, the professionalism of that interaction should be maintained and acknowledged. Processing the interaction through a series of filters is one of the features of the relationship that differentiates it from a social or personal interaction.

The second aspect to be considered is the acknowledgement of the place of processing in social work education. The traditional process recording which lost a lot of support over the years seems to have regained some ground. The introduction of technologies which allow for more accurate recording of content and interaction appeared to supersede process recordings for a time. However, the reflective aspect of the process recording cannot be captured by video or audio recording. The reflective aspect and the processing of information in conjunction with the social worker's personal and professional experiences can only really be appreciated through the eyes of the social worker themselves. In order to access this it is really useful that social workers employ a tool such as process recordings or reflective journals. We will look at ways of using these in your work when we explore reflective practice.

This brings us to the next aspect of social work that attempts to capture and inform the skill of thinking and relates to the development of reflective practice. Reflective practice in social work is recognition that the relationship is a critical aspect of professional counselling and a helping relationship. This relationship is of course two-sided, with the service user and social worker attempting to build a trusting relationship and collaborate together, often around very difficult and challenging issues. In order to achieve this, the social worker must be able to reflect not only on what is going on for the service user, but also what is going on for themselves. The background attitude belief system and experiences of a social worker become a critical part in the ongoing development of the relationship with service users and influences how social workers see service users and their experiences and make decisions about the most helpful approach to take.

Thinking about thinking

To help us think about thinking it is useful to consider different ways of thinking. Figure 4.1 provides a framework to help analyse your thinking. It suggests that you can think about your thinking by checking where it fits in relation to a number of descriptors for thinking. The continuum is designed to promote discussion and highlight differences in our thinking. Each factor is identified as having two opposite ends, A and B, with A representing the critical and conscious end of the spectrum and B acceptance and unconscious the other end. In some instances the B side might not even constitute thinking at all. It would be fair to say that for professional practice you will be aiming for the A end of the continuum.

The descriptors can assist in stimulating consideration on how you are thinking. The skills of thinking will vary in application depending on the time, situation, setting, context and purpose. For example, take the notion of voluntary and involuntary as explained in the example about breathing. This continuum related

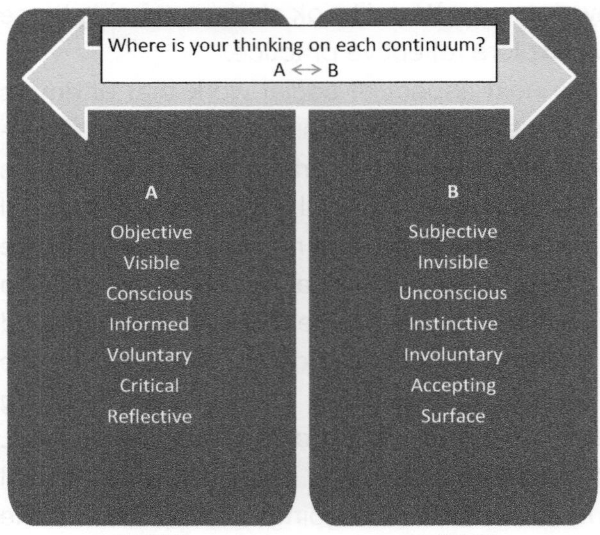

Figure 4.1 Framework for analysis of thinking skills along continua

more to physical actions/reactions. Another way of looking at this is to question how much thought goes into your actions. It is probably not even accurate to view involuntary or unconscious ends of the continuum as actually thinking at all. That makes it all the more difficult to notice if our actions are a result of thinking or may be more accurately described as a result of not thinking at all.

Thinking as part of learning in the earlier example refers to conscious versus unconscious. Of course, the term unconscious in itself epitomises what we mean by being unaware of thinking. Another continuum to consider is how informed your thinking is rather than perhaps being instinctive. This is really interesting to explore, as it draws attention to one of the dilemmas for social work thinking skills. At what point are you so familiar or 'informed' in your thinking that it becomes almost instinctive? Some of the issues about the value of practice wisdom might be incorporated into this debate. If you are so familiar with knowledge, values, etc., then do your actions/responses come instinctively? As with the notion of unconscious competence, this approach to social work thinking is not beneficial. It risks losing sight of how social work is informed and brings us to the continuum of visible versus invisibility. Where are you on this continuum? Are you aware of your skill in thinking and can you provide a rationale for your actions? Have you applied your critical thinking skills or have you been accepting of or compliant with the perceived wisdom? The importance of critical and reflective thinking is well-established in social work (Schon 1983, Redmond 2006, Ferguson 2018) and so we will look at these in a bit more detail later.

Informed thinking

Inskipp (1996, p. 5) emphasises that 'skills need to be broken down into discrete micro skills, learnt and practised. It is not possible to use skills fluently and with confidence by learning about them, but only by having a good model to know what they look like and sound like and then practising them with feedback, probably putting them together into mega skills and understanding how and when to use them according to the theory being used'. Inskipp (p. 6) comments that 'research writing is beginning to indicate that matching or considering client issues with two different theories may be better than trying to use one model with all situations and all issues'. This implies developing familiarity and skills for several models and the ability to match them to the client. It may be that counselling skills have in the past been closely associated with the development of a preferred model of practice informed by one framework. Because of this, it may have been easier to become very familiar with a particular theoretical interpretation of service users' experiences, thus allowing the social worker to develop a level of unconscious competence in their reading of events. This becomes more difficult, as counselling has progressed to support the need for a more eclectic approach whereby the counsellor/social worker may have to consider many different theoretical perspectives and reach a professional judgement about which set of interpretations fits best with service users' needs. This need to have more than one perspective underlines the importance of the thinking skill, as it is this processing of information through the multiple theoretical filters that then generates ideas and plans for change and interventions and indicates what approach to take and which questions to ask and even what to listen for in communicating with service users.

Informed thinking means that as professionals we must have familiarity and understanding of a knowledge base, values, method and skills. In the standard of proficiency for the social work profession, HCPC (2017) requires that they have an understanding of and an ability to apply a number of social work theories and models of practice. This is reflected in standards required throughout the profession. It means that social workers have to be informed by different theories and be able to deliver a range of interventions based on different models of practice. To fulfil these requirements, social workers need cognitive skills which help them to make decisions/select the theory and model most appropriate to a particular scenario. It is not acceptable to rely on one theory/model. The range of theoretical ideas and associated methods and skills are summarised in Table 4.1.

While an in-depth knowledge of all the grand theories and subtheories illustrated is not essential, what is essential is an awareness that they exist. You need to have the ability to recognise their influence, in particular in interdisciplinary/multidisciplinary work. Different theories provide a language for communication and influence how others may understand and interpret the service user's experiences. Within social work some of the theories and concepts have more influence. That influence may depend on what was popular when you studied social work in college or what is viewed as most important in your social work context or may even be personal preference.

Professional culture, defined by Walsh (2013, p. 9) as 'being represented by schools, agencies and professional associations, impact on a social worker's ideas about theory, and practice impacts your theoretical influences'. Different theories offer different interpretations and so provide more options about what needs to happen next; again, this requires some thinking skills on the part of the social worker trying to match theory with needs and also fitting with their own skills, values and knowledge base. Different theories as seen in Table 4.1 also connect to different choices of methods in social work. We have already discussed that

TABLE 4.1 Knowledge base for counselling social work: grand theories, subtheories, associated methods and skills

<table>
<tr><th colspan="10">GRAND THEORIES</th></tr>
<tr><td colspan="3">Biological</td><td colspan="3">Psychological</td><td colspan="4">Sociological</td></tr>
<tr><td colspan="10">Some theories informed by/drawing from the grand theories to be aware of</td></tr>
<tr><td>Genetics</td><td>Physiology</td><td>Neuro psychology</td><td colspan="2">Psychoanalytic</td><td>Humanistic</td><td colspan="2">Developmental</td><td>Radical</td><td>Social learning</td></tr>
<tr><td colspan="2">Behavioural</td><td colspan="2">Cognitive</td><td colspan="2">Cognitive behavioural</td><td colspan="2">Systemic</td><td colspan="2">Social construction</td></tr>
<tr><td colspan="10">Some theories derived from/informed by the above to focus on specific issues/life experiences. These draw on one or more of the above core theories to explain certain experiences or life events</td></tr>
<tr><td>Crisis</td><td>Bereavement</td><td>Attachment and loss</td><td colspan="2">Trauma</td><td>Domestic violence</td><td>Addiction</td><td>Feminist theories</td><td>Offending</td><td>Suicide</td></tr>
<tr><td colspan="10">Methods of counselling social work and therapeutic interventions associated with one or more of the above theories</td></tr>
<tr><td colspan="2">Psychoanalysis</td><td>Behaviour modification</td><td>Task-centred</td><td>Person-centred</td><td>Attachment therapy</td><td colspan="2">Trauma-informed care</td><td colspan="2">Behavioural therapy</td></tr>
<tr><td>Problem-focused work</td><td>Cognitive therapy</td><td>Family therapy
Cognitive behavioural therapy (CBT)</td><td>Solution-focused therapy</td><td>Motivational interviewing</td><td>Crisis intervention</td><td>Narrative therapy</td><td>Group work</td><td>Community work</td><td>Drama
Art
Music
Play
Therapies</td></tr>
<tr><td colspan="10">Skills: Some of the core skills and values which are employed in above methods</td></tr>
<tr><td colspan="10">Talking: responding, empathising, questioning, affirming, reframing, challenging, supporting, eliciting, giving feedback, advice and/or information, influencing. Listening: active, accurate, constructive listening, observing, demonstrating engagement and empathy.
Thinking: managing preconceived ideas, reflecting, self-awareness, cultural/ethnic sensitivity, assessment, planning, and supervision.
Adhering to ethical practice and social work value base (including: dignity, respect, collaborating, social justice and human rights, cultural and ethnic diversity as foundation for reflective, anti-oppressive, anti-discriminatory and anti-racist practice).
NB: For more on theory, see Thompson, N. & Stephney, P. (2018) Social work theory and methods: The essentials. Routledge.</td></tr>
</table>

no one theory has been found to be more effective than others and so this flexibility should not have a negative impact on the work. Walsh (2013, p. 10) in supporting the view that thinking skills are important, states that 'faced with many possible perspectives, and being subject to agency cultural factors, social workers should ideally relay on critical thinking skills to guide their use of theory'.

In a way, this is an attempt to make a case for social work counselling skills to recognise and maintain the connection between practice and theoretical frameworks. Theory is our friend. Theories provide a rationale to support our work, provide alternative ways of understanding what's happening and also generate new ideas about what might be helpful. Theories also provide a connection to an appropriate methodology for intervening as different social work methods are informed and supported by different theoretical ideas.

It may be easy to see the place of thinking in your early career as a social worker. And perhaps some people put pressure on themselves to have these theories, so integrated in their thinking that it's almost as though they don't think about them anymore. Certainly they may be less conscious of thinking about them. However, thinking and drawing on theories is not something reserved for your student days. Thinking is something that happens from the moment you become involved in a case; it continues through every conversation you have with the service user and right through to when you finish a piece of work and think through or evaluate what happened and what the outcome was. When we look at group work we will see even more clearly the importance of thinking as a beginning, middle and end process in all our relationships with service users.

(Case example: for examples of theories and methods influencing your thinking and shaping your responses, see Appendix 4.1.)

Critical thinking

Guiding your use of theory requires the practise of critical thinking skills. Fahim and Masouleh (2012, p. 1371) suggest that critical thinking 'refers to the use of cognitive skills or strategies that increase the probability of a desirable outcome ... the critical person is something like a critical consumer of information; he or she is driven to seek reasons and evidence'. For them, it involves being open-minded and therefore 'willing to examine issues from as many sides as possible, looking for the good and bad points of the various sides examined. In fact, a critical thinker must cultivate a sense of healthy scepticism along with an ability to be open-minded, especially when considering viewpoints contrary to one's own'. Applying the skill of critical thinking in social work ensures that social workers challenge not only their own preconceived ideas but also ideas and interpretations that interpret service users' experiences. Social workers, because of their understanding of and commitment to the 'social', must be able to apply a socially informed critical thinking to their work.

Gibbons and Gray (2004, p. 21) clarify that in social work:

> *critical thinking presumes that each person constructs or makes sense of his or her own reality; is able to recognize the limits of his or her knowledge; and to see knowledge as ever-changing, even shifting and unstable. The critical thinker approaches a question, situation, problem, or issue with an evaluative mindset, wondering about its strengths and limitations, meaning, purpose, truth, validity and a range of possible options to respond as well as outcomes of any actions taken in response to the situation.*

Therefore, social workers must engage in informed and critical thinking. This also highlights the importance of social workers being active in research. This does not necessarily mean conducting empirical research, although that would be welcomed, but it does mean keeping up to date with research in order to ensure that their practice is evidence-informed as well as informed by more established theories. We will come back to this later.

Stages of thinking

Thinking in social work may be usefully described in three stages. The three stages we will explore are: thinking, processing and reflecting, as illustrated in Figure 4.2.

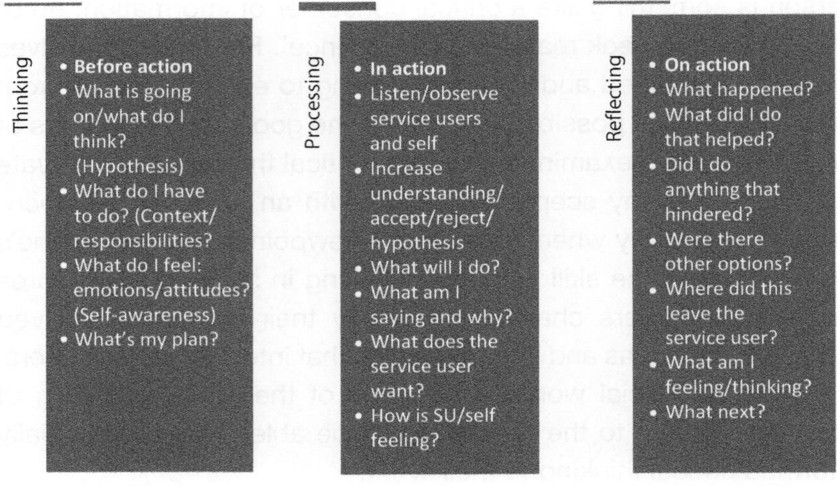

Figure 4.2 Three stages in applying thinking skills

For the purposes of discussion, let's consider that thinking refers to how we apply the skill in the planning and preparation stages of the work (before), processing will relate to thinking as we are actively engaged with the service user(s) (during) and reflecting to the thinking after the encounter(s). When referring to reflective practice the term reflection in action is often used for what we are calling processing and reflection on action relates to reflection after the interaction. Later we will look at reflective thinking as associated with reflective practice.

In counselling the social worker moves through these three stages and employs their thinking skills as they go. Perhaps the informed, objective and conscious aspects of thinking are more to the forefront in the planning stages while a move to more unconscious, invisible and instinctive levels of thinking may appear in the processing stages. This may be explained in part by the challenges associated with processing. It involves thinking about and managing all that's happening as the service user adds their perspective and information to the interaction. We have already mentioned the idea that when you are talking you are not listening and learning. The challenge of thinking and listening should also be acknowledged. This is the core challenge of this processing stage.

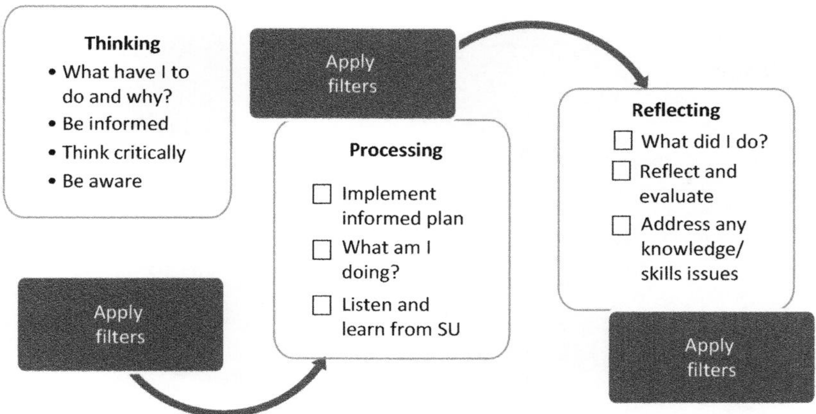

Figure 4.3 Processing stages of thinking through professional 'filters'

Yet Gibbons and Gray (2004, p. 31) remind us that 'good listening, which is central to good social work practice, is related to critical thinking; all possibilities need to be heard and considered before sound decisions can be made'. Therefore, this processing involves adding new information and making decisions about if and how it fits with what you had been thinking before you met the service user. The most basic process is evaluating the information and categorising it. Simple categories would include: what fits or confirms what you were already thinking; what is not supported; what further information you need to make a call on either of these. Other levels of processing may involve ordering information as exemplified in the notion of assessing for signs of risk and signs of safety. In this you process the information into two categories: risk and safety. Processing is a way of taking in information through listening and observing and making sense of it by filtering it through your knowledge base, etc. Figure 4.3 illustrates this idea that at each stage of thinking, processing and reflecting you pass your thinking through a set of professionally relevant filters.

After the interaction between the social worker and the service user(s) there is more time to think or reflect. Part of all these three stages involves using your social work knowledge base, values systems, etc., to inform your thinking, processing and reflecting. There are many factors to be taken into account in these thinking

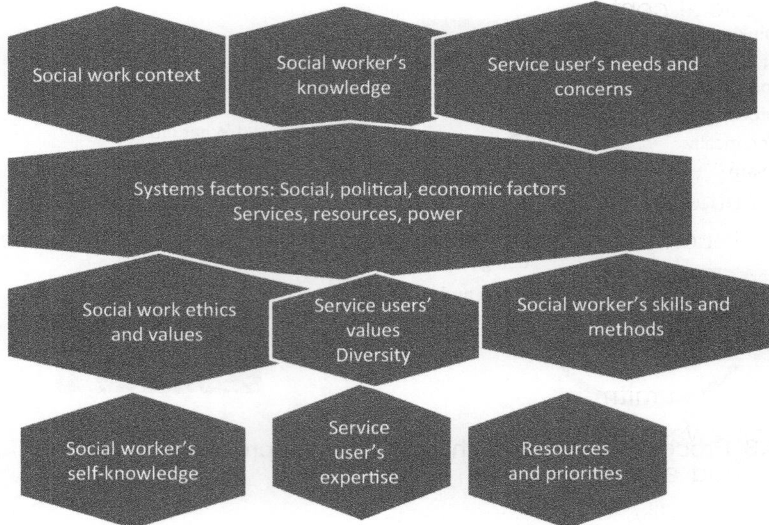

Figure 4.4 Filters for processing social work thinking

processes and these are conceptualised here as 'filters'. The idea is that all your thinking is clarified by going through these filters. This means you know what you need to do and why. It makes your professional thinking transparent to you and then you can make you thinking transparent to others as required.

Figure 4.4 illustrates the key filters involved in social work counselling. The risk is, then, just like driving a car, where processing all of the information in what needs to be an apparently spontaneous interaction can, with practise, mean that you lose sight of all the component parts of what has informed your thinking and actions. Typically, the main victim of this loss is the lack of connection between practise and the theoretical frameworks that inform our practice. That's a bit like forgetting the rules of the road once you have your licence. Not a good idea!

Professionally competent thinking

The level of thinking required in a professional social work encounter differs in quality and content from what would work for you in a social context. It takes years of education to develop a knowledge base to inform this thinking process. The knowledge base involves a broad knowledge of theories of human growth and development which encompass biopsychological and social interpretations of human behaviour. Knowledge of theories then informs methods and skills and what is most appropriate in any social work context (see Table 4.1). As you can see in the filters illustration (Figure 4.4), social work thinking is also influenced by a set of values, by an understanding of the legal context, by the requirements of the agency or service who is employing the social worker, by a commitment to reflective practice which adds a dimension of self-awareness as well as understanding the importance of reviewing and evaluating the interaction both as it happens and afterwards. Ideally, counselling social work provides the opportunity to review and evaluate with the support and guidance of professional supervision. This is therefore a different level of thinking and of processing the ongoing interaction between social worker and service user than would be typical in social interaction.

Context

It might be helpful to say a little more about context. Walsh (2013, p. 9) cites research in the field of health administration (Westert & Groenewegen, 1999), which shows that 'the intervention behaviour of professionals is significantly accounted for by their conformity to prevailing practices in their employing agencies'. In Table 4.1 we considered the continuum of critical thinking and compliance. It is worth checking out when the response to context is more about compliance and when it is informed by critical thinking. While it is of course necessary to be in compliance with legal, agency- and context-driven policy, regulations and guidelines, that does not detract from the professional obligation for critical thinking.

This critical thinking is enhanced by also being evidence-informed. This aspect of thinking involves the ability to access understanding and critically evaluate the evidence from research. Social work is sometimes criticised for a failure to address research both in terms of accessing it to inform practice, but also in terms of conducting research to support practice. The debate about evidence-based practice and evidence-informed practice has been ongoing. This is not a dispute about the importance of research, but a more complex question about what is good research and also some critical thinking about the politics of research.

Research: evidence-based or evidence-informed practice

For social work counselling skills this is particularly interesting because it leaves social work vulnerable to being required to base practice on research that has not been conducted on social worker/ social work activities, but rather on other disciplinary approaches. This runs the risk of not capturing some of the nuances of social work practice. In the second part of this text we will look at a number of applications of counselling skills in practise. The three areas to be explored are particularly interesting in the context of research. Solution-focused work might be seen as a practice lead model where research to support it came later. Motivational interviewing, on the other hand, might be viewed as a research-led intervention which has contributed over time to identifying the importance of some of the more complex interpersonal skills required to build relationships and develop therapeutic outcomes. Finally, we will look at group work. Group work is one of those approaches which although well-established as a core activity in social work, the movement towards evidence-based practice may have created a situation in which the complexity of what works in group work has been difficult to capture. We will address some of the debate around the feared disappearance of group work fuelled at least in part by some of this evidence-based research phenomenon. In social work there has been an attempt to distinguish between evidence-based research and evidence-informed research. This is a very helpful distinction, because it addresses the fact that social workers absolutely need to be able to understand research and apply it in practise as appropriate. However, the distinction allows for the opportunity to critically think about research output and research methodology and in this analysis discover if and how the research has captured the essence of social work interventions.

Case example: the relevance of research evidence

So, for example, in the area of addiction, the dominance of cognitive behavioural therapy (CBT) has been established. In conducting an analysis of approaches to working with couples around addiction issues the evidence to support CBT was very clear (Loughran 2003). However, this review also demonstrated that part of the strength of the evidence was due to their proportionately much larger number of research projects that actually examined CBT. It might be useful to question, for example, the politics of funding and to consider if some success in demonstrating outcomes with a particular intervention makes them more likely to be able to acquire additional funds. A famous research project in the USA called PROJECT MATCH set out to compare three different interventions in the field of addiction (Loughran 2003). Two of these, CBT and MI (Motivational Interviewing) already had a well-established track record for success in the field. The third approach, AA (Alcoholics Anonymous), had little or no such track record and might be considered to have built its success on personal experiences rather than research evidence. Interestingly, in this study, all three interventions were found to be relatively similar in outcome with some small differences in relation to very specific populations. Much of the subsequent analysis and discussion about this research revolved around methodological issues. For the purposes of this discussion, the point being made here is simply that research, while essential and valuable to inform social work, is not necessarily something that should be accepted without question. More recently a well-known researcher and practitioner in the addiction field raised the issue of whether we are actually asking the right questions in research (Orford 2008). These examples are raised here simply to point to the importance of considering research, and perhaps to see the value of research for social work informing practice, but also of the importance of critically analysing and appreciating the more complex issues around research methodology and the politics of research.

Reflective practice

Schon (1983) distinguished between 'reflection in action', which refers to thinking while actively engaged in action, and 'reflection on action', which involves thinking about actions and interactions after they have happened. Both of these forms of reflection are important in social work practice and can be seen to be the components parts of reflective practice. As a recognised and desirable aspect of thinking skills required in social work, it is concerning that little research has been done on if and how such reflection is conducted and supported. In his research, Ferguson (2018, p. 416) found that 'the demands of face to face work were so great at times that workers could not think about or feel that complexity while they were in it, if they were to focus on service users' needs'. In fact, Ferguson (2018) suggests that reflection in action may have been 'turned off' as a self-preservation response to manage strong emotional or challenging encounters. This argument clarifies the vital importance of reflection on action. 'Staff support after practise encounters need to be rigorously reflective, analytic and critical. Reflection on action should also address feelings and sensory experiences that may not have been though about in action (Ferguson 2018, p. 425).

Reflecting on your way of thinking of or making sense of service users' experiences is a critical step in developing your counselling repertoire. You can begin to see that these ideas shape your response to service users. In some situations this shaping of your response isn't something you are aware of. Some theoretical ideas about human behaviour have such currency that we accept them as a given. Hence, what are actually no more than one theory's preferred ways of explaining something becomes accepted as fact. Even a group of relatively new social work students will be able to generate ideas about what is happening in a scenario despite having had little exposure to the range of theories we have identified. This is what I mean by a theory having widespread currency. In order to develop a professional level of counselling skills it is a critical step to find a way to challenge these preconceived ideas. Only when you learn to reflect on what is influencing your own thinking can you then draw on the range of alternative possibilities about what might be the service users' world.

Self-reflection

The skill of self-reflection is one that is hard to recognise in terms of our social communication skills. It may come to your notice if someone says to you, maybe in an argument, 'go and take a good look at yourself'. We could think of this as a form of self-reflection or maybe as a form of conflict. And yet, this notion of looking at yourself and paying attention to what part you might play in a disagreement, for that matter in any situation, is one that deserves attention. Often when faced with a difficult situation, we instinctively take time to think through what has happened and, in particular, take a look at the part we may have played in this. So while self-reflection may not be a well-recognised skill in our social communication, it is nonetheless something that we can turn to when we get into difficulties.

In terms of self-reflection in a professional context it is important that social workers rely on this skill, not just in times of difficulty, but as something that is worth doing on a regular basis. As Thompson (2009, p. 102) states, 'we are, in effect, a tool of intervention in our own right, it clearly pays dividends to have some degree of understanding of that to a resource'. Self-awareness involves having at least some notion of how other people perceive us, how we come across to them. He further clarifies (p. 103) that 'it is necessary to gain feedback from others in terms of how they react to you'. He also emphasises the other side of self-awareness, which he states is that of developing and understanding how external factors affect you. In this discussion, Thompson (2009, pp. 102–103) also acknowledges that 'self-awareness is something that can develop over time. This skill does not come automatically and, given the demanding nature of social work, the longer we go without reflecting on these issues, the more uncomfortable it can be to do so'. He suggests it's important to 'develop this habit ... of self-reflection from an early stage in one's career and continue to keep a clear focus on how we are affecting other people and how they are affecting us '(Thompson 2009, p. 103).

In this consideration of reflective practice we need to take account of both the role of reflection as taking time to reflect on our work and also reflection as a skill in developing self-awareness. This involves reflecting not just on our actions and decisions in our work but also reflecting and understanding the impact the work has on you and that you have on the work. These reflective skills can best be supported and developed though regular professional supervision. The supervision must incorporate all aspects of the supervisor role so that it includes time to reflect and consider your impact on service users and their impact on you. Supervision that focuses solely on case management and accountability will not achieve the same development of this important skill. The more limited form of supervision becomes more widespread where decisions about resources and time constrains are allowed to impinge on the quality of the supervision process.

Process recording in social work

Papell (2015) suggests that there was interest in the process as distinct from the content of social work practice since the time of Richmond in 1917. This supports the position that while knowledge and information is important for responsible social work practice, so too is an appreciation of other factors that impact the relationship with service users and the outcome of that relationship. According to Papell (2015), Richmond recognised the importance of a number of aspects that should be captured in recording casework. These included what was then referred to as social diagnosis, but also the interaction between worker and clients and accounting for the work for agency records. So process recordings served multiple purposes: administrative, diagnostic and educational.

Process recording is enjoying somewhat of a revival in social work education. The development of audiovisual technologies has provided tools to more easily record social workers in action, but these do not capture the thinking process we have been exploring in this chapter. Such devices do not assist in tracking how social workers have applied/thought through the filters we have identified. Black and Feld (2006, p. 141), writing about process recordings, more recently remind us that 'it is important to clarify the difference between the purpose of a process recording on the one hand, and the documentation that agencies need for internal record keeping on the other. Process recording should be viewed exclusively as an educational device to facilitate students learning of analytic and interventive skills, as well as attitudes, values and ethics – all of which function synergistically comprise the essence of social work practice'.

Homonoff (2014) identified that the use of process recording in social work education is mixed. She does discuss some aspects of process recording which may have supported its survival in the education repertoire. Ideally, the process recording provided the opportunity for the social work student to select a case/situation that has raised some questions for them. They can describe the details of the case, the setting, the purpose and goals of the intervention, a rationale for the theories and methods applied as well as their impressions, attitudes, emotional, personal and professional response to the case. The key factor has to be that the person working with the social worker on reflecting on the recording must use this to build trust and openness, just as the social worker needs to in working with service users. (We will look later at the experience of assessment that may be shared between service users and social work students.) Using process recordings in a supportive way can allow students to identify both what they have learned and what they need to learn. Process recording as a learning tool is only as useful as the student and supervisor make it. However, the technique can certainly work to help you identify the thinking filters that shape your work practices and responses to particular service user situations.

Process recordings have developed into more focused activities. They can be designed to focus on one aspect of an interaction and to avoid being overly descriptive. Walsh (2002) builds on the traditional template for process recording by introducing the application of a strength perspective. This ensures that learning takes place in a supportive and strengths-based environment. The process recording should include: the purpose of the interview, the content of the interview, analysis of the content, the role and goals of the social worker (Walsh 2002). The main focus is on the analysis. Analysis of content according to Walsh (2002) should address the assessment, the relationship and treatment (ART). The analysis and development of an understanding of the factors that influenced thinking are of more interest than a detailed description of events. Looking at briefer, more focused aspects of the interaction makes the use of process recordings more feasible.

Vicary et al. (2017) highlight the importance of going beyond first-order analysis, i.e. description, to a higher level of analysis, including interpretation and conceptualising about the interaction. Their work supports the use of electronic journaling, which may be the way forward for reflecting on process in the future.

Thinking about thinking can take a more simplified format as well. In developing your critical thinking skills, Cottrell (2011) talks about applying basic-level critical thinking such as comparing and sorting into different categories. For example, you can select a couple of apparently opposing ideas: problems are about individuals versus problems are about society (basically, which is your preferred way of thinking, psychological or sociological?). Think about where you fit with those opposing ideas. (See Appendix 4.2 and Appendix 4.3.)

When you are listening to the service users do you have a system for sorting the information? The use of risk and resilience in assessment is a good example of this type of thinking. You have two categories and information as it comes in is attributed to one or the other. For example, when you hear there is family support, that might go into the resilience category; if you hear about an unstable relationship, that might be more in the risk category, etc. What sorts of categories do you tend to apply to help you organise your thinking?

More and more in social work we are being asked to identify what it is we do and how we contribute to the well-being of service users' lives. In terms of the focus of this discussion, part of that is a responsibility to know our skills and the limits of those skills so that we can continue to build our expertise. While the traditional process recording may not be a feasible option for professionally qualified workers, there is a need for some template to guide our thinking about our practice before action, in action and on action. Figure 4.1 and Figure 4.4 can be employed to provide just such a template. They can serve to provide a comprehensive set of ideas to direct your reflection on action and to enhance your skill in observing or becoming conscious of your thinking and processing in action. See Appendix 4.4.

Final comments

Thinking as a social work counselling skill is complex yet vital. It can be thought of as having a number of stages which relate to thinking before engaging with the service user(s), thinking (processing) that is going on as you communicate with the service user(s) and then the thinking (reflection) that takes place after the encounter which helps identify what needs to happen when you engage in thinking before the next meeting. In social work, informed and critical thinking alongside reflective practice form core components of professionally competent practice. All of these contribute to the way in which we utilise the other counselling skills of listening and talking, and of course shape how and when we use the other skills we have identified as being embedded in the core counselling social work skills.

5 Questioning

- Looking at composing and asking questions as part of the social work counselling skills repertoire and distinguishing that from asking questions in a social communication context.
- Considering the purpose of questions and the interaction between thinking, listening and the actual delivery of asking questions.
- Exploring the skill of questioning as one of the most difficult skills to employ in a therapeutic way. It is a skill that needs to be developed appropriately and applied judicially to avoid undermining the collaborative relationship.
- Drawing on examples to develop an appreciation of the skills and also providing exercises to facilitate developing these skills.
- Considering research that may inform the application of these skills in practice.

Introduction

Questions can be viewed as simply being an integral part of most social conversations. In fact, we probably ask so many questions every day that we don't even realise that we are asking questions, and even if we do, we probably don't think too much about the different types of questions and their purpose. Typically, social questions are geared towards seeking information. Very often that's just factual information. Sometimes we can be using questions to seek information to help us solve a problem, to ascertain what we need to do next or to simply discover what resources are available to us in relation to some issue we are attempting to address. Other questions may be associated with 'checking out' if we have the correct information about something or even to find out if something we are thinking is actually true or valid. You might have picked up a sense that your partner/child/friend/workmate is annoyed/excited/sad/happy and decide to ask about that; you simply want to know what's going on.

There are many different ways in which we can use questions. Some questions are more like social conventions than really questions. For example, often when people meet they will say, how are you doing? You might notice that sometimes people don't even answer that question and the person who asked the question doesn't pursue an answer. That may be because there is an agreed understanding that it's just an introductory piece of conversation and not really a question that deserves or requires an answer.

Other questions that are typical in everyday conversation are queries; for example, what price is that? Can you give me directions? However, even in a social conversation we also use questions in many more subtle ways. You can ask questions to begin to help solve problems, so questions can be about seeking advice. For example, what do you think I should do about my finances or what's the best way to sort out this problem? These are other ways of seeking information, but this information is to try and help us to solve problems. We can use questions in other ways as well. For example, we can use questions when really, we know the answers already, so technically we are not really seeking information: we are asking a question for some other purpose. An example of this would be if your boss comes into the office and says, when will you have that report? It may be a question about getting a timeline on when that report will be ready, but it could also be a question which is really to remind you that you haven't yet completed the report. So, the tone and the context within which the question is asked also add to our understanding of what the question is about and what levels of meaning it might have. This is true even in social conversation.

In social conversation, when we think about context, it can help us to decide whether some other types of questions are appropriate. For example, we might ask questions about how people are feeling or about emotional situations. Typically, we would only ask these questions when we are aware that it's appropriate. This may mean that you know the person well enough or you have already developed that kind of a relationship where emotional or feelings-type questions are acceptable. Such questions might be asked in other contexts where you don't have a relationship but, for some reason, it becomes part of your job to ask that kind of question. This is partly what we will be looking at when we look at professional questioning.

Staying with social conversation for a moment, there are still other kinds of questions that we might ask. Sometimes we ask questions as invitations to conversation. An example of this in a social conversation might be something as simple as, what did you think of the match? That is an open invitation to the other person to say what it is they have to say about a particular sporting event. It may be that the question is used as an invitation to open a very social communication; the type of question that some people might talk about as just 'social lubrication' almost; it is the kind of chit-chat that happens between friends that allows people the opportunity to talk, to share ideas, to share attitudes about some social event. This kind of question might be as broad as a neighbour asking 'oh did you hear about … (something)'. So, questions in social conversation can be asking for factual information, they can be a social convention, they can be indicative of the fact that you already know the answer and you are trying to invoke a response from somebody else or trying to encourage somebody else to do something for you which you know they haven't done but which they had undertaken to do. Questioning can also be about inviting people into a conversation, being inclusive and even getting down to a level of allowing people the opportunity to discuss their emotions and to give the signal that you are ready, willing and able to have that conversation. So, questions even in social conversation can have multilevel meanings and multiple purposes depending not only on the question itself but also on the tone and the context within which the question is asked.

From social to professional competence in the skill of questioning

In terms of our social conversation, we are probably not even aware of how many questions we ask and also not aware of how we use asking questions to achieve goals in our conversation. However, when using questions in a professional context, we really do need to become much more aware of the power of questions and of the place that they have in terms of helping conversation, and also their potential for creating barriers.

Purpose and delivery

Let's start with some simple ways of thinking about questioning in a professional context. Consider two parallel aspects of questioning as illustrated in Figure 5.1.

We can begin to differentiate the reason or purpose for asking a question. Is it just a social convention to initiate conversation, or is it because we are curious or unclear, or is it more serious? It may be that the goal is to explore an issue or to introduce the need for change; thus, we have concerns or responsibilities that inform why we need to ask questions. The second and parallel consideration is a continuum about the style we employ to formulate and deliver the question. Are you simply asking for information in a casual and invitational way, or is there a need to move to a level of questioning which involves perhaps having a more serious or even professional tone and conveys that this is not social conversation. At the far end of the continuum is the questioning that takes an interrogative tone which may be used to convey or even give emphasis to power differences.

These parallel considerations suggest that it's not only the type of question that you ask but that there are other factors involved as well. We have already mentioned that the tone and the context are important.

First consider the **purpose** of the question from:

convention ⇔ *curiosity* ⇔ *concern*

and then think about the mechanism or **style** for framing the question(s) from:

asking ⇔ *questioning* ⇔ *interrogating*

Figure 5.1 Continuum of purpose and style of questioning

Context

Within the context you need to be aware of the professional setting of the relationship between the social worker and the service user. We have emphasised before the importance of building a relationship between the service user and the social worker. Employing the skill of questioning is another part of how this relationship can be built successfully, but when managed poorly or without the requisite attention to thinking and listening then it can be a contributory factor to the relationship becoming tense, strained or even conflictual. In social work, questions can be used for many different reasons including some of those that we have identified as part of social communication. For Shebib (2003, p. 126), questions are an important tool for gathering data. 'Social workers listen in order to understand, but they cannot understand if they do not have sufficient information – by asking questions they lessen the probability that they will make assumptions'. However, although questions are an important part of the counselling process, Shebib (2003, p. 126) says that 'social workers must consider numerous factors such as the goals of the session, the context in which questions are asked and the individual needs of the client and adapt their questioning techniques accordingly'.

Different styles and types of questions

Often when we're talking about social work and counselling in general, we make the distinction between open questions and closed questions. This is a very important and helpful distinction.

Closed questions

Both open and closed questions can be employed when clearly seeking information. Sometimes information can be acquired with a closed question. Koprowska (2010, p. 87) refers to these closed questions as 'narrow questions'. The definition of narrow question fits with the notion of closed questions and is about questions that can be pretty much answered by yes or no or by very little information, perhaps even a monosyllabic answer. Once you think about a closed question and think about the kind of information a closed question is trying to elicit, you can begin to picture the fact that if a closed question is asked there is going to be a very brief answer and therefore the conversation is going to be imbalanced, with the social worker doing more talking and indeed having to think of more questions to get the information they need. A series of closed questions can begin to look very like an interrogation. The social worker is trying to think of questions to cover the data that they require, and the service user is not giving much thought to the answers because they are factual information that are close to hand. It might be helpful to think of these as prescribed questions as often they take the form of a checklist of some type of formulaic questions aimed less at opening an opportunity to understand the service user and more at meeting requirements to address specified criteria. These kinds of questions don't give the opportunity to the service user to really think about what's happening for them or to explain in more detail to the social worker what the experiences have been like for them. Because closed questions create an imbalance whereby the service user does not get the opportunity to spend a lot of time thinking and talking, it's very difficult for closed questions to contribute to the development of a good relationship with the social worker.

That's not to say that closed questions don't have their place, of course, they do. For example, the purpose and delivery of questioning in assessment are critical factors in how you conduct assessment and even how you record the information gathered in an assessment process. This sometimes does involve asking a series of closed questions. Often these questions are more focused on factual and even demographic data. In social work, you have to consider when asking a lot of questions one after the other, often closed questions which involve possibly very brief answers from the service user, where that leaves you on this continuum we have mentioned. It is easy to shift from a position of being curious and concerned and asking so that you can understand the service user's situation to finding yourself in a situation where you are asking questions very quickly one after the other and where it can become more like an interrogation scenario. As mentioned, sometimes it's useful in assessment to get the closed questions of a factual nature dealt with early in the conversation so that you have the information you require, and it allows you to open up the conversation more with the service user.

Closed questions are also useful to refocus the interview or session. If there are some issues or topics that you need to address and there are time constraints, using a closed question, delivered in supportive tone, can get you back to that topic (but remember that an open question can also achieve that goal).

Closed questions can sometimes be useful to regain 'control' of a meeting/interview. As we have identified, when the social worker is asking questions they have the floor, so to speak; once you have the floor you can direct the conversation. A closed question can be useful to interrupt the flow of conversation that you see has turned in the direction of being unhelpful or even to simply get the serve user to stop talking. Think of it as putting a full stop into the conversation. Be careful about using closed questions for these purposes, because as you will see, other types of questions can achieve the same goal with less risk of undermining the service user/social worker relationship.

It is worth noting the importance of context and expectations. In terms of social convention, sometimes what appears like a closed question actually is viewed by the service user as an opening and opportunity for them to tell their story. So, a closed question (for example, how many children do you have?) may be seen by a service user as an opportunity not just to give you an answer of three children but to actually fill you in a little bit more on the children in terms of age, names, etc., and it may very well be the start of a more open conversation. There is also the possibility that a service user who is very anxious and wants to tell you their story as quickly as possible will simply do that regardless of the kind of questions that you ask. Nonetheless, it is important to remember that asking questions offers you the opportunity to use questions in a range of different ways, not just to seek information but to actually contribute to building your relationship with the service user.

Open questions

The other categories of questions that are often talked about in counselling are open questions. Koprowska (2013, p. 84) refers to these as 'broad questions'. The goal of these broad questions is to elicit more expansive answers. They invite explanation, ideas, opinions and proposals or suggestions as well. Ideally they elicit a more-detailed, often descriptive, answer from the service user.

Open questions can be delivered in many different ways depending on the tone and the context and, again, as with closed questions, it may not just be the style of questions but how often you use them. It is important to realise that the skill of questioning is connected to all of the key skills we are considering as core to social work counselling: thinking, listening and talking. While the actual delivery of a question is clearly part of the talking skill, how you formulate the question, when you ask the question, what you are attempting to achieve by asking that particular question at that time and in that way are more closely connected to thinking and listening. For example, in terms of thinking, different theoretical ideas which then inform an approach or method in social work have different ways of managing the skill of questioning. So you have to apply the thinking filters to formulating and composing a question and then build your questioning by listening to answers/responses and processing these in order to decide what to say next. Having an awareness of how your three core skills operate together to inform the skill of questioning is essential in developing your questioning ability to a level of professional competence. When we look at applying these skills in different models of practice it will become clearer that some practices place a big emphasis on limiting closed questions and emphasising open questions, but also on using not just questioning but reflection as a way of eliciting ideas and inviting service users to talk. We will discuss reflections later on in the book.

Indirect questions

Shebib (2003, p. 137) adds a third type of question to open and closed questioning, which he refers to as indirect questions or questions that are embedded in statements. Indirect questions are a softer way of seeking information. Their wording tends to be less intimidating than more direct open and closed questions. Indirect questions can involve using both reflective information and a question at the same time. Staying with discharge issues for the mother in hospital, you might use a summary of what has been said before to start the question and then add your question. For example: 'We have been taking for a while now and I understand that this is really difficult for you, I'm just wondering now what would be the most helpful way to move forward?' Or: 'We talked before about how upset you were when your mother got sick and how worried you are about what's going to happen next for her, what are your thoughts on this now?' Or: talking to mother and daughter together ask, 'We have had a chance to talk about some options available for when you are ready to leave hospital, have you had a chance to talk together about those?' All these are open questions, but you are giving some indication in the way you ask the question which directs the service user to earlier conversations or shared appreciation of the situation.

Reflective questions

Questions can be used to acquire information and data, but they can also be used in a way that helps the service user to consider or reflect on their situation. Shebib (2003, p.127) suggests that asking a thought-provoking question stimulates clients to begin to reflect. Reflective questions tend to be open-style questions which offer a reflection on something the service user has said, to bring it to the attention of the service user and then to invite the service user to say more about that. This should be distinguished from a reflection. As we will see later, a reflection is offered without being a question and without even an implied question. When you add a question or implied question, it is more accurate to think of it as a reflective question.

Rhetorical questions

As with social asking questions which we mentioned earlier, it is also possible to use questioning in social work for very many different reasons. For example, it might be useful sometimes to ask a question even though you may know the answer already. The use of this style of questioning can be to create an emphasis for the service user to draw their ideas and thinking back to a certain issue. This can often be a useful technique where you are trying to affirm the service user. You might ask a question about something that you already know they have achieved, for example: what did you do that helped you get through a similar problem before? You may already have some ideas about what they did, but it may be very helpful to allow them the opportunity to go over this again and to help them to identify some successes and some of their resilience and strengths and in talking through their answers be facilitated to make connections with skills that they used in problem-solving in the past.

Hypothetical questions

McLeod and McLeod (2011, p. 164) identify another style of questioning. They refer not only to open and closed questions, but they talk about hypothetical questions. Hypothetical questions are intended to encourage a person to consider new possibilities or to think in a 'supposed', 'imaginary' way. This is not unlike some of the solution-focused questions we will talk about later. It is an example of a way in which asking questions can be creative and productive rather than challenging and intimidating. Such a question might be as simple as 'Just imagine that things were going better for you …'

- What do you think would that look like?
- What would be going on for you then?
- What changes would you notice then?

Other styles of questioning are circular questioning and Socratic questioning. Table 5.1 offers a summary of different types of questions.

TABLE 5.1 Summary of range of questions

Prescriptive: set questions required in context including demographic data	Refocusing: drawing back to a topic	Rhetorical: elicit discussion rather than requiring information
Evocative: eliciting positive and negative memories	Goal review: evaluating goals	Emotive: drawing out emotional responses
Explorative: facilitating finding new or unfamiliar information	Challenging: helping to raise difficult points or explore differences	Reflective: providing opportunity for deeper understanding
Elaborative: building more detail about a new tonic, awareness or understanding	Confirming: check accuracy of information/ understanding	Problem-solving: highlighting possible change or steps in resolving problems
Expanding: assisting finding out more about an issue or topic	Directive: leading to a particular topic	Feelings-focused: looking for emotional or feelings-related information
Focusing: helping to look at some related aspect	Content-focused: looking for factual or content-related information	Suppositional: allowing opportunity to develop ideas about what's going on

There is a range of different orientations to questioning which can be used to get information but also to build relationships and enhance understanding of service users' perception, expectations and goals. Questions can draw attention to and elicit deeper understanding of: goals, expectations, perceptions, understanding, awareness, context, need, resources, resilience, self, others, community, etc.

Circular questions

Moving beyond simple open or closed dyadic interpretation of questioning to more complex and sophisticated analysis, we consider linear versus circular questions. Circular questions move beyond seeking information/answers in a linear way, such as asking questions from one source or valuing one person's view or interpretation more than others. With circular questions the social worker 'seeks to develop understanding and gather information about family dynamics by consulting with one member of the family about how s/he sees the relationship between other members. This conversation happens in the presence of the others so that communication is enhanced' (Loughran 2010, p. 105). This form of questioning involves providing a safe space so that people who are involved with each other, as family or in other contexts, can be free to talk openly about their perceptions of what's happening in relation to issues or problems that are the focus of the conversation with the social worker. It allows the social worker to begin to develop an understanding of the issues from the various perspectives of those involved, rather than relying on one version or the story. As with the other forms of questioning, circular questioning requires skilful consideration of what is the appropriate purpose and content of the question(s).

Purpose: focus and goals

Asking questions, then, is not just about seeking information. It is also about trying to create a focus for the interview and to try and build the relationship with the service user. Part of building this relationship may well be to ask questions that help the service user to rethink the situation and to help them begin to recognise what needs to be done, agree goals and identify skills they already have in place to help them in achieving those goals.

Theory-informed question(s)

All questions, whether you recognise it or not, are informed by some idea you have about what's going on or where you want to lead the conversation. This means that it should be possible to track by listening to the questions you ask the theory/theories that are most influential for you and indeed what method or model of intervention you are employing. Without being aware, you may ask questions that already demonstrate your bias or an assumption you have made. This might be where you have some theoretical approach that you give preference to and you ask questions which are directed by the ideas informed by that theory. For example, if you are using psychoanalytic theory you may ask questions about a service user's past, whereas if you are using a behavioural approach you will be putting questions to them that are more about eliciting information about current actions and consequences. These questions serve to give direction to the conversation, but where you ask a question in such a way that you are demonstrating a bias or preconceived assumption then that can be problematic. It is important to be informed by theory and to have a professional level of competence in delivering a specific intervention. However, it is not enough to know how to ask an open question, informed by whatever theory seems appropriate to you at the time; it is also important to ask questions with an open mind. We have discussed the concern that being too embedded in one theory may create unhelpful bias in your thinking skills. This can be demonstrated in how you employ questioning in your counselling interactions.

Faulty questions

Shebib (2003, p. 127) recognises that because asking questions is a very skilful task, it is of course possible for questions to be faulty. Faulty questions are those that 'bias answers, antagonise clients ... keep the interview at a superficial level. Insensitive questions that can disregard client's feelings or leave them feeling judged or abandoned'.

You might ask a leading question where you actually ask a question with the response you require embedded in the question. An example of this might be in a situation where an older mother is in hospital and you believe she should go home to live with her daughter. A loaded question/bias question would be something like 'You're taking your mother home, aren't you?' The service user may feel judged because they are not ready to take this step, or abandoned by you once they realise this is what you want them to do.

It is also possible to ask insensitive questions. If the social worker isn't reading the situation well and they haven't taken the time to build a relationship with the service user, it is possible that they will ask questions either at the incorrect time or maybe in a way that doesn't give the service user sufficient time to respond to the question on an emotional level. Ways that can be helpful in order to avoid this insensitive questioning can be to make sure that you use other skills in conjunction with questioning. For example, you can formulate more sensitive questions having built empathy through reflections which we will talk about again in later chapters. It is important to recognise that questioning isn't something that happens in one part of the interview, it is something that should happen throughout the interview as appropriate. Asking questions is only the output of engaging all three core skills so must be generated through thinking, listening and then talking.

Control

It is also important to recognise that when you are asking questions in the interview the service user is less in control and also is not being given the opportunity to talk while you are asking questions. Shebib (2003, p. 129) says that questions put the social worker in control. While to some extent it is important for the social worker to be in control in order to create a focus and to make sure that information that's required is actually recorded, on the other hand, on the continuum from asking to questioning to interrogation this means that the service user may experience a series of detailed and inquisitive questions as an interrogatory experience. In a worst-case scenario this experience may lead the service user to feel antagonistic towards the social worker. Probably if the service user feels that they are not in control and that they are being subjected to some kind of investigation or interrogation by being bombarded by questions, it's not going to be easy for them to engage in the discussion in a meaningful way.

Direction

Although attending behaviour forms the foundation of the micro skills hierarchy, it is questioning skills that provide a systematic framework for directing the interview (Ivey 1994, p. 49). Questioning is not just about getting specific information and making an assessment, but is also about opening up the conversation with the service user and allowing them to tell their story. Part of this is to facilitate client self-exploration. Ivey (1994, p. 50) says that the issue is *how to question wisely and intentionally*. We will continue to consider open and closed questions as the main techniques for proceeding with the interview. It is important to keep in mind at all times that the questions you ask are influenced by your own theoretical framework and by the requirements of the context within which you are meeting the service user, and they are also influenced by the response of the service user. Remember also that the service user is responding not just to the questions you ask but also how those questions are asked. As we have said, the service user is very likely to respond negatively if they feel you are putting them on the spot or if the questions are coming at them hard and fast. This is one of the risks we have identified for asking closed questions. However, it is worth noting that for some service users who may be very reluctant to speak or find it very difficult to get their voice, a series of very gentle closed questions may begin to open up the conversation for them (Ivey 1994, p. 55).

Exploration

It is useful to move on to consider the purpose of questions in terms of setting the agenda. Asking questions is a very important part of guiding the discussion in the direction which the social worker needs to go. Again, this is a demonstration of the power of asking questions. Such power should be used in an appropriate and supportive way. Part of the smooth flow of the conversation will depend not just on asking questions but also facilitating the service user to answer the questions as fully as possible. Here it is possible to use probing or gentle explorative supplementary questions that help to draw attention to aspects of the answer that need further attention. So, getting the rhythm right is very important. A combination of some closed questions but more open questions and reflections can create a rhythm to the conversation that makes it easier for the service user to get involved and to think about their answers. This combination can have a very positive impact in terms of de-escalating any conflict that might arise and certainly in dealing with the power issues that service users may experience.

Asking questions also optimises possibilities of getting useful answers and full answers to achieve some secondary aims in questioning. For example:

- Reinforcing important issues or points by drawing attention to them with further questions
- Demonstrating to the service user how much or how little they know or understand about the problems that they are having
- Eliciting from the service user for themselves an understanding of the solutions or positive ways in which they have already managed the situation
- Helping the service user understand the appropriate actions that need to be taken or expressing their ideas about actions that they wish to take
- Generating a shared understanding of what's going on and what needs to be done
- Sharing power with service users while still being in control of the interview
- Creating a collaborative and productive environment and atmosphere when questioning is conducted in a skilful manner
- Increasing and enhancing opportunities for contemplation; in other words, it can increase the developing knowledge and understanding of the extent of the problem and the perceived implications from the social worker's perspective, but more importantly from the service user's perspective
- Questioning can elicit not just information, but can be used as a technique for affirming rather than undermining the service user
- Create a supporting rather than a challenging approach to the discussion

- Add to eliciting reflections and in such a way the reflectiveness can deter or dissipate the potential for conflict
- Generate for the service user a sense of confronting themselves rather than being confronted by the social worker

Framework for analysing types of question

We have considered a range of question types that are commonly seen as part of counselling skills. The skill of formulating and asking questions has been clearly linked to the theoretical influences on the social worker asking the questions and listening to responses. In addition, other factors such as context, purpose and relationship between service user and social worker have been highlighted. This is a lot to take on board. Tomm provided us with a very helpful and clear framework for understanding the interaction between these factors and analysing questions (Tomm 1988). In this framework he considers questions along two intersecting continua which address two aspects of questioning:

- Whether the question(s) are meant to be seeking information either to inform the therapist/social worker or the client, or
- Whether the question is designed to try to influence the service user in terms of change. This second axis considers the theoretical influences which underpin, inform and shape the question.

Tomm (1988) distinguishes these theoretical influences along a continuum mapping linear and circular assumptions. Linear assumptions are derived from theories which emphasise understanding problems by tracing them back to the origins of the problem. This typically will include a more cause/effect approach and is more likely to focus on understanding the individual and their contribution to the problem development and maintenance. This also implies that it is possible to identify the 'source/cause' of the problem(s). At the other end of this continuum are the assumptions derived from theories which understand explanations of problem development and maintenance in a more circular way. This means that these theories are concerned with learning more about the context or the system within which the problem develops and is maintained. Such assumptions would then seek to inform questions that look beyond the individual to their interaction with other people within their family, within their peer group and within their community. In this framework, then, it is possible to consider questions which are influenced by a range of different theories and are further shaped by the intent or purpose of the question.

Figure 5.2 illustrates two intersecting variables to consider. One axis refers to a range of questions from focusing on the individual to focusing on broader systems. The other axis relates to whether questioning is primarily about information seeking to orientate the social worker or the service user. Therefore, questions may be about orientating the therapist/social worker or they may be about orientating the service user. Questions may also be about moving in the direction of eliciting or promoting change, in behaviours, feeling and/or thinking. The type of question will also be influenced by whether

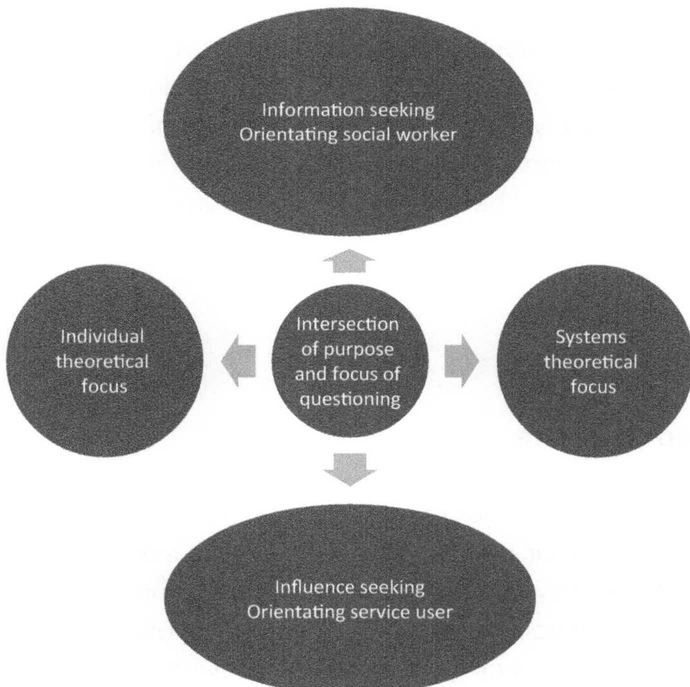

Figure 5.2 Framework for analysing questions

the theory which informs the social worker is one which seeks explanations of problems in the past or whether they are questions about the future, whether they are questions about deficits/failure or resilience and strengths. In this analysis, Tomm (1988) considers that questions based on linear assumptions and which are intended to influence the service user may fall into the category of regulatory and strategic questions. As we have already discussed, this style of questioning can pose challenges in particular to the development of a collaborative relationship between therapist/social worker and service user. This style of question is predominantly investigative or interrogative. This draws our attention to the risk of ignoring or neglecting the orientating-type questions which also seek to understand the problem in a more holistic or systemic way. Orienting yourself involves asking questions to draw on service user experience and expertise. Orienting the service user tends to be about asking questions to gather information in order to make judgements about responsibility and target change. Moving too quickly from seeking to orient yourself to orienting the service user reflects formulating questions which are predominantly influenced by a linear notion that such responsibility will ultimately lie in the hands of an individual. This can inevitably prove very difficult in terms of developing a good working relationship and can ultimately result in insufficient information being gathered before imposing an interpretation of the problem on the service user.

Remember!

One question at a time

One of the particular challenges of asking questions is the tendency to have questions in your head; you feel obliged to ask them and because of that you may find it difficult to move on and follow the service-user lead until you have asked. These questions can have the impact of overly influencing the interview. Having questions in your head that you are anxious to ask can have the effect of closing down some of your listening skills. It can certainly have the impact of influencing what you are actually listening for. One clue to this for you is to consider how often you are already composing the next question while the answer is still being given by the service user. This is a sure sign that you are not fully listening to the answer and therefore you may miss some vital clue that you have not considered yourself before this. So, it is important that when you compose a question you listen for the answer before you actually construct the next question in your head. This does not mean that you have to just follow the lead from the service user exclusively. You may very well have a series of questions that are going to have to be answered at some point in the interview. Of course, this is the case in particular when doing an assessment that has a structured format. However, no matter what the format, it is important that once you ask a question that you are at least open to hearing the answer and that the answer then becomes something of the information that you process. So, remembering again the three stages of talking, listening and processing, once you ask your question, remember to listen to the answer and then process the information. Avoid getting caught up in a question-and-answer communication sequence – it is likely to be exhausting for you and the service user and is unlikely to convey a commitment to building a collaborative relationship. Perhaps more fundamentally a question–answer formula is unlikely to give you the level or depth of relevant information you are seeking and is more likely to generate tension and defensive responses. We have looked at this process in Chapter 4.

Composing the next question should engage your own cognitive skills and good questions should then also engage the cognitive skills of the service user. You may experience asking questions for which the service user has very quick answers. However, a question that the service user has to take time over and consider may be a therapeutic/enlightening question in itself. Such questions may be an initial step towards considering the need to change. Part of processing what you hear in response to your question is about deciding which pieces of the answer fit with the puzzle you are trying to understand. You will make decisions about privileging some types of information in the answer more than others. For some examples of open questions, closed questions and reflection see Appendix 5.1.

Cultural context

It is important, too, to remember the cultural context within which you are asking questions. *Who can ask questions and of whom?* Different cultures may have different approaches to what asking questions means for them. For example, in some cultures, it may not be appropriate to ask questions at all. In other contexts, it may be seen as insulting to question older people or different categories of people depending on their status.

Setting. Other things to consider would be where the interview is happening. For example, it might not be appropriate to ask parents questions in front of their children. In other situations, it may not be appropriate to ask one partner questions about the relationship in front of the other partner. So, these cultural and contextual issues are important in deciding what kind of questions are appropriate to ask and what kind of information is appropriate to seek in a particular setting.

Power. This refers back to the discussion about the relationship between asking questions and the perception of power. In general, the person asking the questions certainly appears to be in a more powerful position. It is worth noting that sometimes for the service user who is being asked the questions the only way to have any power is to not answer, to refuse to answer or to give a tokenistic reply. The kind of answer that you give to a question may be reflective of your interpretation not just of the question itself but of the whole context within which the questioning is happening. The same question might be heard very differently if the tone is a gentle tone, an engaging tone, is in an established relationship and if the atmosphere in which the asking of questions is happening is one that makes the service user feel trusting and more relaxed. All of these issues set an important agenda for asking questions.

6 Assessing and assessment

- Assessing and assessment as part of social communication skills and how that differs from the application of those skills in professional counselling social work.
- Assessment as an ancillary skill incorporated in all the core skills of talking, listening and thinking and the challenge of employing the core skills for the specific purpose of assessment.
- Consideration will be given to assessment which over-relies on talking/questioning and the implications associated with assessment as a judgement.
- Challenging ideas that assessment is not a therapeutic intervention.

Introduction

One of the themes in this book is seeking out the connection between social life communication skills and the development of those skills to a level required for professional communication or social work counselling. We have established that social communication skills do indeed form the base for further skills development. While the capacity to employ these skills for therapeutic purposes clearly requires a different level of competence in the delivery of the skills, it is perhaps more important to acknowledge the part that the thinking process plays in the application of such skills. We have explored this process and considered the place of social work knowledge, skills and value base as core components that underpin thinking in this context. Here we will consider firstly the place of assessment in what we might call everyday life and then look at assessment and the skill of assessing in the context of social work.

Assessment in social communication

When looking at the concept of assessment in everyday life, it is fair to say that we are often the subject of such assessments. Let's look at one possible context for assessment. For many of us, the most familiar context for assessment is what we experience through the education system, although you may have been the subject of assessment of one form or another in other situations, work-related for example or possibly some form of psychological or health-based assessment. Whatever the context, there is something about assessment that raises concerns about being judged, often accompanied by feelings of having little or no power to influence the judgement process. Obviously most of us attempt to deal with this by working to meet the standards required of those in charge of the assessment. Sometimes the assessment may be seeking to place us in some rank order based on psychological profile or set of criteria, for example IQ assessment. In that context there may be little we can do to impact outcomes. If we are lucky these standards will be clearly laid out, achievable, and governed by a process that provides sufficient checks and moderating so that outcomes, even if we are not totally happy with them, do appear to have been reached in a transparent and fair manner.

Formative assessment

Assessment, particularly in the education context, is now more likely to have a formative dimension. Ideally this formative aspect facilitates learning from the assessment process so that we can improve outcomes over time if we are given access to the appropriate resources. In a formative context, then, assessment is something that can be used to suggest attainment of a standard but only with a view to helping the individual to improve their performance. In that type of setting access to resources to respond to and build from the assessment are critical to support the formative nature of that assessment. That involves support and help in preparing for assessment. Whatever the context, assessment does still have a connotation of somehow being a judgement and you are either found to be successful in meeting standards or not.

Less-formal assessing

There may be other ways in which we have less-formal assessment-type experiences. Sometimes in making a decision about a change in our lives we may say 'I need to assess the situation', or 'I need to review my options' or simply 'I need to evaluate what this means for me'. In these more personal self-assessment situations we are not engaged so much in being judged by others but rather are attempting to judge ourselves.

Other aspects of assessment can relate to assessment that acts as a gatekeeper to resources or opportunities. For example, achieving a certain grade in an exam or standard in an interview can be the decisive factor in what opportunities are opened up for you. Assessment can also involve monitoring or providing verification of our achievements. When this is the case and our achievements are recognised and even rewarded there is often a sense of achievement or a reinforcement of our self-esteem and belief in our ability. Used in this way, assessment transforms into a positive experience with the capacity to support success and promote the development of further goals.

So it could be argued that assessment carries with it connotations of being judged, evaluated and measured. If previous experiences of 'assessment' have found us deficient, inadequate or not meeting 'the' standard in some way, then it can be uncomfortable and even intimidating. It could certainly have a negative impact on self-esteem, self-efficacy and overall confidence. Not to mention that it may leave us with a residual dislike, fear or mistrust in future assessment situations. On the other hand, assessment that results in opportunities and success can support self-efficacy and provide positive reinforcement and encouragement.

While in social work we are particularly with more formal types of assessment, it is useful to also consider for a moment the skill of assessing itself. With formal assessments it usually implies that there is some agreed format or set of criteria to be measured against. However, the skill of assessing involves employing communication skills both to gather the necessary information and then to apply the appropriate criteria for judging the extent to which the person or situation meets/fits with those criteria. So listening, talking and thinking are all necessary aspects of the skill of assessing.

In a social context it is unlikely that we will be conscious of the elements that make up our assessing skills. However, you might be aware of asking a friend whose judgement you value to help you make decisions about certain situations, or of valuing a discussion with someone who seems to be able to cut through information and identify the salient facts. All of these are part of assessing skills. When you become more aware of these skills you will see that you are using them all the time, even if it is in small ways. Thinking about situations, decisions or issues in a way that draws on your ability to make a judgement about what is best or necessary in a certain set of circumstances is part of assessing skills in everyday life.

Perhaps it is easier to recognise difficulties in trusting someone's ability to make a good assessment of a situation. Think of comments like 'I don't trust you to make a good call on this because they are too involved' or 'you are too invested in the result here' or 'you are getting too emotional about this to think clearly'. Another phrase I hear is 'your judgment is clouded'. This usually refers to someone's past experiences obviously influencing their assessment. Another example is 'you are being led by your heart not your head', which suggests that feelings and emotions are getting in the way of sound judgement. We are all making assessments on an ongoing basis but are less aware of them until they happen in formal situations and where the outcome of the assessment is deemed to have potentially serious consequences. When we are very invested in outcomes the assessing process may become fraught with anxiety and tension.

Assessment as a counselling social work skill

So where does that leave assessment as part of a set of counselling skills in the context of social work? While acknowledging that in social life we employ levels of assessing skills, in the professional context of social work we are more concerned with the formal role of assessing. This means that we need to look at assessing skills associated with professional judgement as it informs decision-making. Interestingly, there are different aspects to assessments in social work that we need to consider.

First, we will look at some definitions of assessment in counselling and social work, and then we will explore how employing a competent level of counselling skills such as questioning, reflecting, listening and thinking can shape how we manage conducting assessments. We will also look at some factors that may make assessment in social work more challenging. These factors include service users' other experiences of assessment. As we have just identified, the service users' perception and previous experiences of assessment may create barriers. Barriers may be even more problematic in the context of professional assessment depending on the specific reasons for conducting a social work assessment. Regardless of the content or focus of assessment, it is clear that many of us may associate negative connotations to the process of being assessed. It is reasonable to expect that such negative views would be exacerbated in situations where you feel disempowered, fearful and in particular, when the outcome may carry serious and perhaps negative consequences for you and/or your family. Most importantly we will look at what, if anything, can be done to de-escalate the intimidation and threatening connotations of being the subject of assessment. We will also consider if it is possible to employ assessment in a way that builds on some of the identified positive reinforcing aspects of assessment which give access to resources and support self-efficacy and a sense of achievement. Assessment happens in all aspects of social work and indeed in most aspects of professional helping. When a service user speaks to a professional, one of the first tasks is to assess their situation to determine what intervention is necessary and helpful. Such initial assessment simply provides some shared understanding or a map for the interaction. This must be updated as the situation develops over time. The issues, behaviour and goals may change, or in some cases may not change, and this needs to be factored into the social work agenda between the social worker and service user.

Defining assessment

Following on from our discussion about thinking and processing it is logical to take the view that assessment is less one type of counselling skill and more an inherent activity involving the strategic use of many aspects of counselling skills. Assessment can be mistaken for an exercise in asking questions and recording answers. Viewing assessment as just an information-gathering task is very limiting in that it ignores the opportunity to develop a meaningful understanding of the service user's experiences. In fact, assessment should more accurately be defined as an information exchange, facilitated by respectful and concerned acknowledgement of the service user's perspective and informed by social work knowledge and values. It is conducted as part of an ongoing helping process which takes account of cultural and power differences as well as potential risks associated with social inequalities, disadvantage, isolation and oppression. Good assessment involves professionally competent employment of core communication, identified here as counselling social work skills: listening, thinking and talking. It does involve asking questions, but perhaps even more so it relies on the range of listening skills we have discussed as well as the full range of 'thinking' skills. These include weighing up information in the light of knowledge, values and social context. Assessment in this sense is a routine and ongoing activity that should be part of every social work and counselling encounter. As Davis and Jones (2016, p. 83) state, 'assessment can therefore be seen as a set of joint activities that begin the process of change. All elements of change, including strengths and capacities as well as problems and difficulties, are negotiated through dialogue and interaction'. However, assessment in the context of social work has other more specific connotations because of its standing in terms of statutory responsibilities. We will consider some of the factors that may add to assessment in that context being viewed as a different but related activity.

Assessment as an ongoing activity

As an activity, assessment draws on all aspects of counselling, talking, thinking and listening. It is a prerequisite for making decisions about interventions and methods and as such is best employed as part of the process of building the collaborative alliance with service users. Easy to say, of course, and given the potential identified earlier that a service user may already have had some unhelpful experiences of assessment, it isn't without its challenges. Establishing assessment as a part of building your understanding of the service users' situation rather than emphasising assessment as a tool that will provide an objective measure of the service users' risky behaviours is probably a good place to start. Coulshed and Orme (2006, p. 21) define assessment not as a single event but as 'an ongoing process in which the client or service user participates, the purpose of which is to assist the social worker to understand people in relation to their environment. Assessment is also the basis for planning what needs to be done to maintain, improve or bring about change in the person, in the environment or both'.

Therefore, assessment is not about a one-off interpretation of the information which gives an accurate measure of the problem(s) and directs the social worker to a plan of action. Assessment is ongoing, as the social worker and service user explore possibilities about useful ways of understanding the problems or concerns that have brought the service user into contact with the social worker. The assessment process, which is fundamentally a counselling thinking activity, should provide ongoing opportunities to develop shared understandings of concerns. This does not mean that there is agreement about problems or concerns. Shared understanding is not the same as agreed understanding. In fact, the assessment process can serve to illuminate differences of opinion about the identified concerns. It can also assist in highlighting different priorities for change and indeed draw attention to strengths and resilience which might serve to appease the social worker's concerns.

Challenges for ongoing assessment

While the idea that assessment is not a one-off event seems reasonable and constructive, Milner and O'Byrne (2009) voice concerns that in reality there may be less attention paid to building up a picture of what's happening and evaluating plans than the concept of an ongoing assessment would suggest. In their work, Milner and O'Byrne raise a number of issues around good practice in assessment. One of the issues relates to the notion of the ongoing assessment. They cite (Milner & O'Byrne 2009, pp. 51–54), a number of research findings (Kelly & Milner 1996; Scott 1998) which indicate that rather than adding to assessment to build a more comprehensive and accurate picture of a case, subsequent assessment interviews are more likely to simply confirm the initial assessment. This seeking verification of initial thoughts and interpretations of the situation undermines any attempt to create a more collaborative relationship with the service user. If the initial assessment is just that, a preliminary view of what's happening and what needs to happen, then as the social worker and service user grow to know and understand one another better there should be the opportunity for both to see a clearer picture of the situation. This clarity is masked if the social worker is simply trying to confirm their initial ideas.

The ongoing aspect of assessment supports the possibility that the social worker, as they become more familiar with the service user and their circumstances, may have to question their own bias or preconceived ideas. 'No matter how busy they are social workers have to make time to think carefully about what they do, how they are doing it and why they are choosing to do it in a particular way (Davis & Jones 2016, p. 86). So the assessment process is not only ongoing, as the social worker continues to revaluate their ideas about what needs to change through their contact with the service user, but the process also requires that the social worker be reflective and question themselves and their own preferred interpretation of what's going on. This might be a form of self-assessment.

At its best, assessment then becomes an ongoing, reflective activity that the social worker and service user engage in to build their shared understanding about what's going on and what needs to happen. It is an activity which can contribute to building a working relationship between social worker and service user. In the absence of some level of respect and trust, assessment may deteriorate into a process focused on two competing agendas. Department of Education Publication on CAF (2009, p. 23) stated that 'time and care must be taken to ensure the assessment is based on good communication and undertaken with respect for all parties. A "good" assessment is both a good quality process and a good quality product'.

Ideally, assessment should form part of the therapeutic intervention, which is of value in itself. However, in order to achieve this mutuality, the issues of judgement and power have to be acknowledged and addressed. This is not to say that the social worker can relinquish their responsibilities in terms of conducting assessments, but that they can use their counselling skills to optimise opportunities for the service user to contribute their ideas and their feedback on the process.

Inskipp (1996) emphasises the role of honesty in assessment. While she was referring to educational assessment, there is merit in the ideas she espouses for conducting assessment in an honest way, even when there is a power and responsibility imbalance. Given that we are all familiar with what it feels like to be assessed in that educational context, we should be able to appreciate the sentiments she expresses that 'Honesty is about accepting our power and responsibility, being open ... talking with them [trainees] how this power and responsibility can be shared with them and how much remains with us, how much trust we place in them, how they respond to this trust. The honesty is also about giving clear, specific, positive and negative feedback ... and checking that it is heard and understood' (1996, p. 69). 'Those conducting assessment must use all their facilitation skills to help trainees give their best on assessment' (1996, p. 79).

The application of counselling skills to the task of assessment provides a rationale for the importance of taking time to complete the assessment. Through taking time to build a relationship by listening and processing the information you gather, it is more likely that you will facilitate the service user to develop at least some level of trust in the social worker and therefore enhance their willingness to share more information about what's going on.

Conflicting agendas

It is inevitable in some social work contexts that the social worker and service user will have different agendas. The aim of employing counselling skills in the assessment process is to assist in the negotiation of at least some elements of agreement. For example, the identification of a mutually agreed priority, the well-being of the children, might be possible even where those involved see very different ways to achieve this. The agenda or at least one item on that agenda is agreed between the social worker and the service user. Disagreement and even conflict may then focus on the method of achieving that aim. It is important to consider views of assessment that may have negative connotations. As already mentioned, these include ideas about assessment that acknowledge the power and judgement associated with assessment (Inskipp 1996).

Assessment may in fact mean different things to different people depending on the context and their role in the assessment process. In order to negotiate an agreed agenda, the social worker needs to employ their counselling communication skills to provide clarity and openness about the issues of judgement and power. This involves acknowledging their authority and responsibilities and at the same time finding a way to demonstrate that they respect the service user as an expert in their own lives and as the person who will ultimately have to make a choice about change.

Of course, we must acknowledge that in some crisis situations emergency assessments require immediate action and so this is not always going to be possible. But even where crisis actions have been taken, there is usually a follow-up process that can provide the opportunity to review and build on the initial assessment. It may also impact on your ability and willingness to review and change an action or care plan. Of course, any change needs to be done in collaboration with the service user. Many service users that I meet have mentioned that the changing expectations of social workers is a frustrating part of their involvement with social services.

The application of a framework for assessment such as that used in child protection and welfare, the Common Assessment Framework (CAF) in the UK (Department of Education 2009), can provide a clear and more transparent structure. It is important to remember that CAF is not a form but a process based on good communication and respect for all parties. Success in employing such an assessment tool continues to rely on professionally competent communication skills on the part of the social worker. These skills are part of the counselling social work repertoire. Using a standardised tool should facilitate more continuity in assessment with less risk of individual bias. This, of course, is dependent on the continuity and support in training provided. It is important to recognise that the use of any assessment tool is only as effective as the skill of the person conducting the assessment.

The CAF (2009) identifies three domains for assessment: child development, parenting capacity and environmental factors. This draws attention not only to the psychological aspects of assessment, but also to the socioeconomic and political context within which needs arise. Hood reiterates the importance of this aspect of assessment. Hood reminds us (2016, p. 83) that 'assessment takes place within an interpersonal, institutional and socio-political context, and this includes the power dynamics that emerge when people disagree about the problem is and what kind of change is desirable'. So the power differentials are not only between the social worker and the service user but may encompass power issues that impact on the social worker and service user in the broader socio-political world. It could be argued that these environmental or socio-political factors at one time formed a basis for social work practice. Social work's origins in community work saw the profession as advocating for and with service users in negotiating structural disadvantage. Milner and O'Byrne (2009, p. 12), however, voice their concerns that 'while social workers remain within a problem solving narrative which pays little attention to the complexities of assessment it is very difficult for them to make social rather than individual assessments'.

It may be challenging and even frustrating that social work deals in uncertainties. This is nowhere more evident than when it comes to assessment. Social work is supposed to bring the social into the understanding of individual and family matters. After all, the social is an inherent aspect of the social work value system and knowledge base. This often results in drawing attention not only to individual problems but also to structural problems that impact the individuals and their families. It also means that social workers need to take account not only of problem behaviours and possible limitations in coping skills or capacity, but should also consider strengths and resilience. The breadth of the assessment does not necessarily provide a clear and unequivocal answer. As Hood (2016, p. 85) notes, 'in their assessments social workers are often being asked to judge complex situations and deal with uncertainty'. But then service user problems are sometimes complex and this deserves to be recognised, especially if failure to acknowledge such complexity results in pathologising or blaming service users. As Turney et al. (2012, p. 197) highlight, 'It is important therefore that the different domains of the "assessment triangle" are not seen as discrete areas for investigation and that *systemic thinking* is used to explore the interconnections and interactions between different pieces of information' (emphasis added). The importance of taking the social into account in assessment informs the research of Devine (2015), where she points to the barrier created in assessment when the focus is on individual deficits rather than structural disadvantage or inequalities.

Assessment in a statutory context

Assessment is, then, a core part of social work activity, whether this is part of the ongoing development of the social worker's understanding of what is happening for the service user or part of the skill of reviewing and evaluating interventions and action plans. But perhaps assessment is most often associated with the statutory responsibilities for social workers in the field of child welfare and protection. Assessment in this context is undoubtedly fraught with complexities. The outcome of such assessment has far-reaching consequences for all involved. We have already identified some of the challenges to assessment in general in social work.

Assessment in relation to safeguarding is even more challenging. It takes place in an ever-growing and ever-changing legal, policy, cultural and procedural context. Social workers and other professionals are at the same time attempting to assess risk, identify patterns of behaviour, predict future actions while taking cognisance of sometimes contradictory theoretical positions. Different theoretical understandings of what constitutes what is best for children have taken prominence over the years from the long-held beliefs in attachment to more recent recognitions of the place of child and family resilience. One obvious challenge in conducting social work assessment is the growing influence of psychological theory, often at the expense of the sociological or social analysis perspective. There have been attempts to support the inclusion of a broader view on family and environmental factors in assessment. This would allow assessment to fit more as a measure of potential rather than a measure of failure. The CAF does include consideration of 'environmental' factors in the recommended assessment format. However, the extent of the influence of this part of the assessment needs further research. Part of the challenge is that in light of limited resources is the possible temptation to focus on individual responsibility as the target for change rather than tackling issues associated with limited resources available to prevent risk developing. Milner and O'Byrne (2009, p. 19) capture this dilemma in their comment that 'there also exists the tendency to drift not only towards psychological reductionism as a placebo solution to inadequate resources, but also towards risk assessments as a response to continuous public castigation of social work efforts'.

Assessment in this context of children and their safety is particularly vulnerable to public criticism. It is really important that such assessments are done in a transparent and professional way. This involves the social work being fully informed by the legal, policy and agency procedures as required for conducting assessments. What is more difficult to understand is that while as a society we value the safety of children, there is unfortunately always some element of uncertainty. The uncertainty emanates in part from the fact that an assessment is only as good as the information, research guidance, theoretical interpretations, policy and procedures available. This involves attempting to 'balance between diverse needs, recognised risks and restricted resource provision or between considering whether some interventions should be attempted as against the restraints of time' (Milner & O'Byrne 2009, pp. 18–19).

Assessment as a helping/therapeutic activity

A broader definition of assessment should include not only the use of standardised assessment procedural tools but also the ongoing 'thinking' as discussed in earlier chapters. Constantly adding to your assessment an understanding of the service user's situation is essential, whether that's at the stage of initial assessment or after prolonged engagement. This can be achieved by thinking through new information and processing through the filters of theoretical ideas (see Figure 4.3 and Figure 4.4) in a way that generates alternatives, rather than simply validating bias or preconceived ideas.

In his introduction to assessment, Hood (2016) cites a number of definitions of assessment that share the very positive attributes that we would like to consider as assessment. He refers to ideas that see assessment as being about helping people to identify areas for growth, establishing a problem-solving partnership (Walker & Beckett 2011), being part of a basic helping cycle (Taylor and Devine 1993), and planning, implementation and review. For social work, then, assessment can be helping people to identify areas for growth and establishing partnerships as well as ultimately making a judgement on the service user's situation. You can already see why assessment can pose a challenge to building a collaborative relationship.

Devine (2015) identified two models of assessment. She refers to the Anglo-American model which includes: UK, North America, New Zealand and Australia and the Western European model: Belgium, Sweden, France and Germany. She suggests that the 'key distinguishing characteristic of the Anglo-American model relies on a threshold being reached before secondary or tertiary interventions can be justified', while the Western European model provides 'universal services without suspicion and specific risk assessment ... as a means of reducing the load on statutory child protection focussed work and also simplifying the process required to filter families through risk assessment' (Devine 2015, p. 79).

Drawing on the work of Devine (2015), it is possible to make the argument that certain features of how assessments are conducted can contribute or detract from building a collaborative relationship with service users and therefore can enhance or undermine attempts to deliver assessment as part of a therapeutic process. Features of assessment that contribute to enhancing the therapeutic potential of assessment and factors that may undermine that therapeutic potential are identified in Figure 6.1.

Theoretical bias and power in assessment

The practice of privileging the initial assessment also raises problems related to our earlier discussion on social workers' and counsellors' theoretical bias. Bias can be generated by the influence of theoretical ideas about human behaviour and how theory helps, but can also limit us in terms of what we are looking for and how we make sense of the service user's story. The practice of dealing with assessment as a single event may lead to privileging the initial assessment to the detriment of developing an unfolding

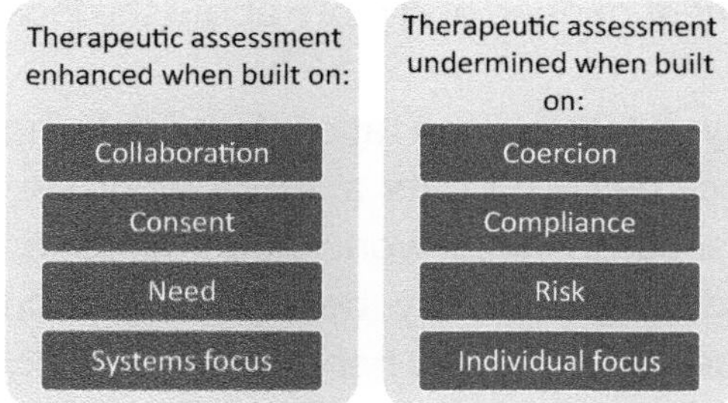

Figure 6.1 Assessment as a therapeutic process

understanding. Milner and O'Byrne (2009, p. 52) cite Sheldon (1995) where he talks about social workers using their counselling and interview techniques to shape the assessment to fit their preferred theory. Taking an ongoing approach to assessment allows for reflection and consultation on assessment. This provides opportunities for social workers to question their initial thinking and generate alternative interpretations. It also should provide the social worker with opportunities to identify ways in which agency preferences influence assessment. Davis and Jones (2016, p. 83) add to this a reminder that 'assessment takes place within an interpersonal, institutional and socio-political context, and this includes the power dynamics that emerge when people disagree about what the problem is and what kind of change is desirable'. Therefore, social workers need to be able to take a critical view on their own practice, but also to question agency and policy factors that may advertently or inadvertently further disadvantage service users.

Assessment as gatekeeper

Assessment can be used for purposes other than developing an understanding of the service user's situation or evaluating risk. Assessment may be used as a tool to establish eligibility for resource allocation. The place of social work assessment in influencing who gets a service also has its challenges. The most difficult aspect of this is where structural factors result in limiting resources to the extent that some people who could benefit from having access to resources are deemed ineligible. The ineligibility may be less about an assessment of need and more about the lack of resources.

Thresholds are often employed to provide a rationale for defining who gets a resource. This includes who gets a social work service. One of the contentious issues in social work is that decisions based on thresholds of predicting risk may be used to ration access to social work services. Where this happens potentially preventable problems may have to develop until they reach a level of risk that is deemed to meet the threshold for service provision.

Assessment that could result in denying a service that the service user wants/needs is inevitably going to require a high level of skill on the part of the social worker. Sometimes the social worker will be faced with accepting that the service user would in fact benefit from the service but does not meet the required threshold. Davis and Jones (2015) recognise that this can create problems for social workers, especially when combined with limited opportunities to advocate on the part of the service user. They suggest (2015, p. 84) that it may even lead to social workers interpreting information in a certain way to assist in gaining access to the services/resources. Such discretionary power is a double-edged sword, as it highlights the risks that interpretation and bias can impact decision-making and outcomes.

On other occasions the social worker may have to attempt to work with the service user to encourage them to accept a service or intervention when the service user is unwilling to do so. The counselling and relationship-building aspect of social work can be undermined by situations where structural factors dictate resource allocation. Here is where the concept of thresholds adds to the challenge. Turney et al. (2011) provided a very helpful review of some findings in relation to thresholds. They reported the following:

> *Limited resources and pressure of work generally result in a tendency to raise thresholds for access to services as a way of rationing responses (Brandon et al. 2008; Sheppard 2009a). High thresholds may mean that children and families with substantial problems and high levels of need do not receive timely help (Biehal 2005). This is a particular issue in cases of child neglect and emotional abuse (Brandon et al. 2008 and 2009; Farmer et al. 2008; Ward et al. 2010).*

Assessments used to gate-keep eligibility to resources or to provide rationale for allocation to those most in need generate further challenges in building a collaborative relationship with service users. Sometimes social workers may be in a position where they are the front-line person implementing policies about the allocation of resources where crisis takes precedence over prevention. Yet if such limitations were not imposed, the social worker's assessment may be that the service user would benefit from the service. The availability of resources is impacted by the social/economic/political influences of the time, which can only be addressed when the social and environment aspect of assessment is fully integrated, not only in the information gathered but also in defining targets for change.

Different settings make collaboration more challenging, but nonetheless engagement of service users remains one of the most important aspects of the social work assessment. Hood (2016, p. 83) says that assessment can be seen as a set of joint activities that begin the process of change. Ideally, the aim of assessment is to work with the service user towards identifying strengths and resiliencies that exist and then agree goals for change. Then the quality of the assessment is predicated on the relationship that can be established.

Talking, listening and thinking

The core cycle of counselling that we have been applying incorporates the three aspects of talking, listening, thinking. Milner and O'Byrne (2009, p. 4) presented a model for assessment that identified five aspects included in the assessment process. These were 'preparation for assessment, collecting information, applying professional knowledge, making judgements and deciding or recommending what should be done'. Of the five aspects, it is interesting to note that only collecting of information focuses on employing the skills of talking and listening. For the remaining four elements of assessment the core skill employed is processing or thinking. Other skills identified include 'being punctual, reliable, courteous, friendly, honest and open' (Milner & O'Byrne 2016, p. 19).

In terms of talking, we can look to the discussion of questioning to inform the activity of assessment. Also important is the skill of being able to clearly describe/talk through an account of the aims and propose, the timeframe for the assessment and potential outcomes. This should also assist in helping the service user to understand what will be included in the assessment. These may include such factors as:

- What other sources of information are available to the social worker
- What options are open to the service user for support
- Clarification on the legal position policy and procedures
- Who has responsibility and for what in the process

Openness and honesty

Openness and honesty about the assessment process is viewed as a skill which can contribute to reducing tension and potential conflict. This is true of the counselling process in other contexts as well. Building the relationship with service users can be complicated, especially when social workers find themselves torn between their responsibility to the agency policy and procedures and their professional perception, which may identify concerns beyond their permitted remit. 'Agency function rarely permits social workers to address major problems rooted in social deprivation, while, at the same time, holds them responsible for attempting to operationalise a care plan that is not founded on realistic social assessment' (Milner & O'Byrne 2009, p. 8).

Openness about the assessment also includes finding ways to communicate to the service user worries that may have led to the assessment. This should include conveying your commitment to listening to their story and attempting to assess not only concerns that might arise but also acknowledging signs of safety, strength and resilience. This can sometimes cause confusion where the assessment gives voice to both signs of risk and safety. However, the skill of processing or thinking will be a key part in interpreting all the information, both from conversation and observation as well as information from other sources and input from other disciplines to assist in providing the basis of an action plan. Ideally the service user should feel they have been heard and that they understand the assessment process. This does not, of course, mean that they will agree with the outcome or be willing to participate in the social worker's preferred plan of action. Where child safety is concerned, despite mutual commitment to the best interests of the child/children, it is not always the case that an agreed view of what is best can be achieved.

Managing these potential professional conflicts requires application of communication skills, specifically thinking and reflecting. These provide a forum for social workers to draw on research and knowledge to support their assessments while at the same time providing access to support and supervision to help them process their own feelings in relation to the situation they are evaluating. Sometimes conflict is interpreted as service user 'resistance'. In many intervention models the notion of resistance has been rejected, which we will explore in later chapters. Forrester et al. (2012) provide a helpful reminder that the context and setting in which assessment happens can contribute to an escalation of this so-called resistance. It is important also to be aware that 'client resistance is not something that solely exists within the client, nor even something that is simply produced by the context of child protection. Rather, it is also to some degree a product of the nature and quality of the interaction between client and social worker. This is crucial because it puts the spotlight on social worker behaviour as both a potential cause of resistance and also our most important tool for reducing resistance' (Forrester et al. 2012, p. 4). As we mentioned, this 'resistance' is exasperated by an assessment process that is focused on identifying individual deficits and neglecting to acknowledge social disadvantage and other social or systems factors.

Writing and recording in assessment

From a counselling and relationship-building perspective, writing and listening are not very compatible activities. Hence, to make it work, you have to work hard on how to incorporate these two seemingly contradictory skills. Most importantly, as a social worker you must be totally aware of your responsibilities in terms of recording the interactions you have with service users, whether this involves filling out specific forms, keeping case notes, completing agency intake forms or other documentation requirements. The fulfilment of these requirements are essential as part of best practice. However, it is important to recognise that unless handled skilfully, these activities may impede or derail relationship-building with the service user. We discussed the connotation of judgement and power that are inherent in most assessment processes. These factors, along with the likelihood that you are not listening as attentively while trying to write coherently, can create barriers to communication.

You need to work on this skill. Following agency protocols is always the best guide regarding how to conduct and record the assessment. While adhering to these guidelines, there may be opportunities to work on following guidelines in the most therapeutically effective way through using writing to build the relationship with service users. This can be achieved by the following: Be well prepared for the assessment. Familiarise yourself with whatever forms or documents you will need to complete, as if you were preparing yourself for an exam. There may be some questions you have to answer and record the answer. The more familiar you are with these questions the better able you will be to ask questions in a way to elicit the responses you need. This includes following the service user's train of thought and helping them to explore the extent of the question to give as full an answer as possible.

In order to make the recording of information a coherent part of the conversation, it is important to explain the purpose of any forms/documents that need to be filled. It can be reassuring to the service user that their answers are (1) being taken seriously, (2) being written down and checked with them for accuracy, and (3) that they are aware of what information and actions are being recorded.

Conducting an assessment where the recording of specific facts is done during the conversation requires developing the skill of acknowledging that you are writing and not fully listening. This means that you need to find a way to shift the focus from listening to writing and back. This needs to have a flow otherwise it will exacerbate the sense of being judged. Ideally, in line with procedures, it is good to explain what forms/information will need to be recorded and how and when this is going to happen in the course of the interview.

Sometimes I undertake form-filling at the start of an interview. This has some benefits in that it gets the perceived formality of writing out of the way, at least partially. However, it does put the onus on the social worker to remember the information gathered on the form. It takes skill to ensure that this does not impede relationship-building. For example, if you find out someone has three children and works part-time and then later ask them if they are still working or, worse, refer to their two sons and forget they have a daughter they mentioned earlier. Just because you have the information on paper doesn't mean you can leave it there, it has to stay with you. In my work with service users developing education inputs for students, one of the issues they identified as being upsetting and annoying was social workers using incorrect name(s) for their children. They saw this as very disrespectful (Loughran & Broderick 2017).

Remember that with the CAF you may have information from other sources which come up in the interview. Again, the point of having shared information is to minimise the repetitious aspect of assessment, especially when it involves a number of different agencies or professionals, so it is important to know how this shared information will be handled in your assessment. Confidentiality should be explained at the outset and the social worker should be prepared to answer any questions the service user might have. This obviously includes being open about the limitations of confidentiality and the process of sharing information.

Another option is to complete forms towards the end of the session. This has the advantage that you have the opportunity to establish a connection with the service user before completing the form-filling, which, as I said earlier, has the potential to create distance between you and highlight power differentials. Again, it requires that you remember information you have gathered throughout the conversation. However, it is often useful to frame the form-filling as a way of capturing key points that the service user has raised, allowing you to check back that you have got it right and also allowing you to clarify the parameters of the assessment.

Of course, the third option is to conduct the recording/form-filling throughout the session. This demands more signposting as to when you are giving your full listening attention and when you are trying to summarise or capture the key factors to be recorded in the forms/documentation. When incorporating the form-filling is done skilfully it can avoid some of the formality associated with focusing on the forms at the beginning or end. To be both productive and constructive, the act of writing must feel inclusive. This may involve sharing the layout of the form either by showing the form or describing key headings to be completed. It is then possible to guide the service user through the steps and check with them if they understand what has been noted and give them the opportunity to add points if they wish. With the development of computer-based assessments the skill involved may be about how you can record information on the computer without alienating the service user. For some, computers will be a very acceptable tool to be used in the interview, but for others it may raise further anxiety about confidentially and who is going to have access to their information.

Being at ease about keeping a record of the interview and filling out any required forms is a first step in helping the service user to be more at ease. Establishing and maintaining a collaborative relationship in a context where there are concerns about risk and the possibility of different views about what's happening and what needs to happen is not going to be easy. It demands high levels of communication skills. However, it is important to remember that a constructive and helpful assessment will demand that the social worker not only listens actively, but also asks questions skilfully. A key part of assessment is the thinking that informs and supports the assessment. This means basing the assessment on a sound knowledge base, informed by social work values and operationalised through counselling skills so as to optimise access to the service user's perspective. It also involves the social worker having the opportunity to challenge any bias or preconceived ideas.

Social worker stress

It is worth noting that research into the factors that impact social work, especially in child welfare settings, are drawing attention to the emotional well-being of the social worker. Being engaged in what is often crisis or traumatic situations can take its toll on professionals. Morrison (2007, p. 246) stresses that 'emotions and power relations are central to social work'. Not only are emotions recognised as central, but standards of proficiency for social work require that social workers are able to recognise and reflect on the emotional impact the work has on them and also to be aware of how that impact may affect their work. In order to continue to work effectively, it is important that social workers pay attention to this, not just in how it might influence their judgement in any particular case, but how it may impede their work more generally. Social workers' employers have the responsibility for supporting social workers. This involves not only identifying social workers who are experiencing stress, but actually creating work environments where such stress is minimised. Social work is built on relationship connections and with this comes engagement with service users who are often in distress. Managing this, according to Morrison (2007, p. 263), 'requires that social workers are not only technically proficient but that they possess maturity in their help-seeking skills and attitudes. Such self-awareness can assist in engaging with service users and promotes social workers' coping mechanisms'.

Exercise 12 Consider these issues in relation to assessment

- Professional competence in the core counselling social work skills: listening, thinking and talking are essential in order to maximise the accuracy, benefits and usefulness of assessment. Agency support and ongoing supervision are essential to continue to develop you skills.
- Employ a need-informed rather than resource-informed assessment process, ensuring that the issue of limited resources becomes the target of change effort rather than only responding to need being limited to what resources have been assigned to meet the need.

- Where assessment is not restricted in this way it is still possible to undermine the social work assessment by not providing the resources identified in the assessment as necessary to address need.
- Take into account individual circumstances or factors that may prove critical to the establishment of a helpful understanding of the issues and apply assessment in a flexible and responsive manner.
- Be aware of and be sensitive to service user sense of powerlessness and of being judged in the assessment process.
- Remember that assessment when handled without due attention to core counselling skills has the potential to damage the trust and relationship-building required to build a collaborative relationship with a service user.
- In the absence of some level of relationship with the service user the assessment may yield at best insufficient information to inform the social worker's thinking, and at worst may provide misleading or conflicting information, thus diminishing the potential for the assessment to form a useful basis for decision-making and planning.
- Formulaic assessment might mistakenly appear to be objective. All social work assessments have some element of subjectivity in so far as they involve interpretation and processing of information. This processing, as we have discussed, can be founded on bias, which gives precedence to one theoretical explanation of that information and ultimately can generate an action plan informed by that bias.
- Note: be cautious regarding allocation of resources and defining the 'problem'. There may be cultural and/or socio-political bias towards privileging the psychological versus sociological analysis in assessment. This leads to the focus on identification of individual deficits (Devine 2015), which undermines the collaborative and therapeutic assessment process. The cynic might say that it is easier to target the service user for change than to acknowledge social,

economic and environmental problems that the agency, the state or others outside the individual/family need to be held accountable for.

- Recognise that core counselling skills are applicable in the assessment process. Having professional competence and of course sufficient support and resources to use these skills will contribute to establishing a working relationship with the service user. Whatever the context, this is a preliminary but essential step in conducting an assessment that yields a helpful and more accurate account of the situation including social as well as individual and family factors where relevant.
- Listening and writing do not go well together. Pay attention to how you can create a collaborative approach to recording during the conversation with the service users.
- Social work in whatever setting is ultimately about helping and is therefore a therapeutic activity. It differs from other interventions in that it should always take account of social dimensions, thus applying a social and critical analysis in understanding service users' lived experiences. This goes beyond the individual to encompass family, community, culture as well as the socioeconomic and political context.

7 Empathy, reflection and reflective responding

- Discussion about empathy including definitions of empathy, distinguishing empathy from sympathy and looking at empathy and developing the collaborative relationship which is at the heart of social work.
- The connection between empathy and reflection will be explored.
- Reflective responding is a counselling skill connected to empathy, listening and questioning. Empathy and empathic listening can be demonstrated through reflective responses.
- Research supports the importance of empathy in counselling. As one of the key ways of demonstrating empathy, reflective responding is then central to social work practice. Research which raised concerns about social workers ability to engage in reflective responding will be reviewed.
- It will then be argued that the skill of employing reflection to formulate responses should be viewed as central to social work counselling and thus be supported and developed. Its place in the core activities of talking, listening and thinking will be considered.

Introduction

Empathy, although widely accepted as a core counselling skill, is one of the most challenging skills to describe. This may be because, despite agreement on its importance, there is less agreement on what it actually means. There has been debate about the nature of empathy and questioning as to whether it is possible to learn to be empathic. Does empathy require only a cognitive understanding or is an emotional dimension also necessary?

This chapter will explore some of these different definitions of empathy. Part of the challenge in finding an agreed definition of empathy relates to some variability in the actual terms used when referring to empathy. Terms such as empathic understanding, empathic listening, empathic reflection and empathic responding are sometimes used interchangeably. For the purpose of this chapter, the skill of being empathic will be considered to be the outcome of employing these other skills. There may be no specific order as to how these skills are employed, but the suggestion here is that empathy is the result of one's ability to listen empathically, then engage in empathic reflection, followed up with empathic responding so as to reach empathic understanding. Achieving empathic understanding requires not just listening and observing to what is going on for the service user, but also communicating that understanding back to them in order to check the accuracy of your interpretation of what's happening. Only then can you empathically understand another person. Shebib (2003, p. 169) agrees that while 'empathy in everyday terms usually means seeing the world through someone else's eyes … empathy in counselling involves both understanding and communication of that understanding'.

Gavin and Seabury (1984) suggest that reflective responses rather than empathy is a term that can be used when dealing primarily with service user's thoughts. In this chapter, however, reflective responses will be considered to encompass both thoughts and feelings. They are presented as a vehicle through which the social worker can transmit or communicate their empathy for the service user's experiences at all levels.

Empathy as a social skill

We all know in our social and personal lives how to judge if someone is empathic. In fact it is probably true to say that close friends are close because they demonstrate at least some empathic abilities. This means that we feel understood by friends and family who are capable of being empathic. Sometimes this involves having shared the same or similar experiences. This sharing may contribute to the sense of empathic understanding. Having empathy with someone usually helps us to know what to say or do in situation where that person needs support. It is difficult to distinguish which comes first, the ability to be empathic or the relationship. Does empathy build a relationship, or does the relationship contribute to the ability to be empathic?

While we can all probably appreciate it when someone demonstrates empathy, it is more difficult to pinpoint what is involved. Nonetheless, we are probably aware when someone is not empathic. This involves feeling that you have not been heard or listened to or understood. Sometimes this comes across when we are being given advice or told what to do rather than someone just hearing us out. It might be the person we are talking to just wants to move on and sort the problem, while you may just want to express your hurt or joy ... it works for both. Empathy in counselling social work is related to the kind of empathy we might experience in a social context. In fact, empathy is known to be an important contributor to building relationships in social work. We will look more at the importance of empathy in social work next. To explore more about empathy in a social communication context, see the example described in Appendix 7.1.

Defining empathy

In social communication the differences between empathy and sympathy may not be clearly distinguished. However, from a counselling perspective it is a very important distinction to make.

Sympathy

Shebib (2003, p. 181) provides an account of sympathy which emphasises that sympathy is about 'a concern for other people's problems and emotions and is related to our own emotional and behavioural reactions. Although it is intimately connected to another's feelings, it is in fact our own reaction. Empathy is objective appreciation of someone else's situation; sympathy is more about your own emotional response'. It is appropriate at times to express sympathy, to let someone know when you feel a response to their situation because it shows your human qualities, but it is essential for social workers to separate out their own emotional reactions so that they don't detract from the service user's feelings and needs.

Empathy

The traditional emphasis of empathy has been on understanding emotions and feelings. Empathy was one of Rogers' six conditions for a therapeutic relationship (1957). He defined (p. 99) empathy as 'the ability to sense the client's private world as if it were your own, but without ever losing the "as if" quality'.

However, broader definitions of empathy also allude to the more behavioural and cognitive aspects of empathy. As Shebib (2003, p. 169) puts it, 'the primary target of empathy is to reply to feelings, but in the process counselors typically capture elements of client's thoughts and situations'. Neukrug et al. (2013, p. 13) hold that 'Rogers' empathy as a way of knowing about another included not just emotional but also cognitive and communication dimensions'. Add to this the difficulty in explaining empathy from two different perspectives: what it means to the social worker and then what it means to the service user. In reality, empathy is only empathy when the service user feels understood. Myers (2000, p. 149) reminded us that 'if the therapeutic relationship is to be fully explored, it makes sense to listen to the voices of clients as they report their experiences of being heard'. This means that the social worker has to seek supervision and practice reflectivity in order to be alert to whether they have been successful in their attempts to be empathic. This involves taking feedback for service users, whether that is direct comment from service users or indirect through observation of the service user's reaction to your attempts at empathy. It is possible that you might think you have got the service user's perspective when in fact you are still imposing your own interpretation on the situation or experience. Given what we have discussed regarding the power difference between service users and social workers, such misuse of empathy could be destructive to the relationship. Miller (2018, p. 36) defines empathic understanding as 'an accepting and compassionate way of being with people that invites openness'. The skill of being empathic in counselling requires not just empathic listening and developing your understanding of the service user's experience, it also requires that you demonstrate that empathy. It is in demonstrating your empathy that the service user has the opportunity to let you know if indeed you have actually succeeded in understanding their experience, perception and/or feelings. If the service user feels understood and accepted then the relationship can be strengthened and this facilitates the development of openness and trust.

Empathy or identifying with someone

There is also the question of whether it is actually possible or even desirable to fully understand someone else's experiences or feelings. Even two people who go through the same experience do not necessarily have the same experience. So, for example, two people who experience having their children in care may have had very different experiences of that and very different feelings about it. In addition, the social worker, whatever their level of skill in being empathic, can never fully know what it is like to 'be in the same shoes' as either of the service users. As Miller (2018, p. 5) highlights, 'empathy involves not only attention to and also connecting with other people, an active interest in understanding what he she is experiencing ... It is not the same as identifying with a person'. He goes on to clarify that empathic understanding does not need such identification or shared experiences. In fact 'identifying with somebody because of similarity with you can interfere with accurate empathy: what they are expressing lies to close to home for you to understand how it may differ from your own experience' (Miller 2018, p. 5).

Defining empathy as part of social work, Compton and Galaway (1999) clarify that 'empathy is the capacity to enter into the feelings and experiences of another – knowing what the other appeals and experiences – without losing oneself in the process. The helping person makes an active effort to enter into the reception frame of the other person without losing personal perspective'.

Neukrug et al. (2013) propose building on basic empathy by adding the ability to: reflect deeper feelings, point to discrepancies (e.g. feeling two different ways about something), use visual aids, analogies and metaphors to demonstrate understanding and to use targeted self-disclosure.

Basic empathy

Carkhuff (1969) talked about different levels of empathy. He distinguished these based mostly on the extent to which the counsellor detracts from or adds to the client's sense of being understood. The five levels were: subtractive, slightly subtractive, basic empathy or interchangeable response, slightly additive and additive. Ivey (1994, p. 146), in discussing Carkhuff's levels, reminds us that 'as the counselor attempts to move towards additive responses [*higher level of empathy*], the risk goes up. Risk in this case means risk of error. You may have excellent listening skills but when you seek to add you own perceptions you may be out of sync with clients' needs'.

Basic empathy refers to giving back what was said without adding emphasis or attempting to move forward the shared understanding of the service user's feeling or experience in order to bring a deeper level of meaning.

Accurate empathy

One distinction that can be made is between empathy and accurate empathy. For empathy to be effective and helpful it needs to resonate with the service user. This requires that you are reasonably accurate in your interpretation of what you are picking up from the service user. For Miller (2018, pp. 35–36), accurate empathy is 'more a way of being that emerges over time and included underlying attitude ... You develop accurate empathy with and for people by taking the time to listen deeply and understand layers of meaning and feeling that they are willing to share with you'.

Miller (2018, p. 4) commented on accurate empathy, clarifying that 'to some extent empathy is innate, but accurate empathy is not. Yet most people most of the time assume that their interpretations are accurate and then act accordingly, which can be the source of great deal of misunderstanding and conflict'.

Advanced empathy

Empathic responding is connected to the use of reflecting emotional/feeling content. With empathy, however, your aim is that your reflection will help to build a connection with the service user by demonstrating that you do understand or at least have been listening to the emotions expressed. You may also use reflection to put words on emotions you have observed or have interpreted as being there and use reflection to put words on them and bring them into the service user's awareness.

Rogers (1986, p. 376) in Neukrug et al. (2013, p. 32) said about reflecting feelings: 'I am not trying to reflect feelings, I am trying to determine whether my understanding of the clients' inner world is correct. Advanced empathy suggests being able to hear and reflect deeper feelings than the client was able to verbalise, or being able to synthesize meaning across previously discussed topics'.

In Carkhuff's (1969) levels, advanced empathy would be at the higher level of skill. It involves taking more risk to try to progress both a shared understanding and to deepen the service user's own understanding of what they are experiencing, emotionally and otherwise. This can sometimes be about expanding emotional literacy. It is very difficult to discuss feelings because our emotional language is often limited. Add to this the wide variety of levels of feeling and the multiplicity of words used to describe those feeling and you can appreciate the challenge. When someone says they are depressed, just what does that mean? Are they clinically depressed, distraught, sad, upset or off-form? Can you be sure that even if you are both in the same range identifying an emotion that you are both tuned into the intensity of the emotion being experienced? It is useful to work on your own emotional vocabulary in order to enhance your skill in demonstrating empathy. Having a broader range of terms for emotions to capture different levels of intensity also provides scope to use these to evoke a deeper level of emotional awareness or to help defuse levels of intensity.

Research

Empathy is generally accepted as being closely associated with positive outcomes in counselling. It is therefore something that social workers need to pay attention to.

Demonstrating empathy is linked to supporting and developing a strong collaborative relationship with service users. For Rogers (1957), empathy was fundamental to developing the therapeutic or collaborative relationship and he claimed that demonstration of empathy was connected to positive outcomes. Shulman's research (2009) concluded that empathy contributes substantially to overcoming the challenges of developing a counselling relationship. His research also confirmed empathy as a powerful helping tool. More recent research has supported these findings, with Bohart and Tallman (2010, p. 93) reporting that 'overall empathy accounts for as much and probably more outcome variance than does specific intervention'. Service users confirm the importance of empathy. Cooper (2011) reports research findings where clients themselves identified that feeling understood was one of the most important benefits in counselling/therapy.

Empathy can be learned

Despite the concerns raised in Forrester's (2008) research, which found that social workers were not employing their reflective skills and therefore pointing to concern about use or lack of use of empathy, it is clear that empathy is a skill that can be learned. According to Neukrug et al. (2013), research into how emotions and experiences activate the brain led Gerdes and Segal (2011) to suggest that empathy is trainable in that this innate response can be developed. They proposed that careful attention to clients builds new neural pathways that facilitate empathic ability while also allowing counsellors to become aware of behaviours that limit empathy. This is further supported by Clark (2010) and Kuntze (2009), whose work is referred to in Neukrug et al. (2013, p. 39). They state that 'the ability to make basic and advanced empathic responses is a developmental process that usually takes time, practice and continuous supervision'. Greeno et al. (2017) also found that that empathy can be learned but that it is more effective when live supervision is provided.

Exercise 13 Developing empathy

Empathy is a skill that combines talking, listening and processing. In a social communication situation, for example among friends, the skill of being empathic may appear to be spontaneous and instinctive. However, it is possible to learn quite a lot about how empathy works and how the skill can be developed by becoming more observant about your interactions in everyday life. Take time to notice when you are feeling listened to and understood. Whats going on, how is the other person managing to convey this sense of empathy in their communication with you? The level of competence required in order to utilise this skill in a more formal professional setting can then be built on from that initial understanding.

Empathy in a professional context

Empathy in a professional context is, therefore, more challenging. Some people take the view that in order to be empathic you need to have gone through the same experience yourself and that somehow having experienced similar things is going to help you to understand somebody else. I have a cautionary note about this. The risk is that just because you have been through a similar experience doesn't mean that it had the same impact on you or has the same meaning for the service user at this point in time. In addition, many social workers will be working with people who are in very different life situations, very different life stages and dealing with very different challenges. So, if the ability to be empathic was dependent on having gone through the experience yourself, then it would be pretty difficult to rely on that as an important counselling skill. Empathy can be learned and developed, but does involve taking the time to listen to the service user, to process the information, to ask questions that facilitate exploration of their feelings and their thoughts. As we have seen, empathy is not just about feelings. Empathy involves understanding people's feelings, but also trying to have some sense of how people are thinking and what sort of thinking and feeling is informing their behaviour. As a social worker, therefore, you cannot rely only on the information that you gather through your counselling skills and listening skills in conversation with the service user, but you can also build on experiences that other service users have revealed to you over time. It is almost as if you have a bank of understanding that other service users have helped you to build over time. In addition, you also have theoretical information about likely scenarios that are going to impact on different people in different stages of their lives and also in relation to particular problems.

Exercise 13 Developing

So, let's just use this example about somebody meeting you for coffee and starting the conversation by saying they are very upset. Let's say you are working with young people and you are perhaps meeting with somebody in a resource centre or somebody who has had some problems with the law, whatever the context. So, you meet with them and they open the conversation by saying they are really upset. It is most unlikely that saying to them, 'Oh, I understand, I've been through the same myself' is going to be experienced as an empathic response. It is much more likely that before you are able to consider any meaningful or accurate empathic response other than being supportive and concerned, you are going to need more information. Hence, empathy is something that develops from listening to the service user and from facilitating them in exploring what is going on for them and being able to feel relaxed enough or at ease enough to be able to share some of their thoughts and feelings about events with you as a social worker. In this context, sometimes it is actually helpful to say that you don't know what it might be like for them in the situation, but that it would be really helpful if they could help you to understand what it is like for them. In Norcross (2010), he gives an example of a situation whereby sometimes if a service user actually doesn't want to talk and feels that they are under pressure to talk and that, in fact, that is the most difficult and challenging thing for them, then being empathic may involve just acknowledging and accepting that there are some things at that particular point in time that they don't want to talk about. He suggests that it may not be very helpful to express an empathic understanding by saying 'I can understand that it is really difficult for you to talk about this right now, but I think it is something you really need to do'. This sort of contradictory message may indeed convey the fact that you at least understand the difficulty, but how effective it is as an empathic response in terms of supporting the service user may be somewhat less clear.

As we mentioned, it is important to test your emotional literacy. This can be done with a simple exercise. This is something you can do with one other person or with a group of people to try to develop your understanding about simple phrases that are used to express feelings. It might be helpful to consult Table 7. 1. This will give you some ideas about naming emotions and different levels of intensity. Plutchik (2001) developed this language for emotions and

TABLE 7.1 Plutchik's eight basic emotions and three levels of intensity

High intensity	Mid intensity	Low intensity
Rage	Anger	Annoyance
Loathing	Disgust	Boredom
Grief	Sadness	Pensiveness
Amazement	Surprise	Distraction
Terror	Fear	Apprehension
Admiration	Trust	Acceptance
Ecstasy	Joy	Serenity
Vigilance	Anticipation	Interest

Adapted from: Plutchik (2001).

presented a more complex set of ideas which includes attempting to name and explain mixed emotions and complementary and contradictory emotions. Examples of mixed emotions might be loving and hating someone at the same time, complementary ones might be being fearful and worried, while contradictory might involve swinging from joy to disappointment over some situation.

Exercise 14 Practise emotional vocabulary

Once again, let's use this idea of somebody simply saying 'I'm really upset' or 'I'm really upset about work'. Set up a situation where you are talking to one other person and, if possible, there should be a number of observers. Two or three would be great, but it is also something that you can do with just one other person. So, the person with whom you are working or practising this skill can just say something to you about how they are feeling. It doesn't really matter what, but for the sake of simplicity let's say that the first thing they say to you is, 'Oh, I'm really upset about work'. This person is either a colleague or somebody that you know through work and you may or may not know very much about the context. That doesn't really matter, because the point of the exercise is that you are going to try and understand your preconceived ideas about 'upset at work' and what that brings to mind for you and see how that matches or fits with what is really going on for the person. So just to sharpen your skills in this, a simple way of dealing with it is that when somebody gives you the statement, you are allowed to say do you mean that you are annoyed at people at work and they say yes or no. So this means that you can just ask lots of closed questions. It is an exercise not in how you convey your empathic understanding but rather in checking how empathic you are. Often when I do this exercise with a group of student social workers they are able to empathise with each other pretty quickly and are quite accurate when they say 'do you mean …'. It is never really clear whether this is because they share so much during their training and understand each other and have relationships with one another at that time, or whether it is that their situations are so similar, or I suppose there is always the possibility that they are trying to help each other out and are less likely to say no, that's not what I mean. For the purposes of learning, though, it is very important that the person who is conveying the information about how they feel is prepared to say no when the social worker is not actually hitting the point correctly. So if somebody says to you 'I'm very upset', does that mean that they feel distressed? Does it mean that they feel angry? Does it mean that they feel frustrated? It is very useful to look at different feelings and try and understand different levels of feelings. For one person saying they are upset might mean that they are absolutely devastated. For another person saying they are upset might mean that something inconvenient has happened. So the words we use are not always a very good guide for accurate empathy. You need to take those words in the context of what you know about the person and also check exactly what that means for the purpose.

So, let's take another example. You are sitting down, you are working with a colleague and you offer them the opportunity of just expressing some sentiment that they are having. They say 'Oh I'm feeling very depressed'. You then need to ask some exploratory questions about what that might mean. If you are unfamiliar with the situation you may have no idea of:

1. What level of depression we are talking about? Are we talking about just upset, sadness, annoyance or are we actually talking about some more serious level of depression?
2. Secondly, you have no idea what the depression or sadness or upset is about.

So, in this exercise, you can ask all those questions in a way that allows you to check whether you are on the right track. This exercise needs to be conducted in a way in which the person who is expressing their sentiment understands what is going to happen and the limitations of the ability of the person practising the skill to meet the needs that they may have at the time. Hence it is important that if you are involved in assisting in this exercise there is a facility to deal with somebody who may in fact through their exploration discover some more upsetting or difficult challenges that they are having in life. This can happen in any context in training or development and is something that we should be aware of ethically. So, using this kind of exercise is a very simple way of just checking how much we are tracking our ability to understand people in terms of their thoughts and feelings about issues. It also gives us an opportunity to challenge ourselves and to really begin to appreciate the various things that influence how we think other people are thinking or feeling. When you do this exercise, you will begin to see how you can draw on other theoretical ideas; in other words, if somebody is feeling depressed, is that because they have suffered a loss? What kind of things do we associate with depression, what kind of things might make sense in the context which the person has expressed this feeling? It is also possible to see how you draw on your experience of other people having gone through similar situations when you are trying to understand the person who is with you now. You might be thinking that other people that I have worked with in this setting or in these situations feel this way or think this way. So, the experience that we build up from service users is critical in helping us to amass the greater appreciation of the range of things that people might be feeling or thinking when dealing with difficult situations.

Empathy, therefore, is both the skill of thinking things through and being able to track and understand people's thoughts and feelings and what is going on for them, but it is also a communication skill. This means that being able to track or understand or have a sense of what is going on for somebody and in the true definition of empathy take a look at the world from their perspective is one side of empathy.

The next piece, which is equally important, is how you express that empathy. Expressing empathy, therefore, can happen in many ways. You can use your other skills to convey your appreciation or understanding of how somebody is thinking or feeling. You may ask a question which follows on from what you think is going on. So, you may ask a question like tell me a little bit about what is going on for you. You might ask a simple open question that helps the person to elaborate what is happening and therefore builds on your understanding. Or you may use a reflection or a summary in which you try to summarise what you have learned and help the person to put a name to their feelings in relation to what is going on for them at the moment. This kind of advanced empathy, where you put a name on somebody's feelings when they haven't been able to put a name to it themselves, is something you should do with caution. When using this, you need always to make sure that if you are getting it wrong you notice the non-verbal and verbal responses that people give you as clues to say you've got it wrong and then immediately go back to exploration.

Reflective responding

In discussing reflection in this chapter we are going to look at it as a communication skill that forms part of the skill of talking. Reflection is essentially a response to information gathered through listening. The information is heard and processed through thinking filters and the resultant response is formulated as a reflection rather than a question. The decision to use reflection is based on the needs of the interview/conversation at that time. The information that forms the basis of the reflection is thought by the social worker to have relevance to moving either the relationship with the service user and/or the discussion in a positive direction. In considering reflection in social work counselling we will explore the importance of access to appropriate supervision in facilitating the development and maintenance of all aspects of the skill of reflection. Reflection as explored in this chapter falls into the category of a talking skill, while other aspects of reflection such as self-reflection and reflective practice were considered as part of the thinking skill in Chapter 4.

Reflection as communication skill

It has been relatively easy when discussing other counselling skills to see how they are used in a social context. However, reflection may be one of the communication skills that is less often heard in social interaction. This does not mean that it is an unhelpful method of communicating, but rather may indicate that it requires a level of skill and genuineness in order to deliver it in a meaningful way. Reflection is often connected with the expression of feelings. Perhaps the absence of reflection is connected with different cultural views and feelings which should be expressed. It may be that talking about feelings is viewed as a very personal matter in social communication and so may be more evident in relationships that are well-established and have greater levels of intimacy or depth. Perhaps it is less likely that we utilise reflection skills to elicit a deeper level of sharing about feelings in more informal social contexts. Reflection of feelings is only one part of what the reflective skill can be used for. Reflection can also be used in the form of summarising our understanding of what's happening and redirecting the conversation. In social conversation when attempting to summarise conversations or check our understanding it's more likely we will simply ask the questions, 'Have I got this right? Is this what was going on?'

Reflection as a social work counselling skill

Reflections represent a way of formulating communication which is neither a question nor a demand or even advice. Reflection in this sense is more like a statement. It is a statement designed to demonstrate that their social worker/counsellor has been listening, has picked up an understanding of some of the issues for the service user and is using the opportunity to communicate back to the service user a reflection of what it is they heard. This form of reflection provides a very helpful change from communicating and seeking answers to questions. We will explore this further later in the chapter.

When you think of reflection you may think first of all about your own reflection as in the image you see, for example, when you look in a mirror. What is so interesting is that the image you see is not just a clear and exact picture of what you look like, it is shaped to some extent by what you think you might see, or what you have seen in the past or even what you think others see. It involves judgement of what you want to see and even what you would like others to see. Because of these other factors, sometimes the reflection is distorted. Often for people experiencing difficulties in life, this distortion emphasises failings. You might even tie this to a notion of poor self-image. Have you ever had the experience of looking in a mirror or perhaps without looking in the mirror feeling and thinking that you were not looking well for whatever reason. No matter how much others contradict the reflection/image you see, it probably makes little difference to your feelings and the reflection you see.

Working from this sort of idea of reflection you can see that empathy in a way is about finding out what a service user sees, how they experience themselves and the world. Reflection is helpful in that you can simply let the service user know what you hear them saying about themselves and checking if that is right. Sometimes this alone will help the service user to question the reflection or image they have been working from. However, the more complex reflection allows you to work in a subtly, empathic and constructive way to help the service user to question for themselves the reflection/image/ideas that they have begun to believe of themselves.

Sevel et al. (1999, p. 20), in their discussion of social work skills, suggest that 'social workers connect with their service users through the use of empathic responses such as reflection of feelings, paraphrasing and attending behaviours'. For them, reflection of feelings requires the social worker to restate and explore service users' comments about their feelings. A related skill is that of paraphrasing in which the social worker provides a brief account of what the service user has said in their own words. A response from the service user can confirm or reject the emerging understanding that the social worker has incorporated into their paraphrased version of the service user's account of what's going on. Both reflection and paraphrasing play an important part in counselling; in particular, they both offer an alternative to the questioning we have looked at in Chapter 5 and they also provide an opportunity for the social worker to demonstrate their understanding of the situation so far. It allows the service user to provide confirmation or correction to that understanding as required.

Of some concern is the work of Forrester (2008), who investigated social work and the communication/counselling skills identified among social workers. Forrester looked at the skills being employed by social workers in practice and found 'some evidence of basic skills, including: expressing empathy, using open and closed questions and avoiding non-Motivational Interviewing, but considerably less evidence of competence in the more complex skills of using reflections, exploring important issues and managing the interview' (2008, p. 1310).

Reflection is often associated with the work of Carl Rogers. Interestingly, in reviewing the work of Rogers it is argued that rather than focusing on reflection of feelings, Rogers in fact did paid attention to reflection in terms of understanding meaning. This suggests that Rogers was interested in reflecting content and meaning as well as feelings. Ivey (1994, p. 125) suggests that classic reflection of feeling consists of a number of dimensions. Firstly, a sentence stem: unfortunately, stem sentences such as 'I hear you say you feel' or 'feels like' have been used so often that they can almost sound like comical stereotypes.' However, you will want to practise a stem sentence as a starting place for your reflection; often using the service user's name simply helps you to soften and personalise the sentence. Next, a feeling label and emotional word is added to the stem. He gives the example of 'John, you seem to feel badly about ...'. The third dimension is a context or a brief paraphrase. His example is 'John, you seem to feel badly about all the things that have happened in the past two weeks'. The words *about*, *when* and *because* are only three of the many that add context to the reflection of feelings. The fourth dimension is the tense of the reflection. He differentiates between present tense and past tense and suggests some clients might find the past tense easier. The final aspect is what Ivey refers to as 'checkout'. This simply means checking out that the reflection is accurate. While Ivey's dimensions are helpful in constructing reflections, it is important not to undo the benefits of composing a reflection by converting them to a question at the last minute. By this I mean as in Ivey's example, if you ask John 'and I got that right?', then you're basically providing John with a closed question rather than opening up the conversation.

Some of the main benefits of reflection are that it offers an alternative to questioning, it demonstrates that the social worker is listening attentively and empathically, it provides an opportunity for the service user to keep the social worker on track in terms of understanding, and reflection can be used in a variety of ways to progress the conversation without interrupting the service user's train of thought. Reflection should build on what the service user has been saying, even if the social worker's intention is to draw the service user's attention to either some specific aspect of what they have been saying or even to draw them away to another aspect of the issue altogether. Reflection can then be used to create a connection between two different aspects of the issue being discussed and so help the service user to make that connection, or at least not feel they have become lost in the conversation. Reflection requires some risk on the part of the social worker in that composing a reflection involves a willingness to convey the level of understanding that they have acquired at this point in the conversation. Being wrong can involve not getting the correct understanding of the service user's concerns or alternatively having missed out in the reflection something that is vital in the eyes of the service user. This means that when composing a reflection and delivering it to the service user, it is an important to do so in the context of having built a sufficient relationship to enable the service user to correct any wrong interpretation and misunderstanding that is developing.

Simple reflections

Reflection can take the form of a very simple repetition of what the service user has said, not in the form of a question but in the form of a very brief statement. Motivational Interviewing has utilised reflection as a core component of its approach. We will discuss this later in the second part of this text. However, it is useful at this point to refer to Miller (2018, p. 27), who gives a detailed account of forming reflections. For him, reflections are used to demonstrate reflective listening. A good reflection is a statement, and in order to create this statement he suggests 'you must eliminate any word at the beginning of your sentence which signifies a question, such as Do you? Can you? You must also be sure that you don't use the tone of your voice to indicate a question. Depending on the language, it is important that the inflection of your voice does not imply a question but rather a statement. So an English inflection of your voice goes down rather than up at the end of sentence'. Miller (2018) suggests that you try some statements such as: 'You are talented? And then: You are talented. Can you hear the difference?' He also makes the point that reflections might seem strange, because in a way you're giving a guess about what your understanding is at that point, so it might seem more appropriate to ask a question. However, reflections can be very effective and provide an important alternative to getting caught up asking a series of questions.

Complex reflections

Rollnick (n.d.) talks about two types of reflection. First are simple reflections, which he suggests are just a rephrasing of what the client has said. He then talks about complex reflections. These are more about extending what a client said. However, in a complex reflection, extending what the client says must be done in a way that does not elicit resistance on the part of the client. Rollnick mentions the use of understated language and its importance in constructing complex reflections. He comments on the power of using reflections to consider change without building or eliciting resistance and doing this through the use of understated, non-threatening language. This involves making a choice to use language which allows for consideration without necessitating full commitment to the change. Complex reflections can be used both to reflect what the client has said while at the same time moving the conversation in a new direction. This allows the counsellor/social worker to connect the client and at the same time present a reflection that facilitates the client considering change.

Example

Let's consider a complex reflection to draw your attention to a possible dilemma for social work and in particular for you as a social worker. Starting with a *context setting reflective summary* such as:

> we have been looking at social work counselling skills such as reflection and have seen the evidence that these are important in building a relationships with service users, this is going to involve developing and using the skill of reflection in your work.

Alternatively, we might try a *double-sided reflection* to draw attention to the conflicting information in the research that social workers are not using reflections, although the skill of using reflections has been shown to be a very useful way of helping to reduce 'resistance' and conflict and helps to engage service users and promote collaboration. The idea is to present the conflicting or incompatible sides of the issue in a non-threatening, thought-provoking way so that the person receiving the two-sided reflection can take time to consider the implications for them of this conflict.

And yet:

(A) Forrester (2008) has shown that social workers are not using reflections as a skill in their practice, while Miller and Rollnick (2013) have provided evidence that the use of reflection skills creates less resistance and is more likely to build positive relationships to help service users move towards considering change.

OR

(B) Miller and Rollnick (2013) have provided evidence that the use of reflection skills creates less resistance and is more likely to build positive relationships to help service users move towards considering change, and yet Forrester (2008) has shown that social workers are not using reflections as a skill in their practice.

Can you see any difference between the reflective summary or the double-sided reflection? Can you see any difference in impact of the A or B version of the double-sided reflection? Is it possible that because B mentioned the lack of social work engagement with use of reflection last that it focused attention on that, and maybe leaves the receiver thinking of this more than the other part of the reflection, OR does providing the more negative connotation that social work is not doing reflections first is better? What do you think?

Then of course you could decide to move on to change it all to an open question by saying:

So, as a social worker, where does that leave you?

Note on combining reflections with questions

In Motivational Interviewing, which we will look at in Chapter 10, the aim is to preferably use refection and open questions and rarely use closed questions. Miller (2018) suggests one question for every two reflections, but preferably even more use of reflections. It takes practise, perhaps because we don't tend to use or be aware we are using reflections in social communication, or perhaps because as we have discussed before, asking questions is just more comfortable.

Paraphrasing and summaries

Woodcock Ross (2011) identified two additional skills that can help in demonstrating empathy and active/accurate listening. These are paraphrasing and summarising.

Paraphrasing as defined by Cameron (2008, p. 51) cited in Woodcock Ross (2011, pp. 33–34) as 'an attempt to combine in a coherent and meaningful sentence, reflections about client's feelings, the situation and/or their behavioural responses to it. Paraphrasing is designed to encourage exploration'. However, paraphrasing does more than provide a brief sentence about what the service user has said, it is much more powerful than that. Paraphrasing allows the social worker to be selective about what gets included. This means that using a paraphrase can accommodate a slight shift in meaning or direction. This is accomplished as much by what is not included. For example, by leaving out references to deficits, the social worker can paraphrase emphasising strengths and not deficits. In the same way, including some aspects of what the service user said but not necessarily all can be a form of editing, and allows the social worker to influence the direction and focus of the subsequent discussion.

Paraphrasing can be used as intermittent signposts to help keep the discussion on course. The use of a paraphrase can allow the social worker to pick up on a point made by the service user and indicate this as a new direction in the conversation. Because they are brief, they tend to fit into the conversation without distracting from it.

Summarising is defined by Woodcock Ross (2011, p. 34) as a response that 'involves integrating broader themes at the end of the discussion of particular point'. Summaries, then, tend to be longer and touch on a broader range of ideas and information that has emerged from the discussion. A summary can be a useful way of doing a check to ensure that you are still in tune with the service user's main concerns and that the service user is clear about what the conversation/interview has covered so far. Summaries serve the purpose of signposting the key points/issues that have been addressed and as a reminder of what needs further attention. Because they tend to be a bit longer than a paraphrase, they can break the flow of the discussion; this may be experienced as disruptive, so use with caution. Of course, it also means that a summary can be used to tie up a point and move on to another area that needs to be addressed.

Final comments

Practising your core talking skills is vital. It's like practising moves in football, or scales on the piano, or any other skill. You need to be able to formulate and use open questions, closed questions and a wide variety of reflective skills as required. This means that you can do so fluently, like speaking a new language. There is growing concern that social workers are not delivering on this fluency in their counselling skills repertoire (Forrester 2008). Hence, practise, practise and practise!

Exercise 15 Practise, practise, practise

This exercise works better if you have someone who knows what you are practising and can give you feedback. Alternatively, you could record yourself practising and listen back to it. If you do this, it's best to have a clear idea or observational sheet detailing what to hear and see how well you managed to deliver. With some methods, for example Motivational Interviewing, observational/coding tools are available to check your adherence to the skills required to deliver a MI intervention.

Practise your response scales: closed questions, open question, simple reflection, complex reflections.

Sit in a circle with 3–6 other social workers. One needs to play the role of a service user (to give everyone an opportunity to practise, you can take it in turns to be the service user).

Brief the role player: The role player should take a couple of minutes to fill you all in on the situation: who is the service user, some facts about their circumstances and the reason they are talking to a social worker. Once the scene is set, you are ready to practise. Try to respond spontaneously to the questions/reflections. Say more or say less, whichever feels most realistic. Remember, this is not a real interview, this is set up to give your colleagues a chance to practise core counselling talking skills … not solve a case!

You can swap the role player after the first task or wait until the three tasks are completed, then swap and go again.

Task one: Open question and closed question

To get started, you can ask one closed and two open questions in any order. Each social worker takes it in turn to ask their three questions in succession. Once you've asked them, then the person next to you follows up with their questions, and so on until all the group have had their turn.

Review: Each person should confirm if they achieved the task by checking with each other for feedback. Here is where it can get tricky. I usually videotape these exercises because people often think they asked open question but that might not be the case. People may intend to ask open questions but it comes out as another closed one. Discuss what happened. It is always important to ask the service user role player what they thought of the questions as this is a good way to get feedback. If you have an audio or visual recording even better to really see if it worked.

Task two: Open questions only

The next task on the practise scale is asking three open questions in succession. There is an added skill to practise this time: you must include some reference to something the role player said in their last response in your next question. When you are taking over from the previous social worker this means you have to include something in the response they received in your next question. This task serves to ensure that you are listening to the role player; if you don't, it will be difficult to meet the task of including what they say in your next question. It also means that even if you have something you want to follow up on from earlier you still have to tie it into what was just said. This is also the beginning of building your skill in listening and refection as it directs you to follow up on something the service user has said in order to formulate your open question. Very good practise! Use the same method and get feedback, and again a recording makes this a much more effective learning opportunity. Watch out for open questions eliciting new and more descriptive information

Reflections:

Just to give people some materials to practise formulating reflections it is helpful if the role player gives them a bit of information to go on, i.e. not giving monosyllabic responses … it is practise.

Now do the same exercise and only use reflections. You can use simple or complex reflections. Take a bit of time if you need to formulate your reflection. If you don't have recording equipment it might be worthwhile having one person in the group act as an observer and even take a note of the reflections offered. You will need this to look next at what type of reflections were offered: simple, complex, feeling, content, etc.

In the real world you will want to use all three of these 'notes' on your talking scale … and be able to deliver them in a way that generates a harmonious and engaging 'tune' (conversation).

(This exercise is informed by many experiences of training over my career, but I want to specifically acknowledge my Masters in Social Work skills, MI training and Relate counselling skills training.)

Empathy has an important part to play in building the essential collaborative relationship between the social worker and the service user(s). Being able to demonstrate your understanding of the service user's world shows respect and conveys commitment to listening and appreciating the service user's perspective. A paraphrase can allow the social worker to pick up on a point made by the service user. Developing the skill of empathy is nonetheless demanding. It requires practise as well as self-awareness, feedback and preferably live supervision. The ability to demonstrate empathy is linked to the skill of employing reflective responding. Research has raised concerns that social workers have not been paying sufficient attention to developing and practising these reflective skills. It is unclear if this is connected to heavy workloads and time pressures which force workers to focus on asking questions and giving advice, or whether it has to do with agency misunderstanding of what social workers actually do. It may also be related to conflicting demands in social work education, which places emphasis on the regulatory and legal context rather than the actual skills required to engage service users in a collaborative and constructive relationship. Whatever the reasons, it is critical that social workers are supported to regain/develop their counselling skills. Fluency in using counselling skills is not an added extra in social work, it is a minimum requirement to meet the standards clearly delineated in the Framework for Professional Competencies, to ensure that social workers have the time and the skills to engage with service users to provide the support and services required.

8 Affirming, advising and motivating change

- Looking at changing ideas about what helps in terms of the shift from confrontation to affirmation.
- Addressing some of the challenges to being affirming, including looking at 'overselling' the positive. Making connections between appropriate affirming and coping.
- Explore the role of helping and giving information and advice and questioning our perception of these as being helpful.
- Looking at the place of supporting and motiving change in the context of developing counselling skills and considering motivation in the counsellor and/or in the service user.

Introduction

In this chapter we are going to look at different directions or goals that you might choose when conducting an interview with the service user. Selecting the three examples of how you might use your counselling skills as referred to in the chapter title: affirming, advising and motivating change already demonstrates the orientation and preferences of the author. These particular three are associated strongly with two of the particular methods we are going to look at more closely in the second part of this book. However, they provide excellent examples of how you can utilise your counselling skills to give a direction or take the interview in a direction that is informed by particular theoretical ideas. In these examples, we will explore how thinking, listening and talking and your core counselling skills shape the conversation.

Affirming

Before we look at how you might utilise this idea of affirming in a professional social work counselling setting, let's look for a few minutes at your own experience of affirmation. Probably of all the things we discuss in this text, convincing anybody of the importance of affirmation is the least challenging. Just think for a few moments about your social communication experiences and consider whether you surround yourself/engage in conversation with people who are affirming or who are critical of you, your behaviours and your values. We are not talking about being open to criticism, but rather we are talking about the sense of people being supportive of you or of putting you down. Hopefully you will all have had experiences where important people in your lives have affirmed you and your beliefs, values and actions. If you can recall what this feels like, even when you are struggling, that somebody was able to recognise the positives in you and took the time to help you to recognise them as well. If you have had such an experience you will recall that telling you that you are good enough or that you are able to do something is not very effective. It's more effective to point you in the direction of the success or strength and to facilitate you to revisit that for yourself even when you're struggling. As we discuss, in using this skill of affirming you will see the importance of basing the affirmation in concrete examples so that they don't come across as condescending or as simply ignoring or diminishing the struggle of the problem. Let's consider the connections between the three core skills, thinking, listening and talking, in relation to affirming.

Thinking: a number of theoretical frameworks that social workers need to be familiar with underpin the idea that affirming service users is a useful and helpful direction in which to take an assessment or an interview. For example, in behavioural theory there is the view that reinforcing a behaviour action in a positive way is likely to create a situation where that behaviour or action will be repeated or replicated. This means that by identifying the behaviour and affirming that behaviour it is likely that the outcome will be that that the behaviour will be recognised as helpful and may therefore be repeated. This holds true of identifying particular values. By drawing attention to a value or set of values the social worker can elicit discussion of those values. The outcome of such a discussion would hopefully be to affirm for the service user that these values were important, helpful and therefore support the service user to hold onto those values and engage in behaviours that are consistent with the value system that you have affirmed.

While behaviour theory works on the basis that a discussion or identification of positive behaviours and values is likely to result in strengthening or reinforcing them, other theories hold different views about why such affirmation might be useful. For example, social construction theory highlights the importance of the way in which we all construct reality. Put in simple terms, this means that as the service user and social worker engage in conversation/interview/assessment it is possible to develop alternative pictures or understandings of what is happening in the service user's life. If you are employing such a theory to inform your counselling skills, then it is highly likely that you will recognise the importance not just of addressing the problem-orientated focus that the service user or for that matter social worker might hold at the beginning of the conversation, but that it is equally important, if perhaps not more important, to begin at least to find the alternative version of the story. This involves identifying, recognising not just the problems but also the strengths, resilience and attempts to resolve the problem that the service user brings to the situation. Again, this involves first of all the social worker paying attention, both listening and thinking, so that they actually recognise and hear this side of the story, and then that they shape the response in ways that affirm these positives so that they too become part of the story (talking).

These are two examples of theoretical frameworks that underpin the importance of affirming positive behaviours and values while conducting a social work interview. Two applications of theory to social work counselling skills which we will discuss in Part II have contributed to providing at least some evidence that affirmation is an important aspect of helping when engaging with service users. Motivational interviewing, which is generally regarded as having a strong empirical evidence base, and solution-focused work, which has in the past been criticised for not establishing such an evidence base, seem to share the fact that practitioners from various disciplines who use these approaches believe they are useful, positive and helpful. This is mentioned here because it helps to demonstrate that while an evidence base and research are important components of establishing the relevance of particular theories, so too the practice experience of utilising these approaches can encourage practitioners to continue to use them. For social work this may also have been influenced by the compatibility that exists between social work values which emphasise the importance of respecting service users and the use of affirmation as a therapeutic intervention.

Listening: in terms of looking at affirmation as part of the output of employing your thinking skill, you can see how thinking is influenced by evidence, theoretical frameworks, as well as practice experience. These things combined are likely to result in a social worker approaching their work from a particular framework, which is already going to indicate how and for what they are listening. To utilise the skill of affirming they need to be listening out for opportunities to identify positive behaviours and values. We have already explored something of the impact of theoretical privileging and listening and later in Part II we will see more about how your theoretical or method preferences are already in play even before you meet the service user. What you hear is mostly likely to be connected to what you are expecting to hear, which means that different theories and methods focus our attention on the ideas that they favour or privilege in their explanations of behaviours. In my experience, to be used effectively, the skill of affirmation must be based on information that emerges from the discussion with the service user. If you don't have examples from the service user to support identifying particular behaviours and values in such a positive light, then attempts at affirmation can all too easily appear to be condescending or unfounded. If affirmation is heard as condescending by the service user, it is likely to be counterproductive. Therefore, while the thinking aspect of using affirmation is critically important in setting the framework to recognise an example of a positive you are looking for opportunities to affirm, this must also be supported by active listening. It is the skill of active listening that helps you to identify specific opportunities in which to employ this particular skill and to establish credible examples to support the affirmation. We will consider an affirmation with and without such support in the next section. It is important to note the importance of your listening skill, as this is what allows you to notice strengths and resiliencies that the service user mentions, often accidently and almost always without acknowledging its importance to them as a resource. This inability to notice or acknowledge one's own strengths, resilience and resourcefulness can be exacerbated when the social worker follows the same train and gets caught in a deficit-led approach to the assessment or interview.

Talking: tracking the connection between thinking, what influences our thinking and listening, we can set the scene for how thinking and listening combine to inform your response. This hopefully also shows how the theoretical framework, your practice experiences and your value system work to shape your ideas. This highlights the importance of understanding and recognising the influence that preferred theories and frameworks have on what you hear, what you see and then obviously on what you say.

Implementing the skill of affirming

- Let's say that theory and practise are directing you towards identifying positive actions, behaviours and values.
- Add to this your skill in listening, which helps you to identify strong examples of success resilience and strengths in your discussion with service users.
- Then you have to decide how you're going to talk about this.

As you might expect from our discussion, it's more likely that you will try to construct either an open question or some form of reflection to elicit further conversation as a way of conveying affirmation.

Closed questions are likely, even when attempting an affirmation, to be experienced as interrogative rather than support.

In working with mothers who have experienced problems associated with substance use (Loughran & Broderick 2017), I had the opportunity to learn more about the challenge of meaningful affirmation from service users. These mothers valued their children and were very distressed to think they might have let their children down. They were also upset when social workers did not appreciate the importance they placed on being good parents. However, they were also very sceptical of social workers who, without knowing them, made affirming comments. Receiving an affirmation from someone who knows you or whose opinion you value will clearly be more likely to have an impact on how you see yourself, which is the aim of affirmation. Alternatively, if the social worker can show that they are basing their affirmations on some legitimate evidence, then this too may help the service user to consider/contemplate that point and make it more likely they will take on board the affirmation rather than dismiss it. Bland et al. (2006) found that service users complained if they felt social workers were not genuine and that they felt they were able to recognise 'fake'. Given the importance of genuineness in building the relationship, it is clear that care needs to be taken in using affirmation in a meaningful way. If you do not have information to support an affirmation, the best approach is to ask an open question and help the service user to explore further whatever point/example you think might yield some helpful information to support an affirmation. You may already have something that you noticed/observed/heard and feel confident you can use that as an example to support an affirmation. This may allow you to attempt to convey the affirmation as a reflection.

Take, for example, that in discussion you have discovered that despite challenges the service user may have in relation to parenting their children, it is very evident that they hold responsible parenting as an important value in their lives. They talk about how important their own parents were to them and in some cases how an aunt or grandparent provided the security that they needed. They are clear that they want to do this for their own children.

Steps in affirming: In my view, closed questions can easily come across as interrogation or challenging. So my advice is to AVOID them, especially if they sound like, for example:

Closed question: Do you think responsible parenting is important?

Closed question: Do you think you are a responsible parent?

With affirmation a good *first* step is to ask open questions. This allows you to explore in more detail positives that can form the basis of an affirmation. This involves *thinking* that such positives exist and then making sure you *listen* for them. We will see how this is employed in different models of practice in Part II. You will need to have gathered a good sense of the service user's positive behaviours/values in order to be able to draw on them in building an affirmation that comes across as real and genuine.

Once you have some evidence to support your affirmation you can move on to using reflections to help the service user look at these possibilities. If you decide to utilise some form of reflection, you can see that you are applying an interpretation on the discussion which is attempting to shape the value of responsible parenting as being significant or important. You can imagine if you attempt to do this you need to have an example of what you have heard or seen so that the service user can begin to reflect or contemplate on how they have been able to convey this impression to you. This does not mean that there are no problems about parenting, but rather is an acknowledgement that despite such problems, the value of parenting may still be evident.

Examples of some possibilities of affirming and just how that might play out in terms of what you say:

Open question: Tell me a little bit about what responsible parenting means to you.

Open question: You mentioned that your parents always tried their best for you, tell me a bit about what that meant for you.

Or

Open question: From what you are saying it seems that you think getting an education is really important for your children, what other things do you think are important for them?

Reflection: Responsible parenting is important to you.

Or

Reflection: You have been working hard to give your children a better life.

Complex reflection: Although we are here today discussing some difficulties around parenting you believe that being a responsible parent is very important.

Or

Complex reflection: You have been having some struggles with your children but whatever happens you want them to be safe and healthy.

Warning: what you need to avoid is doing a 'hard sell' on affirmation. This happens when you believe in the service user, their strength and resilience, but they cannot see it. In responding to the service user's lack of awareness of what they bring, you try harder to convince them that they are strong, resilient, etc. This doesn't work in my experience. It may seem strange that someone gets more 'resistant' when you are in fact trying to say 'good/positive' things about them, but nonetheless you being enthusiastic about the service user's abilities is simply failing to use your skills to lead the service user to discover their strengths for themselves. When a person has become overwhelmed by a sense of the negatives in their life it takes skill to help them begin to pay attention to the positives. Be respectful of this struggle. The more you try to sell the idea, the more reluctant they become to accept your viewpoint. A similar reaction can be seen in managing advice.

Advice

As with the idea of affirming, it is fair to say that we have probably all had experiences of seeking or being given advice. Let's look at the difference between seeking and being given advice.

Thinking: You will need to process advice-giving through a number of the thinking filters we have identified. For example, consider self-reflection and your attitude and experiences of giving and receiving advice. In your personal/social/everyday life, how does this work for you? Let's consider a situation where you are trying to make a decision; you're not sure what to do. In reality you probably already have some ideas and may want support for your own idea, or maybe you really are unsure. Do you want somebody to simply tell you what to do? Sometimes it might feel that way, but in reality how often do you simply do what somebody tells you? Have you ever had the experience where you just wanted to talk through what's going on for you, but did not necessarily find it helpful for somebody to tell you what to do? It can be hard to follow advice, even if it becomes clear that the advice is good/obviously correct. In reflecting on this myself, I realise that sometimes I simply want advice. In these situations it's usually that I have identified somebody I consider to be an expert or who has information. For example, if I'm sick I go to my doctor and I'm going because I want an answer. I don't think I'd be impressed if I was asked what I thought myself. Admittedly, this does not mean that I always follow the advice. Probably I'm more likely to follow the advice if it fits with some of my own ideas, or if I'm really struggling and realise I have no idea what the best thing to do is or I feel vulnerable. In this situation my trust and belief in the doctor will play an important part in influencing how/if I follow the advice. The status of that person will be an important influence on what I do next. So also is the aspect of advice that involves having the information to make an informed decision. Sometimes it's not about advice with regard to what to do but rather to gather the information to better inform your own decision. So if it's about seeking information and instead you get advice this may be experienced as somehow disregarding your own ability to take on board the information and make the right choice for you.

What is the theory behind giving advice? This raises a challenging question for professionals; is it your responsibility to deliver information and advice, or is it your responsibility to create a situation where is more likely that such information or advice can be heard? If you simply deliver information/advice without creating a context or environment in which you have paid attention to making it easier for the other person to hear what you're saying, then have you delivered on your responsibilities? Taking in information is a cognitive task and as such requires a degree of openness to new facts or ideas. It is our cognitive skills that facilitate decision-making and our ability to make rational, well-informed choices. Walsh (2006, p. 141) reminds us that we need to consider the service user's willingness to consider alternative thoughts or ideas. If there is no openness or interest in receiving these then you will not be able to take them into account in making decisions or plans.

Social construction or radical theories refer to the important issue of power that we have discussed in earlier chapters. If you are in a position of authority or power over the service user they may feel they have no choice but to appear to listen. It may create a situation where their only sense of ownership is to appear to comply and then reject your advice.

Listening: there is a difference between somebody giving advice which is unsolicited as opposed to someone having sought advice. Additionally, if you have not only sought advice but had to put effort into getting that advice then perhaps you are more likely to be in a positive frame of mind for accepting the advice. For most people, I think being given advice from somebody whom you feel hasn't really listened or doesn't understand what's going on for you is usually difficult to take. As a student social worker in supervision I recognised that thinking early in the interview that I had the answer to a problem or an issue which has puzzled or challenged the service user for some time was disrespectful. In my experience, usually if you think you have an answer early on in the discussion it's probably because you don't really know what the problem actually is and it definitely points to you not using your listening skills. It is only through appreciating and listening that you can formulate ideas about what might be useful, and even then creating a situation in which your ideas can be heard is just as important as having the information or ideas in the first place.

Talking: in terms of giving advice there are a couple of important barriers to keep in mind. These barriers are ones that you should be able to connect with your own experiences. One barrier that is important to take account of is allowing your concern to translate into giving premature advice. This is most likely to be experienced as undermining, as it suggests the answer to the problem was easy to find. Sometimes when working with students it seems they conduct role plays where, within a few minutes, they are giving advice or 'solving' the problem. When we reflect on this, it is useful to consider if the idea or advice has emerged from preconceived ideas about what's going on and also to consider to what extent, in the role play, the student was actively listening or to what extent they were just waiting for the opportunity to give advice and solve the problem.

Standing back and facilitating people to discover their own solutions can be challenging and difficult in particular as service users may indicate that they just want to know what to do or feel that they simply have no options. In all likelihood, just like the rest of us service users don't really like being told what to do, they prefer to feel empowered in their own ability to come up with an answer that fits with their experiences and expectations and therefore works for them. Using your thinking and listening skills enables you to compose an appropriate response. In motivational social work that response is usually operationalised by using open questions and reflections to elicit interest in information and preparing the way for the service user to seek advice.

Another barrier may be the social worker's real and genuine desire to be helpful. This concern to solve the problem or give an answer is often fuelled by the very reason somebody becomes a social worker. By this I mean people are usually attracted to social work because they want to be helpful, they want to make people's lives better. Further barriers to consider might be the implication of the context within which the social worker is meeting the service user. In some settings there may be an expectation that the social worker will in fact direct the service user to specific actions, associated with the issues of power and service user autonomy. This may create a situation where the social worker in a very tight timeframe has to deliver advice or specific information without having the opportunity to take the time to generate an interest in such advice. As I mentioned earlier, it seems that we are more likely to follow advice when we have actively sorted ourselves. So a barrier to giving advice is not having/creating the time to develop a curiosity, motivation or an interest in new information to inform decision-making. After all that, advice is about. It is construction of a potential problem-solving behaviour based on informed decision-making. From the point of view of using your talking skill, the real risk here is that you overuse talking, giving information and advice to the detriment of actually listening and thinking. Talking will not generate change, especially if it is not connected to the lived experiences of the service user and their desired goals and values. The challenge in social work is often that the service user is non-voluntary; they have not sought help and therefore may be less ready to engage in hearing advice and taking that into account in terms of setting goals or making decisions. This is connected to motivating change, which we will look at next.

Later chapters will look at the place of advice-giving/finding solutions in social work counselling skills. As we will see in motivational interviewing, Miller and Rollnick (2013) have developed a formula for generating openness to information seeking: elicit–provide–elicit. In my experience, both social worker and service user can misunderstand what solution-focused work is actually about. They may think it's about the social worker very quickly providing solutions. This, of course, is not solution-focused work, and we will discuss that in Chapter 9.

Motivating change

One point that I think is useful to make that really helps to explain a little bit more about the challenges in holding back from offering giving unsolicited advice is to consider the concept of the wheel of change, as formulated by Prochaska and DiClemente (1982). This concept of the wheel of change is well-known in social work, but for the purposes of further exploring the challenges of giving advice and motivating change it is useful to apply wheel of change not to the service user but to the social worker. The notion of the wheel of change suggests that there are a number of stages in the process of change: pre-contemplation, contemplation, decision, active change, maintenance. Motivation is enhanced when someone is actively contemplating change or is further along the stages of change, such as planning or actively changing. It is useful to illustrate this in the form of the wheel as it was originated.

We know that in many social work settings we are likely to encounter people who are at the pre-contemplation stage or possibly in early contemplation. Think for a few moments about where you as a social worker are on this wheel of change. Take into account the fact that you appreciate the full context within which the service user's issues have emerged. Often times you may be encountering service user at a time of crisis when changes are urgently needed. Alternatively, there may be legal or health reasons why change really needs to happen. It's very difficult to accept that no one can change somebody else, even when you are in a situation where not changing brings with it unwanted and negative consequences. Ultimately it is the person who makes the decision whether they change or not. Again, this speaks to some unrealistic expectations placed on professionals to try to bring about change for service users, especially in the absence of having the time/resources to build a relationship and establish trust. Cooper (2011) shows that there is a direct connection between motivation and outcomes. He found that key to enhancing motivation was the quality of the counselling relationship. However, in this context we are just going to look at the pressure on social workers to already be in change mode and this may essentially undermine the importance of taking time to build trust and a collaborative relationship. What this looks like on the wheel of change is that the service user is likely not to be thinking of the need to change or just getting to a point of considering change, i.e. the first two stages of change, while the social worker is already focused on active change. It may result in a situation where the social worker is reacting to the urgency for change while the service user is trying to come to terms with recognising the need to change or managing their ambivalence about being told they need to change. This leaves the service user and social worker in two very different places and increases the difficulty for both in finding a way to develop a shared understanding of what's happening and what needs to happen. Using your counselling skills to enhance or elicit motivation or interest in change is challenging in these circumstances.

It is useful to also think about what we know about motivation. Behavioural theory would point to the possibility that motivation to change is increased by previous success in changing. If we have an experience of being able to make changes it is more likely that we will know what behaviours will help with change. Success builds a repertoire of skills for change.

Cognitive theory talks about self-efficacy or the belief in our ability to change. If we believe change is possible then it is more likely to happen. Motivation can also be perceived as an inherent personality characteristic. You might say that someone is a very motivated person or perhaps has a driven personality. For the purposes of counselling social work, this is a very limiting perception as it suggests that motivation is given an almost static quality. For social work it is helpful to think about motivation as something that can develop or be developed in response to different situations. It can be enhanced in response to the collaborative interaction between the social worker and the service user using listening and talking skills. Because we will look at this more in Chapter 10 on motivational interviewing it is sufficient for now to note that motivation can change in response to many circumstances, including: belief in success, fear of failure, urgency of the situation, perceived negative consequences, importance or value placed on change versus staying the same. In motivational interviewing, Miller and Rollnick (2013) use the concept of ambivalence to explain that change is not always easy because often we are drawn to stay as we are even when we are also considering the need to change. Ambivalence is normal and should not be treated as a deficit or failing. Respecting the process required to bring about change through building trust and collaboration involves employing all the elements of thinking, listening and talking skills.

PART II

The application of counselling social work to methods

Rationale for exploring the application of counselling social work skills and motivational interviewing, solution-focused work and group work

These methods were chosen because they address readiness to change, enhancing motivation to engage in the change process and help to build optimism about change by working with strength, resilience and previous success. In other words, the predictors of positive outcomes, before other methods can be utilised to more effect.

In reviewing research on counselling and psychotherapies, Cooper (2011, p. 56) highlights the findings of Asay and Lambert (1999). They presented what works in the therapeutic encounter by estimating the percentage improvement in clients as a function of therapeutic factors. In their work they found that 40% of the variance in outcomes was accounted for by what they called client variables and extra-therapeutic events, 30% by the therapeutic relationship, only 15% to the techniques or method employed and 15% to the placebo or expectancy effects. This research supports the position that the actual method is less important than the therapeutic relationship that is established in any form of counselling intervention. In addition, Cooper (2011) then summarises his findings on counselling and psychotherapies research in general and identifies that while client factors are the strongest predictors of therapeutic outcomes, these can be further refined to focus on levels of motivation and involvement in therapy and the links between having a positive but realistic attitude towards outcomes and the process of therapy. These factors do not preclude the likelihood of better outcomes where a service user has higher levels of psychological functioning, which was also found to be predictive of better outcomes. However, the identification of the predictive importance of motivation and a positive attitude are important rationales for giving further consideration to two counselling methods: motivational interviewing and solution-focused therapy, which specifically address these factors.

The general finding of no difference in the outcome of therapy for clients participating in diverse therapies has several alternative explanations. First, different therapies can achieve similar goals through different processes. Second, different outcomes do occur, but are not detected by past research strategies. Third, different therapies embody common factors that are curative, although not emphasised by the theory of change central to any one school (Asay & Lambert 1999, p. 29).

9 Applying social work counselling skills in Solution-Focused Work (SFW)

- Look at what solution-focused work (SFW) actually is.
- Review core theoretical influences on solution-focused work.
- Consider what the research tells us.
- Describe the key features of solution-focused work as a method of intervention.
- Explore the connections between solution-focused work and the social work counselling skills discussed in Part I.
- Draw on solution-focused work to consider examples of applying social work counselling skills that are compatible with solution-focused work.

Introduction

Understanding theoretical influences is important in understanding how different methods of intervention have emerged, how they work and what methods will be helpful in interactions with service users. In this chapter we will consider these in relation to solution-focused work (SFW). Because our interest is on counselling social work skills we will focus more specifically on how these influences shape the application of social work counselling skills in this method of intervention. First, let's describe briefly what SFW is about. For more information, read De Jong and Berg (2002) and Ratner et al. (2012).

What is SFW? A brief summary of key assumptions

In practice, SFW can be used in a range of situations. It is considered a brief form of therapy/counselling and this is a purposeful position informed by the view that positive change can happen inside, outside and independently of the therapy/counselling setting. Brief is not necessarily prescribed by a specific number of counselling sessions or conversations, but typically the aim is that the SFW conversations will provide sufficient support, confidence and clarity about goals to enable/empower the service user to move forward themselves. It is designed to be helpful even in only one meeting, but there is usually an explicit invitation to return should the service user decide that more would be helpful. The method is future-, strengths- and goal-focused. The term 'solution-focused' should not be mistaken for an approach that seeks to give solutions to the service user. Quite the opposite! The method is premised on the view that the service user already has the solutions or at least the beginning of what can build solutions. It is the social worker's job to facilitate conversations that identify, access, amplify and support service user's strengths and coping skills and then help the service user to make the connection between these and achieving agreed goals.

To further describe the method, let's look at the underlying assumptions of SFW. These assumptions shape the interaction between the social work and the service user and distinguish SFW from other approaches or methods.

A summary of some key assumptions that underpin SFW

- It is not important to understand the 'cause'
- Problem discussion can be actively UNHELPFUL
- Goals are always important
- There are ALWAYS exceptions (e.g. times when something is doing something that works)

- Do more of what is working
- Even the smallest change can set a solution in motion
- Clients cooperate; the idea of resistance is not helpful
- All clients are motivated towards something; it's your job to find out what that is

(Adapted from Ratner et al. 2012, pp. 21–23)

Exercise 16 Think about the concept of 'cause'

You should take some time to think about or discuss each of the assumptions, because it is important for you to really think through the implications of accepting these ideas before you will feel comfortable applying them in practice.

Take the first one; it is not important to understand the 'cause'.

This suggests that discussion of what has 'caused' the 'problem' that brought you into contact with the service user is not helpful. Consideration of the term 'cause' gives rise to many questions. Questions informed by a social construction perspective on how we assign meaning might be:

1. Do you think it's possible to work with someone without 'knowing' the 'cause' of their 'problems'?
2. Is it helpful to talk about problems and what the service user sees as the 'cause'?
3. For whom is it necessary to identify a 'cause': you and/or the service user?
4. Is it possible to track down and confidently identify the exact 'cause' of a problem?
5. Who says it's a problem? Who says that it is the 'cause'?
6. For whom is it a problem?
7. Who gets to say what the truth is or the most accurate/appropriate meaning of the 'cause' or the 'problem' actually is?

8. Does your status/power position dictate whose version of the 'cause' will be accepted?
9. If so, how can a service user influence this process?
10. If the 'cause' is in the past, can you change the past?
11. If the 'cause' is someone else's behaviour, can you change someone else?

Summary of skills employed in SFW

There are a range of skills embedded in the core listening, thinking and talking framework. All of the skills described and discussed in earlier chapters form part of the broad repertoire of skills which may be useful in conducting solution-focused (SF) conversations/counselling. De Jong and Berg (2002) identified some specific skills that they identify with the SF method. These can be summarised as:

- Listening
  - Getting details
  - Empathy
- Responding/talking
  - Echoing service user words
  - Open questions
  - Summarising
  - Affirming and complementing
  - Exploring client's meaning
  - Amplify solution talk
  - Leading from behind
- Thinking
  - Challenging preconceived ideas
  - Reframing

(Adapted from De Jong and Berg 2002, pp. 20–51)

We will explore some of these in more detail later. For now it's enough that you have these in mind as you consider theories and how they inform thinking in SFW.

Theories, methods and skills

Different theories support different intervention methods. Ideas about how to interpret the information you get from the service use, what factors to focus on in attempting to bring about change and how best to achieve this all depend on the underpinning ideas that influence the method. Figure 9.1 presents a brief overview of the theories, concepts, methods and skills associated with SFW. We will refer to these throughout the chapter.

What this means for us in practice is that we have to think about what we are doing and why we are doing it. We then also need to have an understanding of what specific communication skills will be necessary to deliver that intervention method. It also means that in appreciating the differences in the application of theory and skills we need to notice these differences and practise new ways to use our core communication skills so that what we think, listen for and say fit with the aims and rationale of a specific method we want to employ.

Solution-focused work, like many other methods, is informed by a number of theoretical ideas. Theories that resonate with SFW include aspects or concepts from social construction theory, systemic theories, behavioural and cognitive theories. Of these, it is probably social construction theory that provides the framework for many of the distinguishing features of the method. It is the emergence of an understanding that meaning is created, communicated and interpreted between people and in a social context that provides the underpinning rationale for SFW. This is often used in conjunction with the systemic commitment to explore service users' experiences. The emphasis is then on a social rather than an individual perspective and on service users' strengths rather than deficits or limitations. Elements of behaviour and cognitive theories can also be found in SFW (Loughran 2010). For example, the SFW understanding of what works in identifying and achieving goals is very informed by behavioural principles and the methods approach to supporting positive self-worth has a familiar cognitive theory basis.

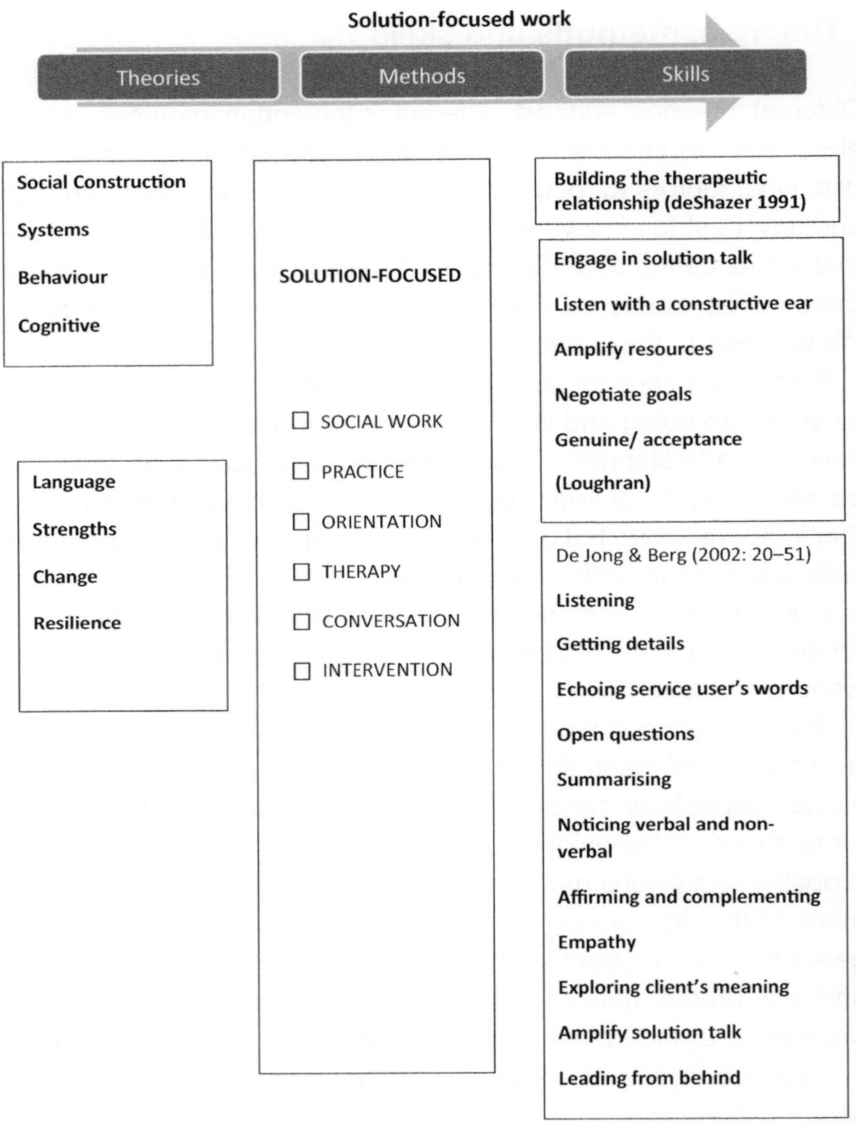

Figure 9.1 Brief overview of solution-focused work

Research and SFW

There is widespread support for the view that while there are diverse forms of counselling/therapy, positive outcomes continue to be associated with what are termed common factors. These common factors focus predominantly on the quality of the therapeutic relationship or therapeutic alliance (Asay & Lambert 1999, Duncan et al. 2010). Cooper (2011, p. 53) reiterates the view that 'different therapies are about equivalent in their efficacy because they all share the same key ingredients, albeit not the same technique'. Those ingredients are most often associated with a set of nonspecific factors common to all therapies, predominantly the quality of the therapeutic relationship. Some aspects of the service user's perspective are associated with the successful development of this relationship, but the focus from the counsellor's perspective is usually on the ability to engage the following attributes: empathy, warmth, acceptance, affirmation and encouragement (Asay & Lambert 1999, Duncan et al. 2010).

We will consider the place of the therapeutic relationship in SFW before looking at three aspects of counselling skills as they apply to SF social work: listening, thinking and responding (talking). Each of these will be broken down into a number of specific examples of how they are applied in SFW.

- The therapeutic relationship
- Listening: listening with a constructive ear, engaging in problem-free talk, noticing exceptions, strengths and resilience
- Thinking: employing theoretical versatility, applying SF assumptions to move from problems to solutions and the skill of reframing
- Responding (talking): asking questions, goal-setting, empathic responding

Exploring core skills as applied in SFW: employ listening, thinking and talking to demonstrate genuineness and acceptance

Building the therapeutic relationship: A therapeutic relationship, the SFW recognises the importance of the relationship between therapist/counsellor/social worker and service user. This therapeutic relationship is described by deShazer (1991, p. 74) as 'a negotiated, consensual, and cooperative endeavour in which the solution focused therapist and client jointly produce various language games focused on; exceptions, goals, and solutions'. This is in line with the idea of developing a relationship with a service user based on an exploration of their 'exceptions' and goals rather than employing empathy to understand how they feel about their problems. We will look more at empathy in SFW later. However, it is only if you accept this paradigm shift that the SF approach becomes plausible and you can then employ the core counselling skills in this different sequence of exploration and solution-building. Building the therapeutic alliance the SF way depends on the social worker uncovering a positive way to view the service user's world and acknowledging/focusing on their attempts to manage in that world. This is done through finding exceptions, the times when the service user is doing something that works or at least works better. In SFW there are always examples of this and we will look later at the skills employed to help the social worker find/notice these exceptions. The search for the positive is at the centre of a respectful and genuine positive regard for the service user and it is this that forms the cornerstone of the SF therapeutic relationship.

Exploring listening skills as applied in SFW: identify resources, amplify resources and connect to solutions

Listening

In addition to employing the listening skills mentioned earlier, SFW provides a somewhat different slant on listening. This is best described by the work of Lipchik (1988) in her article 'Interviewing with a constructive ear'. This approach to listening is consistent with the counselling skills we have already discussed; it is concerned with paying attention to verbal and non-verbal communications, with what is said and not said and it draws on noticing and observing as well as 'traditional' listening. In SFW the influence of social construction thinking has particularly impacted the skill of listening. Through a social construction lens we are more aware of the risks of hearing not only what is said but of only hearing what we are listening for. Hearing only what we expect, or alternatively processing what we hear in such a way that we dismiss what doesn't fit with our ideas or expectations, proves to be a serious limitation on effective listening. In cognitive theory we refer to self-defeating thoughts or negative thoughts which can overwhelm a person. By adding the social construction perspective it is clear that these negative interpretations or thoughts can be created in a social context and so both the service user and the social worker/counsellor can contribute to the development or creation of the negative perspective by selectively hearing only the negative and then building an understanding or an interpretation of what is important based on this incomplete account. It is like only hearing one side of a story and that side is full of the negatives. This can be presented as a problem-saturated version of what is happening. Lipchik (1988) describes the skills required to counteract this selective listening. She suggests listening with a constructive ear which seeks to capture the story of strengths, resources and resilience. Based on her four stages of constructive listening we can identify the following steps:

- Identify exceptions – pay particular attention in conversation to the service user's account of events in which they side-line, ignore or dismiss their success or coping. Because SFW holds the view that there are always exceptions, that means times when the service user is coping or managing the problem or doing better because the problem is less intense. It is the role of the social worker/counsellor to assist in identifying these. The way to do this is through active and constructive listening.
- Amplify exceptions – once you hear an example of a strength/success/coping then draw the service user's attention to it by asking open questions to find out more about it, be curious about the success: how did that happen, what did you do to make that happen, etc. This brings the exception into the conversation and thus amplifies it and makes it real and tangible.
- Highlight solutions – having identified the exception, rather than simply saying, that's great, or you are doing really well, you have drawn the service user into an exploration of the exception so that they do not think of it as something you have imposed but

rather something you helped them to recognise and accept. Now you are on the way to harnessing this as a resource for building a solution. Highlighting the connection between the exception identified and the solutions only works if the service user is helped to see the strength for themselves, it is not as effective if it seems that 'you are only saying that to make me feel better'.

- Reinforce solutions – the aim, then, is to employ the skills associated with goal-setting to help move from the exception to linking it to a possible pathway to resolving problems, i.e. building a solution. The SF method takes the view that it is easier to do more of what is already working than to try to do something that is completely unfamiliar and may be outside the service user's experience. It is also considered that doing more of what hasn't worked in the past is going to have the same results, so it is critical to elicit these solutions from the service user's experiences.

Exploring thinking skill applied in SFW: reframing, reflection and acceptance

Thinking

In considering applying the skills of thinking in SF we will look at what SF draws from its theoretical base to influence the processing of information gathered through listening. As part of this we will also explore the skill of reframing. This skill can be applied in SF work to assist in shifting from a problem focus to a solution focus by supporting the worker to reconsider the problem-focused information and seek or uncover a more positive solution-focused perspective.

Reframing and theoretical versatility

To be able to address this paradigm shift we need to first engage our reflection skills and second be open to questioning our preconceived ideas, what I referred to earlier as explanations that are generally accepted. In a discussion of this openness to learning, Robinson (1974) highlighted the notion of four levels of competence which is useful in this context. He proposed that when we don't know we don't know that is unconscious incompetence; then we realise we don't know so we are at conscious competence. When we learn what is required we can begin to develop a level of conscious competence; and eventually when we don't know that we know we are at a level of unconscious competence. This is like an automatic response when we are not aware that we have actually used our competence to inform what to do. You may think that the goal should be to develop knowledge and skills to this level of unconscious competence. For social work and counsellors in general this aspiration is, to my mind, faulty. It neglects to take account of the fact that no matter what we know or what level of experience we have, once we engage in professional conversation with service users there is an unknown factor, the service user's perspective. This means that we need to remain conscious and vigilant about what we think we know and how we are allowing our knowledge and experience to influence the interaction with service users. It is only then that we can respond to individual differences and engage in a truly therapeutic alliance with each service user we encounter. Walsh (2010, p. 56) suggests that the SF helper must make sense of the context, role, knowledge base and ethical dimensions before deciding if, and then how, to use SF in their work.

It is tempting to say that before you engage your counselling skills you need to engage in this thinking process, but that would be misleading. In actual fact, as we have discussed, this thinking process is part of your counselling skills repertoire. You start with having an understanding of your own perspective on human development and what is important in understanding and explaining people, their experiences and challenges in life. You will probably notice that your preferred theoretical explanation will be informed by some of the grand theories we have already discussed. Social work originated in a more sociologically informed arena. Social work, with its focus on the 'social', is concerned with the social context and with attempting to address the ways in which society and culture impact individuals, families and communities. The influence of the psychological grand theories is a much more recent phenomenon. With practise and experience you will see the links between the grand theories and the next level of theory including systems, cognitive behavioural and social construction (review Table 4.1). From there you can connect to a specific method of intervention/ counselling that fits with your understanding of people, problems and change.

A personal reflection on theoretical orientation

When I started in social work our course was very influenced by systems theory. In the early days it was quite a prescriptive set of ideas. For example, there was the idea of the functional and dysfunctional family and the importance of prescribed roles in the family. I worked as an addiction social worker/counsellor and so this informed ideas of the day that considered the possibility that addiction was functional in holding the family together. It seemed that as social workers we could use this theory to make an assessment on whether a family was functioning in a positive way or if they were dysfunctional. We won't go into the validity of this thinking here, but it helps to make the point that it provided a set of ideas about how to read and understand service users' experiences. At that time I worked with a clinical psychologist who was a committed behaviourist. He saw things very differently.

What was most helpful in these divergent positions was that we had to become much more transparent about how these theoretical perspectives were shaping our ideas about what was happening for and with service users. In an attempt to share my view of the importance of understanding family systems, I brought him out on a home visit. We discussed the impact of family relationships and the social context within which the family managed the addiction. He contributed ideas about learned behaviours and factors that might be reinforcing the addictive behaviour. The most obvious difference was of course that I was looking at families and he was looking at individuals and both perspectives were valuable. The outcome was that we both had to question our own perspectives and learn to appreciate another perspective. This enriched our interaction with service users and generated a whole range of possibilities that we were able to engage when trying to formulate ways of helping our service users. Given that there is little evidence that one method is absolutely superior in dealing with all problems

(Asay & Lambert 1999), versatility in our thinking is really helpful to inform what we need to do next.

Figure 9.1 suggests a range of theories that seem to inform solution-focused work. For SF work predominantly the ideas emanate from the social construction philosophy. deShazer (1991) found this to be useful in supporting the shift from concentrating on understanding the problem to being more interested in solutions. It was this paradigm shift that allowed us to think of problems as constructed through language, which then open up possibilities that problem construction may in itself be part of what needs to be addressed.

In practice, I have found that many social workers find the idea of being solution-focused very attractive. Maybe it appeals to social workers' values in terms of respecting individuals and empowering them. What is sometimes less obvious is the influence of other theories in blocking the adoption of a social constructionist perspective on what we see or hear from service users. You need to be clear about what ideas you are using to help you understand people's experiences, in particular how you understand or explain their problems.

To help us engage in this critical reflection, Berg (1994) suggests that we exercise the skill of reframing. You can do this in small ways; for example, when you think someone is annoying. Consider alternative ways of describing and understanding what might be happening; you/they are anxious/under stress/ambitious/concerned/worried; they are trying to impress; or have great ideas that you just don't agree with at that time.

Exercise 17 Challenge your thinking by applying the skill of reframing to the case of Jack (Appendix 9.1: Case example: Jack)

Steps in applying the skill of reframing

- Think about your current interpretation of the client's troublesome behaviour

- Train yourself to think about a number of alternative interpretations
- Pick one of these, the most plausible and best fit
- Formulate a sentence that describes this new positive interpretation
- Give feedback to the client on this
- The reaction will tell you if it fits for the client
- A good fit will bring visible change in your client

(Berg 1994)

There are a number of assumptions that inform SFW and that reflect the influence of social construction theory. It is useful to consider what you think about each of these assumptions. Do you think they are helpful, limiting or unhelpful? Adherence to one theory limits possibilities for you and for your service users.

Exploring talking skills applied in SFW: demonstrate respect, accept, affirm and encourage. Ask open questions, reflect alternative interpretation or understanding and reinforce positives (George et al. 1999)

In discussion with other professionals, concerns often emerge; for example, about not exploring the cause of the problem (see Exercise 16). SFW does not emphasise this aspect of counselling conversations. Consistent with its social construction roots, SFW takes the view that any explanation of the cause of a problem is just that, one version of what might be the cause. It further works on the premise that time spent trying to get to the cause of the problem is valuable time spent away from moving on from that problem to a future in which the problem holds less importance for the service user. It may be that there is a draw for helpers to understand the cause and indeed to attempt to understand the problem. It may be that as helpers this problem discussion offers some reassurance that we know what we are doing and where we are going with the conversation. However, in SFW this sense of having direction should come from the negotiated goals established early in the conversation. These are goals that fit with the service user's hopes for the future and therefore goals that may help to engage the service user in the move towards positive change.

De Jong and Berg (2002, p. 17) clarified their position on problem discussion (some added comments in italics). They explain that they '"ask how we can be useful to you" (*goal setting question*). Clients generally respond by describing a problem of some sort and we ask for some detail (*addressing service user expectations of counselling and respecting their need to name the problem*). However, we spend much less time and effort here ... ask for fewer details ... and do not ask for possible causes.'

Engage in solution talk: The SF method values the strength and resilience demonstrated by service users, but it goes further than that. SFW, drawing on social construction theory, takes the view that there is always evidence of strengths and solutions in all cases if you just look and listen for it. We will consider what might block us from seeing this other interpretation of reality. Social construction theory supports this assumption by recognising that truth is not an objective reality but rather is dependent on the language employed to describe 'the truth', and also whose voice is privileged in the telling of the story of what is true. In other words, some people's version of what's happening will be given more value than others' and some will fit with preconceived ideas and beliefs and so will be given more credence. This speaks to social workers' value systems regarding issues of power, inequality and social justice.

For the SF social worker starting out with the assumption that there are always strengths, resilience and solutions means that it becomes possible to: take time to engage with the service user's life apart from the problem. Rather than focusing on a discussion about the problem, it is seen as valuable to instigate conversation about life apart from the problem. For many service users this may be an uncomfortable experience to start with. Service users come to a counsellor/social worker because they or someone else has identified that they have a problem. There is almost a shared understanding or social contract which is underpinned by a joint expectation that the focus of discussion will be the problem. The service user will probably feel they are expected to talk about the problem and in fact may have experiences of being viewed as resistant or uncommitted if they do not engage in problem description and discussion. If the social worker does not employ their counselling skills as informed by the assumptions of SFW, the service user and social worker may start talking about the problem and find it difficult to move away from the concerns that emerge. If, however, the social worker accepts that diverting at least some of the discussion away from the problem will give an opportunity for strengths, successes and solutions to be identified, they can use the core counselling skills to ask questions and use reflections that draw attention to other aspects of the service user's life. It may be that the service user has had previous problems that they resolved, or that they have interests, values, abilities or social networks that could be key elements of a solution story. These can get drowned out in the problem-saturated story.

This process of 'editing out' aspects of experiences or life stories is an important part of understanding the SF method. It is only if the social worker recognises that this can actually happen that it is necessary to actively redress the imbalance caused by editing out the positive which gives precedence to the problem. This skill is engaging in solution talk. It is not easy as the social worker has to continue to build a therapeutic relationship with the service user. This relationship requires that the service user feels listened to and that they feel that the social worker respects their experiences. It is quite challenging to continue to demonstrate your interest in and respect for the service user's experiences while skilfully redirecting them to a part of their story that they have lost sight of or in some cases a part of their story that has never been accessible to them before. Sometimes this can be achieved by differentiating between the start of the 'helping' process or counselling per se and what might be seen as 'a bit of casual chat before we get started'. Service users may find it easier to accept that it is OK to chat about their interests, jobs, etc., before you get started on the problem. The SF method was initially influenced by the observation that if you can establish this more positive conversation then the service user is more likely to become engaged and even optimistic about change.

Stories about strengths, success and resilience are not always easy to find. A number of factors may influence the attachment to the problem story. For example, for the service user it may depend on how often they have had to tell the problem-saturated story before or on their acceptance of the socially defined exceptions that a problem focus is more likely to get you the service. For the social worker it may be that because their theoretical preference is to explore the problem as a prerequisite to finding the cause of the problem and resolving it, it is more difficult to respectfully divert the conversation away from the problem. The term 'solution-focused' does infer that someone is staying focused, and in light of the strength of the problem-focused pull it is often up to the counsellor to provide the focus towards the solution story. However, it is important to keep in mind that while the social worker may ease the direction of the counselling towards solutions, it is the service user who must be facilitated to identify and engage with their own solutions.

Change

Solution-focused work holds the view that change is happening all the time. This underlying theoretical construct of change supports the premise that change while it is happening all the time may go unnoticed. Change is in fact inevitable (deShazer 1988). It is the failure to notice change that contributes to the construction of ideas such as individuals being stuck or resistant to change. In SF terms this signifies the absence of noticing, not the absence of change. These unobserved or undervalued changes include minor adaptions that service users make to survive in the face of difficult situations, small successes in terms of managing life's challenges and resilience born of resisting problems and drawing and building on social supports. Through a social construction lens it becomes possible to notice these as resilience and resources, to amplify them and then to harness them to work towards a set of goals and a better future. Change, it is argued, can arise from either a difference in how a person views his or her world or by the person doing something different, or both (George et al. 1990, p. 4). These possibilities also reflect the influence of both cognitive and behavioural theories on SFW.

Social construction theory is important in offering different perspectives on change.

Exercise 18 What about change?

Ask yourself what you think about change: is changing something difficult or easy? How can you make changes, why would you make changes? Do we change because we want to or because someone has put pressure on us? What sorts of circumstances create a situation where we are more likely to change? Do we resist change, in particular if we feel it is being imposed on us? These are all great questions to generate our thinking about change. How we see change and how we have experienced the need to change in our own lives will impact on how we interact with service users around change. If you understand that change might be difficult then you will handle it differently than if change is something you have experienced as easy. The methods we are looking at all have a different take on change.

Explore talking/responding skill as applied in SFW: use of a range of questions

Negotiate goals by asking goal-setting questions: the miracle question and scaling question

Responding

Having engaged constructive listening and thinking or processing skills, the next step is to follow through with a response. There is a range of responses the fit within the SF framework. These can be broadly categorised as questions and reflections. SFW is really helpful in identifying an array of different types of questions which can be distinguished by their purpose embedded in the formulation of the question. They also provide interesting ideas about how to get more detail from the service user. Because the focus of these questions is on strengths and positives the assumption is that it will be easier and of course more helpful to get details of successes rather than failures that might emanate from questions about the problem.

The questioning skills in SFW are congruent with the overall approach and so typically include:

- *Coping* questions – questions to elicit information about times when the service user is coping or at least coping better. Finding out more details about what the service user already knows about finding and harnessing solutions that fit with their perspective, skills, abilities and priorities.
- *Exception-finding* questions – questions which focus again on times when things have been better. Like the coping questions, these draw on the assumption that the problem fluctuates in terms of intensity and duration and that the problem is not occurring all the time. So these questions direct attention to times when an exception is happening instead of the problem. The problem(s) does not retain the same hold and finding out the exceptions to experiencing the full intensity of the problem is another vehicle for working towards solutions.
- *Instead* questions – based on the view that change is happening all the time, that it is inevitable, instead of questions are formulated to address the idea that it is easier to track changes by following what is happening rather than what's not happening. It is seen as more useful to talk about the presence of something rather than the absence. An example might be following a discussion where the service user identifies as a goal that they don't want to be stuck at home all the time. You might ask: what will you be doing instead of staying at home all day?
- *Relationship* questions – while SFW might not be known for addressing emotional content (we will look at changes in this later), there is still evidence of its family systems and systemic roots. Relationship questions are an example of this connection.

They attempt to get a picture of who else might be involved in the solution. For example, when talking about goals and describing in more detail what life will be like when the goal(s) are achieved, a relationship question might be: when things are better and you are going out more who will be the first to notice this change in you? These questions are very powerful because they give the social worker information about how/if the service user is connected with family, friends and other networks.

Case example

In asking this type of relationship question in my early SF days I had not done sufficient listening and eliciting to be able to assist a service user to tune into a more positive picture of his life. I asked a young man who would notice that he had turned a corner and was getting his life back on track. We had what felt like quite a long silence as he thought about the question before replying that he couldn't think of anyone who would notice. I realised without asking a problem-focused question that he was quite isolated, even more than I had realised. In true SF style, it was the service user himself who rescued my question. After some further thinking, he decided that the first to notice would be the doctor who referred him to the social work service. We then had a useful conversation about what the doctor would notice and through reframing his responses we were able to consider the possibility that perhaps he would impress a professional with his capacity to change.

- *What else* questions – again typical of SF, but need to be used with care. Too many 'what else' questions may become intrusive and may be seen as disrespectful of the responses the service user has already given. However, when used skilfully they are invaluable, simple ways to elicit more detail about what's working, what the service user wants in the future and allows both service user and social worker to get a much fuller description of the service users' perspective. The detail can then be used almost as a rehearsal for the service user as they talk through what a specific day or interaction in their preferred future would look like, step by step. This type of detailed rehearsal of what would be happening when things are better can make the changes seem more possible and more attractive. Some of these 'what else' questions can also be helpful in developing the goal-setting that is an essential aspect of SFW.

- Service user (SU) in response to 'instead of' question: 'I'll be out of the house more'.
- Social worker: 'So you will be out of the house more, what else will you be doing?'
- SU: 'Well I suppose I'll be meeting other people'.
- SW: 'And anything else?'
- SU: 'Maybe I'd have to talk to them'.
- SW summarises: 'OK then you'll be out of the house, meeting people and talking to them, is there anything else you might like to be doing?'

- You now have the start of a list of possible goals that the service user most likely has some familiarity with. Any or all of them are positive steps that would make them less isolated. You can follow on by checking out which of these might be most important, interesting, or a higher priority for the service user (looking at preferred goals) or check which aspect of the preferred future the service user already has the skills necessary to engage with (looking at exceptions).
- *Goal-setting* questions – goal-setting is a core skill in SFW. In fact, the method is probably best known for two of these goal-setting questions. Given the centrality of goal-setting we will look at these two formats in more detail: the miracle question and the scaling question. We have looked at questioning in a separate chapter as it relates to core counselling skills, but its use in SFW provides additional options on the application of the skill.

Goal-setting questions

Other theoretical influences which can be seen in the method developed by deShazer and Berg include the commitment to setting goals which would be strongly associated with behavioural theory. The construction of well-formed solution-focused goals mirrors that of behavioural theory. Well-formed goals are a key aspect of SFW. The characteristics of goals include (Berg & Miller 1992): goals need to be small rather than large, achievable, relevant to the service user, perceived as involving work and clearly described in concrete behaviours.

In practice I have found that setting goals can be a painful and difficult part of the work with service users. It is particularly poignant when the service users are struggling to think about any future where things are better for them. Without a sense of some hope for the future it is considered difficult for the service user to really engage in working on problems or accessing solutions. It is part of the skill of the SF worker to (re)capture that sense of hope through the skills of identifying exceptions and resources and amplifying these and affirming the service user. While the behaviourally informed focus on goals is a central part of SFW, there is also the acknowledgement that it may be necessary to help the service user change how they are thinking about the problems. This draws on both cognitive and social construction theories. Understanding how these two inform the method provides a vital map of where to go in the therapeutic conversation. Cognitive theory helps to explain how we can engage in self-defeating thinking while social construction can help us to understand how this negative thinking can be concocted or created though societal problem definition and views of what is acceptable.

Two goal-setting skills have emerged from SF which have influenced many areas of counselling social work. Arguably the most famous of these is the miracle question.

Miracle question (de Shazer 1988, p. 5) *(a form of hypothetical question)*

'Suppose that while you are asleep tonight and the entire house is quiet, a miracle happens. The miracle is that the problem which brought you here is solved. However, because you were sleeping you don't know that the miracle has happened. So, when you wake up tomorrow morning, what will be different that will tell you a miracle happened?'

The question captures some important aspects of the therapeutic value of goal-setting. It opens up possibilities; they don't even have to be realistic initially as they serve the purpose of introducing hope for a better future. In following up the miracle question by eliciting details of the concrete behaviours that will happen after the miracle, it becomes possible to work with the service user to sift out the realistic, doable behaviours and to begin a process of rehearsing for a life where things are better. Coping/instead of/what else questions can be employed to explore this detail. As ideally some of the after-miracle behaviours are already evidenced or small elements are evident, it becomes the social worker's job to notice these and by affirming the service user's goals to negotiate agreement of mutually important goals. This is particularly important where the goals of the service user do not necessarily address some concerns raised by the social worker. The aim of this question can be achieved through less-dramatic alternative configuration of the question.

Follow-up questions can include:

What will you be doing differently? (Finding more behavioural details)
Who will be the first to notice? (Relationship question)
What will they see you doing that will be different? (Behavioural and relationship question) When they see you doing (name what is being done differently) how will they respond?

In my experience, many concerns and issues have been raised in discussions with social workers about this question. For example, is the idea of a miracle culturally bound, is the term miracle suitable to raise with all service users, does it have religious connotations? Further, does the question imply that it would take a miracle to bring about change? This was not the intent of the question, but one can see the possible interpretation. Such an interpretation is the opposite to the intent of the miracle question, which strives to release the service user from the confines of being stuck in the problem to allow them to hope, wish for and describe their preferred future. The fundamental aim of the miracle question is to allow the service user the freedom to imagine the better future, without necessarily committing to the change. It instils hope and by doing so plays a part in building the therapeutic alliance which is at the core of professional helping.

Ratner et al. (2012, pp. 93–94) offer alternatives to the miracle question which still retain the hope-promoting essence of the miracle metaphor. They suggest questions such as 'What are your best hopes for therapy?' and comment that once the notion of hope was introduced to the very first question, 'miracles' proved less necessary. Ratner et al. (2012) also explain that the description of the preferred future is not a solution in itself, but rather provides a starting place to ask follow-up questions about what difference it will make to the person's life. These questions can then help to establish quality-of-life outcomes that become the focus of the counselling.

The scaling question

'Scaling questions have a great versatility. They invite clients to put their observations, impressions and predictions on a scale of 0 to 10' (De Jong & Berg, 2002, p. 108). The idea is that 0 represents things at their worst or a time when the problem is more pressing, while 10 represents things being better or potentially the problem being solved. By asking the service user to pick a number on the scale 0 to 10, information is provided about their perception of where they are now in managing the problem and working towards a change.

In practice I find that social workers like the scaling question, but the challenge is not to overuse or rush it. Asking a sequence of scaling questions might give you a sense of where the service user is at with a number of issues, but I find this less helpful than employing the scaling question as a pivot to anchor drilling down to the service user's perception of the likelihood of change, and how realistic they are about what will be needed to make the changes.

Before asking the scaling question, I think it is important to follow some of the SF format of asking about problem-free times, asking coping and exception questions and establishing some parameters about the service user's goals. Through this process the social worker should have a better sense of the service user's resourcefulness and resilience. Getting to this may involve doing some reframing with the service user to assist in helping them to access an alternative perspective, it may also involve employing a curiosity stance to facilitate the service user to explore times when they coped better, were less caught by the problem or even remembering times when the problem wasn't there. In other words, the scaling questions are not stand-alone but fit in with the overall SF method and require some preparatory work. Behaviour theory criteria for goal-setting are a good guideline to keep in mind when working with the scaling question. For me, then, the scaling question is not a starting up question like the other goal-setting questions. It is more suitable at a later stage in the first meeting and can be helpful in checking in about progress at subsequent meetings. The scaling question is a tool to help gain a more concrete picture of where the service user is and where they want to be and what they think is involved in getting there. With this in mind, it is useful to be clear about what you mean by 0 and 10 on the scale.

Let's go back to our service user who was having problems about isolating themselves at home. You might pose the scaling question about getting out of the house. However, this is only relevant if you already know that the service user actually wants to do this and sees this as part of a preferred future. Also you would ideally have some understanding of skills they can draw on to achieve this. Think about goals being achievable. Selecting a goal for the scaling question which is neither desired nor has any evidence of being achievable would be counterproductive. So having established these you might ask:

SW: Cathy, you have been talking about wanting a time when going out becomes part of your everyday life and I realise that you have been able to achieve this sometimes, for example in meeting me today (sometimes it's helpful to summarise some of the successes you have identified in preparation for asking the scaling question, it can help to remind the service user of exceptions), so on a scale of 0 to 10 with 0 being the worst things were when you never left the house at all and 10 being what you describe in the future, where you would be able to go out without worrying about it at all, where do you see yourself today?

If the answer is 0 then you may need to ask how Cathy was able to prevent things getting worse than a 0 (using your questions to elicit the more positive perspective).

If the answer is 1 or 2 or more then ask:

SW: What do you think you have done to manage getting to 2 (or whatever the number is)? You want to begin to get some detailed and concrete examples of what the service user thinks is involved in achieving the goal, if this brings to light some ways in which the service user is unrealistic about the goal or what it might take to get there, you can focus on the parts that are realistic and achievable, acknowledge them and amplify them by getting more details. Both the social worker and the service user can get a lot of valuable information from this question. There are a number of options to follow.

SW: (Offer summary of what SU has identified.) Being at 2 has involved you getting out and seeing me and also deciding to try to go to the shop at the weekend and going out to the garden now and then, so what would 3 look like/what would you be doing at 3? Again affirm and amplify the SU ideas by summarising what they come up with, focusing on those ideas that are potentially realistic, doable or even already evident.

After exploring this you can move on to check what number would they be satisfied with if this is appropriate. As you work with the scaling question you continue to follow the assumption of the method looking for exceptions, identifying and amplifying success, resources and resilience and help to make the connections between these successes and eventual solutions. Remember to engage your counselling skills to affirm, reflect and summarise what you hear.

Empathy: De Jong and Berg/Lipchik

Within SFW there has been some variation of opinion about the place of empathy in the method. De Jong and Berg (2002) draw on Biestek's principles of social work practice (1957) to explore the connection between controlled emotional involvement and empathy. This echo's Rogers 'as if' concern that while connecting with service users feeling is important, it is also important to recognise that these feelings belong to the service user and not to the social worker. de Jong and Berg (2002, p. 38) agree that 'empathy has a well-established place in working with clients'. They clarify that for them there are different types of empathy and different ways of expressing this sense of empathic understanding. They recommend 'an empathy of natural interruptions which can include a knowing nod of your head, paraphrases, summaries that convey your understanding of the significance of what the person is saying, respectful silences and adopting a compassionate tone of voice. Empathic affirmation is also useful, but not where this is used to amplify negative feelings that may drive the person further into aspects of their life that are least helpful for generating positive change' (de Jong & Berg 2002, p. 41). This view of empathy is consistent with the underlying assumptions of the method. Reflecting on negative thoughts and feelings would be seen as giving emphasis to them and supporting a deficit perspective. While it may be important to acknowledge these thoughts and feelings to support the development of the therapeutic alliance from the SF point of view, helping the person to recognise, acknowledge and give a voice to positive thoughts and feelings that have been lost or hidden by the problem is a method that can make a difference.

This alternative or, perhaps more accurately, additional dimension to empathy demonstrates that hearing what is not said as well as what is said can be utilised to convey empathic understanding while at the same time compassionately shifting the focus away from the problem to solutions. Even within SF practitioners there is some difference of opinion on just how empathy should be employed. Lipchik (2002, p. 20), one of the early proponents of SFW, moved away from the deShazer and Berg approach to incorporate a more emotionally empathic dynamic in her work. She believed that a SF method could accommodate more attention to the emotional world of the service user. For her, emotions are part of every problem and every solution. The cognitive behaviour influences on SFW have limited the talk about feelings. Including the emotional element contributes to conveying that we understand what service users are telling us in more depth and so is helpful in building the therapeutic relationship. In supporting her argument for more recognition of emotions, Lipchik (2002, p. 62) draws attention to developments in the field of neuroscience which support the view that cognition and emotion are separate but interacting and that both influence actions.

This debate about empathy raises questions defining the parameters of what might be experienced as empathy by service users and also by broadening the skill and purpose of empathic responding beyond that initially conceived by Rogers.

Final comments

SFW provides a great example of counselling social work skills in action. The method clearly draws on the core skills of listening, thinking and talking/responding. It employs these skills with a different purpose, which is informed predominantly by social construction theory. This results in an adaption of the skills to fit with its theoretical influences, which places more emphasis on certain aspects of the skills, such as questioning and goal-setting. Fundamental to applying your skill in a way that is consistent with SFW is the adoption of the shift in paradigm from problems to solutions. This requires active engagement in challenging your thinking skills so that you can listen for and respond to versions of the service user's experiences that may have disappeared from view. Exercise 19 will help you to work some more on this challenge.

Exercise 19 Applying your thinking skills in a solution-focused way

You can do this exercise alone, but it's more fun and probably better learning if you have two or more people involved.

1. Read the case about a young man called Jack (Appendix 9.1).

2. Take a note of what parts of the story resonate with you and how you explain what you think is going on.
3. If there are aspects of the story that cause you to be worried or concerned, identify what is worrying and why.
4. When you have looked through the case and developed your ideas about what's happening, and maybe even some ideas about what needs to happen.
5. When you have discussed your perceptions of what's going on for Jack, read and review the edited version of the case in Appendix 9.2. Does the edited version bring up new ideas for you, does it change some of the points you raised, can you track the difference that the SF interpretation offers Jack's story?

10 Counselling social work skills and Motivational Interviewing (MI)

- Provide a brief description of the theoretical frameworks that inform motivational interviewing.
- Review the core counselling/therapeutic skills employed in MI.
- Consider the compatibility between MI and social work values and practice.
- Look at implications of social work-focused MI research.
- Explore the emergence of motivational social work.

Introduction

The theories informing MI are very persuasive and the method appears familiar. Because of this, it is often seen as a simple but not easy way of working with service users. The way in which these familiar counselling skills are orchestrated is, for me, a hallmark of an MI-adherent intervention. In this chapter we will look at the theories that inform MI, then we will talk about MI as a method of intervention and finally we will explore the application of core social work counselling skills discussed in Part I, in the MI world.

Motivational interviewing (MI) was developed by William Miller and Steve Rollnick (2013) in the early 1980s. At that time it was specifically looking for ways to work with people who were experiencing problems with alcohol and other drugs (AOD). In their opening chapter of the most recent edition of their book, Miller and Rollnick (2013) refer to the approach as conversations about change, reflecting the diversity of language employed when discussing these helping methodologies.

MI retains the influences brought to it by Miller, who attributes much of his early thinking about the method to the humanistic ideas embedded in the Rogerian therapeutic alliance. Miller and

Rollnick defined MI as 'a directive, client centred counselling style for eliciting behaviour change by helping clients to explore and resolve ambivalence' (1995, p. 325). As the method evolved the connection to Rogers can still be seen in the inclusion of the concept of guiding in the definition 'motivational interviewing is a collaborative, person-centred form of guiding to elicit and strengthen motivation for change' (Miller & Rollnick 2013, p. 137). This is particularly evident in the decision to make more explicit the underlying spirit of MI. 'The influence of Rogers as reflected in a core belief in the importance of unconditional acceptance is identified as one of the four elements of the MI spirit' (Miller & Rollnick 2013, p. 17). 'Along with a commitment to collaboration, compassion, evocation and acceptance, the four pillars of the MI spirit clearly encompass much of the person-centred principles espoused by Rogers's client-centred work' (Miller & Rollnick 2013, p. 22).

Theoretical framework

Humanistic theory and the therapeutic relationship

Building the therapeutic relationship has a central place in MI. This is informed by MI's humanistic theory foundation and it permeates all aspects of the MI spirit. It is consistent with humanistic thinking that through valuing the person and acknowledging their autonomy you are more likely to engage with them in collaborative partnership. All the core components for developing a therapeutic alliance as identified by Rogers (1957) are therefore found in MI.

The connection to the therapeutic alliance including: empathy, warmth, acceptance, affirmation and encouragement (common factors identified in Asay & Lambert 1999, Cooper 2011) are evident in the formulation of the MI spirit. Perhaps because of its connections with Rogers or maybe because MI represents a shift away from more traditional confrontational approaches, it seems to fit well with the social work value base. Social work and MI share the belief in the importance of accepting and respecting the individual. They also value autonomy and a belief in the individual's strengths and resourcefulness as well as a basic belief that people want what's best for themselves and their families, even if this proves problematic at times. The principles of MI such as expressing empathy, respecting client autonomy and being collaborative are congruent with social work values and ethics (Wahab 2010). Empathy, a core social work value and fundamental MI principle, is an important component of the process that strengthens the therapeutic relationship (Miller & Rollnick 2013). Later in this chapter we will look at how the application of counselling skills supports this relational aspect of MI as a method.

A summary of the theories, concepts and skills for MI is presented in Figure 10.1, which will help to guide us through the ideas and concepts in the chapter.

Concept of change

As already mentioned, MI emerged at a time when interventions and treatment in the addiction field were premised on the need to confront faulty defence mechanisms such as denial and resistance. These ideas were rooted in the psychoanalytic theories of the day. Also of influence was the disease concept of addiction, which promoted total abstinence. Around this time, Prochaska and DiClemente were developing their ideas about therapy and what might support change. In 1982 they presented their ideas about a more integrative model of change. Their model was compatible with the work being developed by Miller (1983). Both recognised motivation and the quality of the relationship between counsellor and client as key preconditions for change (Prochaska and DiClemente 1982, 1983 and Miller 1983). It is not surprising then that MI and Prochaska and DiClemente's Trans Theoretical Model (TTM) of change should work well together. Such was the perceived connection between these two that Miller and Rollnick (2013) have had to clarify that MI is not TTM. In fact, while early iterations of MI did draw on some of the ideas of change from TTM, more recently MI has focused more on the language of change formulated around concepts of talk that sustains behaviour and change talk (Miller & Rollnick 2013).

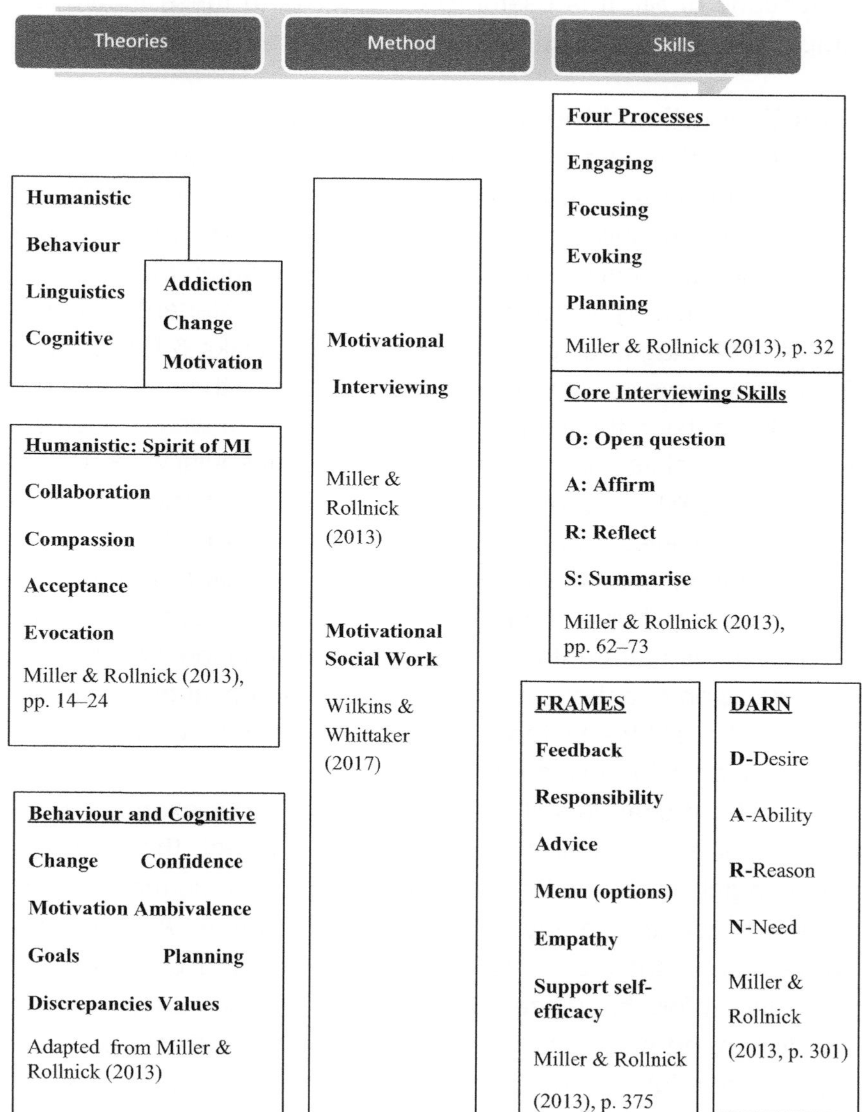

Figure 10.1 Brief overview of Motivational Interviewing

For the purpose of setting the scene to consider social work applications of MI, it is useful to consider both these theoretical perspectives on change.

Trans Theoretical Model (TTM) of change

This theory of change has found much support in a range of helping settings and social work is no exception. In summary, it proposed that change is a process and that this process involves moving though a number of stages from pre-contemplation, contemplation, making a decision, action and maintenance; sometimes a sixth stage, relapse, is included (Prochaska & DiClemente 1983). This purports to provide a comprehensive theory of change applicable outside the field of addiction in which it was conceived. One example of its use in analysis of a different social work setting is Gelles' (1996) critique of the family preservation movement. In his analysis, Gelles suggested that one contributory factor to the failure of family preservation services was the lack of attention to the pre-contemplative stage of some families. He suggested that this undermined attempts at working towards change. Families not at the decision or action stage of the process of change would not be able to benefit from intensive input because they were not ready for to engage with the idea of change.

The TTM of change still informs ideas in MI, for example ideas about ambivalence (Miller & Rollnick 2013). In fact, the stages of change highlight that to be ambivalent about change may be indicative that you are already moving towards change. 'Ambivalence involves simultaneous conflicting motivations and can therefore be an uncomfortable place to be' (Miller & Rollnick 2013, p. 157). This discomfort can be harnessed to help a service user consider why change might be necessary and/or helpful, and such contemplation is the second step of this conceptualisation of the change process in TTM. We will explore how this might translate into application of skills in terms of responses to ambivalence later in this chapter.

Another way in which this theory of change can be helpful is in working with social workers to consider how they perceive their own place in the change process.

Exercise 20 Stages in the wheel of change

Draw the wheel of change and the stages of change on a whiteboard and talk through the meaning of the stages and what they entail. (See Appendix 10.1.)

1. Have a discussion about professional interventions. Consider at what stage of change social workers meet service users. In particular, identify the frequency with which social workers encounter service users who are still in the pre-contemplative stage, i.e. they have not yet considered the need for change.
2. Consider how social workers themselves think about change. Think, for example, about the challenges when faced with a crisis situation where perhaps a service user is at risk. You may find that the social worker is ready for action; they recognise the risk and vulnerability of the service user and want/need things to change now.

It is very striking to mark the place of the service user on the wheel and then the place of the social worker. They are almost at opposite sides of the wheel. For professional helpers who value starting where the service user is at and who recognise the value of the relationship, this illustrates that being in such different places regarding change is an immediate challenge to the development of any level of cooperation between them.

Linguistic perspective on change: change talk

MI's shift in focus from TTM to change talk is evident in the 2013 edition of Miller and Rollnick's text book. This shift is attributed by them to the influence of psycholinguistics and defines change talk as 'any self-expressed language that is an argument for change' (2013, p. 159). Conceptually opposite to change talk is sustain talk, 'any speech that can be uttered on behalf of change can also be spoken as an equal and opposite reaction on behalf of the status quo' (Miller & Rollnick 2013, p. 164). This also represents another set of theoretical ideas that inform MI.

Cognitive behavioural theory

Miller and Rollnick (2013, p. 134) are very clear that MI is not a form of cognitive behaviour therapy as it 'does not involve teaching new skills, re-educating, counterconditioning, changing the environment, or installing more rational and adaptive beliefs. It is not about installing anything, but rather is about eliciting from people that which is already there'. However, in putting motivation to the forefront, it is useful to have an appreciation of cognitive and behavioural ideas about what motivation is. Some CBT concepts that are consistent with MI are as follows:

- Achieving any goal and experiencing some success can in itself enhance motivation
- Change can happen in response to extrinsic motivating factors (e.g. pressure from outside), but sustained change is more likely where the motivations becomes intrinsic (internalised)
- Understanding of cognitive process associated with, for example, ambivalence, value systems, discrepancies or cognitive dissonance

The influence of these behavioural and cognitive theoretical concepts is still evident, but there has been a growing emphasis on the 'MI as a clinical communication method and as a guiding style of enhancing intrinsic motivation' (Miller & Rollnick 2013, p. 131).

Method

MI: a communication method and guiding style

MI is designed as brief intervention. Miller and Rollnick (2013) suggest that two sessions of MI can be helpful, but that if a person is not motivated to engage with the change process then further MI might not be helpful. MI can also be introduced or reintroduced at different stages in counselling depending on the need to enhance motivation or work with ambivalence about change.

Despite the fact that MI places an emphasis on adopting the spirit of MI and the relational foundation, it is also clear that there are techniques and processes that are embedded in the method which help guide the practitioner. As Moyers explains:

> *There are two critical elements that make up the MI approach, the first of which is the relational factor ... The second critical element, or technical factor, is the focus on evoking and strengthening a particular kind of language within the MI session. This language, called change talk, is the spontaneously occurring speech from the client that favors a desired change.*
>
> (Moyer.s 2014, p. 358)

Getting to this change talk also involves engaging with the four processes identified in the MI as a method of intervention.

Miller and Rollnick (2013) refer to the four processes of MI: engaging, focusing, evoking and planning. These processes reflect the theoretical underpinning of MI, particularly in the emphasis on engaging. While always consistent with these humanistic influences, focusing, evoking and planning demonstrate traits found in behavioural thinking in terms of how to move towards implementing change. The usefulness of drawing on these other theoretical ideas is most evident when talking about a person who has moved into what TTM would term the actions stage. For MI that would mean that there was a shift towards change talk. Once the service user has moved toward this, MI recognises that it might be useful to draw on behavioural or cognitive behaviour theory and methods. Miller and Rollnick (2013, p. 301) state that 'MI combines well with a variety of other treatment approaches and may enhance retention and adherence'.

MI has developed a number of strategies to assist in building the therapeutic relationship, enhancing motivation and eliciting change talk. The first of these refers to working with a person who seems to have shown few or no signs of change talk. In the TTM of change this would be a pre-contemplator. Like many of the MI strategies it is described by its acronym.

D – Desire
A – Ability

R – Reason
N – Need

The theoretical basis of this relates to the concept of discrepancy, which has been part of MI since the start (sometimes called cognitive dissonance). Discrepancy means that there is an imbalance between what's happening at present and what the person would like to be happening either now or in the future. This, in practice, may concern a discrepancy, imbalance or mismatch between present behaviour and future goals or between present behaviours and one's value system. Ultimately, discrepancy can lead to some level of discomfort with the status quo. If the discomfort/discrepancy is strong enough or persistent it can be an impetus for change. For someone not displaying change talk, it might be assumed that they are not experiencing discrepancies in their lives, and yet through exploration it may be possible to help them to discover and articulate discrepancies. Miller and Rollnick (2013, pp. 243–253) provide a detailed account of discrepancy and how it can be harnessed for change. It is useful here to acknowledge that there are alternative responses to discrepancy which may detract from change talk. They raise a number of reasons why discrepancy might not lead to change:

- The change required is seen as too much and so motivation to attempt it is low
- The change required seems to be outside of the service user's ability and again this may be demotivating
- The service users may have adopted an ability to avoid thinking/contemplating on the discrepancy, being able to put it aside so then it isn't dealt with and so does not motivate change

(Miller & Rollnick 2013, pp. 243–253)

There is probably a certain level of discrepancy that we can each tolerate. In fact, we may have to learn to tolerate some discrepancies in our lives. It becomes problematic when this tolerance allows us to engage in behaviours that are unhealthy or unhelpful to ourselves or others. Not unlike the crisis theory of change, which suggests that in a crisis feeling out of your depth and unable to cope can be the trigger motivation for change but if the crisis is diverted, handled by others or in some way dissipates before we change then the necessity to change to manage the crisis also dissipates (Loughran 2010).

DARN then helps the counsellor to draw attention to four factors that might help to harness discrepancies to motivate change. Bringing possible desires, reasons or need for change out through supportive conversation, along with discussion of ability to make changes, DARN hopes to highlight discrepancies that have been masked. Where there is little sign of such discrepancies Miller and Rollnick (2013, p. 248) offer two suggestions. Firstly, 'a good starting place is to assume that discrepancy is already there and search for it'. If this doesn't help then try 'instilling discrepancy' which 'is a process of sitting together and considering reasons why the person might consider change'. This can be achieved through using the core counselling skills such as open questions and reflections. Understanding this connection between discrepancies, motivation and change is helpful in implementing the DARN strategy. It also helps to recognise commitment language. Hohman (2012, p. 85) reminds us that the strength of the commitment language is a predictor of outcome. This is represented as DARN-CaT, adding signs of commitment and taking steps as indicators of stronger commitment talk.

A final set of skills we will mention in MI was developed based on research which identified six common components to effective brief interventions. These were given the acronym FRAMES. This provides a guide to conducting an intervention. Using FRAMES involves providing feedback to the service user, working on the basis that ultimately the service user has responsibility for change or not changing, while advice is helpful it should be done using the Elicit–Provide + Elicit guidelines, this is likely to be assisted by outlining a range of options again including not changing but with some discussion of possible consequences of each as understood by the service user. The interview must be conducted demonstrating empathy though empathic listening and responding and finally supporting the service user's sense of self-efficacy or belief in their ability to make change.

F – Feedback
R – Responsibility

A – Advice
M – Menu (options)
E – Empathy
S – Support self-efficacy

(Miller & Rollnick 2013, p. 375)

These acronyms (see Figure 10.1) provide brief summaries of sequences of counselling skills that can be used to deliver effective interventions depending on the level of engagement with the process and the service user's position with regard to motivation for change.

Applying social work counselling skills

Listening

We discussed the importance of knowing what you are listening for and the impact that can have on what you hear. MI involves searching for change talk and discrepancies even when they seem to be absent. It also involves hearing them when they might be masked by some of the barriers to change discussed above, e.g. fear of change, lack of confidence in ability to change, etc. These are all part of the listening skills that are core to counselling and social work. Active and accurate listening skills are essential in the implementation of DARN and the other strategies in MI. The difference is less about what you do (listen and respond) and more about connecting what you do with why you are doing it (thinking) and of course utilising the core 'talking' skills for MI such as open questions and reflective response.

MI's OARS

Hohman (2012, p. 35), in a discussion of the engagement and assessment process in social work, refer to the use of 'the MI assessment sandwich. This involves the first 20 minutes of an assessment/intake interview being focused on use of OARS, the middle part of the interview focusing on standard agency protocol and the final 20 minutes using MI skills to elicit ideas about change and planning'. Miller and Rollnick (2013) devised the acronym OARS to explain the core counselling skills applied in this interviewing/counselling process.

OARS refer to the basic counselling skills employed in setting up communication with the service user that is consistent with a client-centred orientation and building a therapeutic relationship/alliance and which match with social work counselling skills:

O – Open questions
A – Affirmations
R – Reflections
S – Summaries

(Miller & Rollnick 2013, pp. 62–73)

These skills are designed to enhance the client's sense of agency, to create a collaborative relationship between client and counsellor, and to demonstrate empathy (Miller & Rollnick 2013). Each of these has been discussed in earlier chapters; however, we will look now at the central role they play in MI. What is important to recognise is that these core counselling skills which should be part of social work professional formation can be applied in MI as informed by the theoretical influences outlined.

Processing

The complex nature of processing for a professional helper has been discussed in Chapter 4. We will consider here some particular elements of this processing that are involved in MI and how these impact social work practice.

Social work counselling skills and MI

'MI involves quite a complex set of skills that are used flexibly, responding to moment-to-moment changes in what the client says. It involves the conscious and disciplined use of specific communication principles and strategies to evoke the person's own motivations for change' (Miller & Rollnick 2009, p. 135). Social work also involves listening to service users. It may not specifically focus on the concept of ambivalence but it does recognise that change may be difficult. Given its concern with both the individual and the social, social work is more likely to take cognisance of the systemic or social aspects of problem development and maintenance. Although this involves applying a broader lens to the interpretation of issues/problems, facilitating the service user to tell their story remains critically important. So social work and MI want to engage service users and once engaged help them to consider change. For this the skills of open questions and reflective listening or reflective responding are the most helpful.

Rollnick et al. (2010, pp. 1243–1244) provide a helpful summary of three core activities involved in MI for the novice counsellor/practitioner. They identify three basic activities:
Practise the guiding style: this involves following three principles. To engage with and work in collaboration with patients, emphasise their autonomy over decision-making, and elicit their motivation for change. These are operationalised through some of the core counselling skills we have discussed earlier.

- Asking – open questions
- Listening – reflective listening and express empathy
- Informing – by asking permission to give information and then checking what implications might be

Rollnick et al. (2010) add that it is important to elicit rather than instil motivation for change. One option is to assess importance and confidence and this can be done by the use of scaling questions. Not unlike the type of question we explored in SF work.

On a scale of 1 to 10, with 1 being I have no confidence and 10 being I'm very confident, where do you see yourself today? You can follow this up with open questions and reflections to help the service user to think about what gives them confidence and what, if any, experiences they have had to date that could help build their confidence.

Given that we have already looked in some depth at the issue around giving advice, it is worth noting that in MI they have a very particular position on this interaction. They think not of advice or

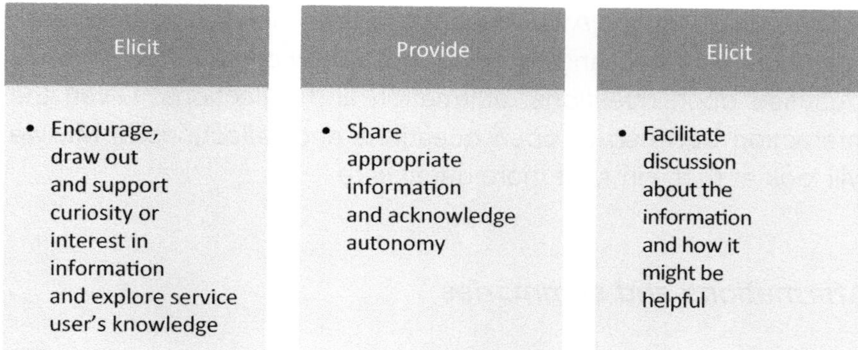

Figure 10.2 Steps in information exchange. (Adapted from Miller and Rollnick 2013.)

information-giving but rather of exchange information: the style of exchanging information is very important in MI because of its basic premise that the service user is expert in their own lives and of course because of the commitment to valuing self-determination, often referred to in MI as the client's autonomy. A formula consistent with eliciting information and motivation from the service user is employed. Hence the social worker elicits interest in or at least openness to hearing information, encourages service users to talk about their own knowledge and skills and what they may have tried already, then provides the information and follows up with checking what, if anything, that information or advice means to the service user. In MI it is referred to as Elicit.

The final step is make decisions about change or setting goals. This is done by responding skilfully to the patient's language and by eliciting change talk. Rollnick et al. (2010) acknowledge that the biggest challenge is usually with the shift in style and attitude involved and in particular trying to let go the 'righting reflex', which is a tendency to identify a problem and solve it for the person. Make it right.

Social work counselling skills and MI

The skill of talking/responding in MI draws on the core skills identified in OARS.

O: open questions A: affirmations R: reflections S: summaries
In exploring talking and listening in social work we have already identified open questions, affirmation and reflections. Given the interaction between of open questions and reflections in MI, we will look at these in a bit more detail here.

Affirmations and summaries

We have already discussed affirmations in some depth in an earlier chapter, but again it is important to note that they have an acknowledged place in MI. Summaries could be described as the skill of capturing the key aspects of the service user's contribution and editing that in a way that checks you have understood what is important to the service user while allowing you the opportunity to focus and direct the next step in the conversation.

Open questions and reflections

In fact MI is quite prescriptive about the interplay between open questions and reflections. We have discussed open questions and reflection before. Open questions are invitations to speak. They may provide some direction to the conversation, but essentially they allow the service user scope to take the discussion to wherever they think is useful. In MI, open questions followed by an appropriate response or series of appropriate reflective responses are considered to be the most effective way to engage service users. In MI the use of reflective responses is connected to reflective listening, which is the skill required to gather the information to inform your reflective response. Reflective listening can be seen as part of the listening set of skills that includes empathic listening and the reflection offered is then part of the skill of responding/talking. Miller and Rollnick (2013, p. 60) clarify that 'in the engaging process the primary purpose of reflective listening is to understand the client's dilemma, to see the situation trough the client's own perspective. There is no particular direction involved'. Limitations about questioning have been discussed already. In MI, Miller and Rollnick (2013, p. 61) caution that 'because questioning is a less demanding skill(for the counsellor) than empathic listening it is easy to fall into the question–answer trap, asking a series of questions instead of following and reflecting the persons' statements'. The MI way is that once you ask an open question you should respond with a reflection.

The place of reflection is further developed in that different uses or designs of reflections are used for different purposes in MI. In the process of evoking change or change talk 'reflection and other fundamental counselling skills are used strategically to accelerate change' (Miller & Rollnick 2013, p. 60).

Reflections, which are an identified skill in counselling, have a particular place of importance in MI because the method and its research have demonstrated that reflection is the most appropriate way to engage service users and to elicit motivation for change. This, it would seem from Forrester et al.'s (2008) research, is something that is not evident in social work practice despite the fact that social workers are expected to engage service users and work towards change. We will come back to this dilemma at the end of this chapter.

Types of reflections

Engaging reflective responding is central to MI. Miller and Rollnick (2013) provide a very helpful expansion of the multiple formulations of reflective responses, including the following.

Simple reflection

This involves 'a simple acknowledgement of the client's disagreement, emotion or perception' (Miller & Rollnick 1991, p. 102), which can permit further exploration and diffuse argument. This can be a reflection of content or a reflection of feeling. Accurately understanding and then articulating emotions is very challenging (see discussion in Chapter 7). That is why using reflection is so helpful. With a reflection you can make an informed 'best guess' at what the feeling/emotion might be and at the same time demonstrate an openness to 'getting it wrong' and being corrected by the service user.

Complex reflection

By being more strategic about the reflection you can be selective about what you choose to reflect. It is possible to shift the focus away from sustain talk or even to offer a reframe by reflecting on a different aspect of what was said or by adding a new dimension to what was actually said. A complex reflection adds something to the original statement by the service user. This might be a different angle or a different emphasis.

This reflection shifts from the service user not wanting to quit to the suggestion, delivered through a reflection, that the service user may be concerned it won't work. This avoids argument and gives the service user an opening to consider (reflect on) the different slant offered by the MI worker.

> C: I don't want to quit
> T: You don't think that would work for you.
>
> (Miller & Rollnick 1991, p. 104)

Amplified reflections

'To reflect back what the client has said in an amplified or exaggerated form – to state it in an even more extreme fashion than the client has done.

> C: I just couldn't quit. What would my friends think?
> T: In fact, it might be hard for you to change at all.'
>
> (Miller & Rollnick 1991, p. 104)

Double-sided reflection

'Acknowledge what the client has said, and add to it the other side of the client's ambivalence' (Miller & Rollnick 1991, p. 105).

> SU: I know that Ed worries that I'm drinking too much but that's because he isn't a drinker himself. I've told him that I've cut back anyway but he won't give up.

> SW: You think that Ed has no reason to be worried at all but on the other hand you have been trying to cut back yourself.

Affirmations

The skill of noticing and drawing attention to positives in the service user in order to support or affirm those strengths.

It is also worth taking into account the difference in 'depth' that can be associated with reflections. It may be helpful to use the language of a lower-intensity sense of the emotion than what you are actually picking up. Miller and Rollnick (2013, p. 59) clarify that 'skilful reflection moves past what the person has already said, but doesn't jump too far ahead [it is often useful to understate slightly what the person has offered] if you overstate the intensity of expressed emotion, the person will tend to deny and minimise it'. So, for example, if the service user is expressing rage (not necessarily naming it) in order to de-escalate the situation or to check out just how rage-full the service user is, you might reflect:

Understating:

SW: This is really making you angry.
SU: That doesn't even begin to describe how mad I am about this
OR
SU: Yes, you are right about that I am angry and sometimes I feel like I can't keep my anger in.

Overstating it might look like:

SW: You are in a rage about this.
SU: Well I wouldn't say that, it's a bit annoying maybe

Empathy

Empathy and the skill of demonstrating empathy are important in MI. Again this fits with social work values and skills in working with service users we have already discussed. What is particularly interesting is that MI has been researching the place of empathy and its importance as part of the helping process. Moyers and Miller (2013) asked the question, 'is low empathy toxic?' They found that 'high-empathy counselors appear to have higher success rates regardless of theoretical orientation. Low-empathy and confrontational counseling, in contrast, has been associated with higher drop-out and relapse rates, weaker therapeutic alliance and less client change' (p. 878). This gives further evidence that it is important to support social workers not only in learning the skills required for empathic responding but that they need to have support to practise and develop those skills if we are to build an evidence-based best practice.

Guiding

'MI can be viewed as being a refined form of the naturally occurring communication style of guiding when helping someone to solve a problem (Rollnick et al., 2010). 'Guiding involves a flexible blend of informing, asking and listening, and skilful clinicians do this in practice, as do good parents and teachers. As such, MI resembles a familiar approach to helping, but in a refined manner that uses reflective listening in guiding the person to resolve ambivalence about behaviour change. Learning MI involves retaining clarity of purpose and calmness in the face of often irrational and seemingly contrary motives, and using thoughtful reflective listening statements to facilitate change' (Miller & Rollnick 2013, p. 136).

Motivational social work

'In motivational social work (MSW) the role of the social worker is to listen for the client's ambivalence expressed though change talk and sustain talk and to reflect their desires, abilities, reasons and needs back to them so they can hear and process their own reasons for change. MI can be used in a variety of social work settings where the aim is to create change, and where clients are ambivalence about change' (Teater 2014, p. 125). She clarifies that 'MI was developed to be focused on the client and to employ the principles of empathy, unconditional positive regard and congruence (Rogers 1957), yet to encompass a more guided approach in helping the client resolve ambivalence in the direction of positive change' (Teater 2014, p.125).

Galvani and Forrester (2011) reviewed social work interventions in relation to drug and alcohol problems and they noted that a high proportion of effective interventions involved MI as a basic communication style (although usually as part of a complex social work intervention). This supports the argument that social work and MI are compatible. But it does more than that! MI has been successful in articulating the skills required to work effectively with service users around change. This has been achieved through explicit formulation of communication and counselling skills that engage service users and facilitate working with them toward change backed by robust and compelling research. On the other hand, social work, despite its long tradition, continues to struggle with both expounding a clarity about what it offers, how it works and even if it works. The development of an MI-based social work practice has the potential to assist in addressing these issues for social work.

MI has gained support in social work attributable in part to the profession's search for evidence-based practice. Authors such as Hohman (2012) have presented MI as part of social work practice. It is a way of working with service users that both meets the evidence base requirement and fits with social work values. In their online resources, Islington Social Workers refer to motivational social work (MSW) as 'grounded in principles of Motivational Interviewing (MI), Task Centred Social Work (TCSW), and Motivational Risk Assessment and Management (MRAM). MSW is a relationship-based model of practice that aims to reduce resistance and ambivalence in service users'. They further suggest that in addition to the four processes of MI already discussed, MSW adds 'being purposeful, child-centred and clear about concerns'. Again, consistent with MI, they highlight the importance of self-determination or service user autonomy. 'An important principle of MSW is self-determination – that only the service user can create and sustain meaningful change. The social worker can be a change agent, a support, a coach, and a facilitator – but cannot make the necessary changes'. This more systematic application of MI principles is a welcome move for social work; however, there should be a note of caution. As we described MI at the start, it is informed by humanistic theory with some influence from cognitive and behavioural ideas. What is less evident is the more critical discourse of systemic, radical or social construction theories. These theoretical frameworks are important in social work practice as they provide conceptual tools to step back from seeing only the service users' responsibility for change and direct at least some attention to the social context, referred to in the beginning as the 'social' in social work.

Of course it is important for social workers to be given professional support to enable them to deliver an evidence-informed service. Social work connecting with MI is hopefully a progressive move. It may serve to give further recognition to the fact that building collaborative relationships with families and engaging service users' intrinsic motivation can best be achieved by employing core counselling skills that have long been part of the social worker's repertoire. For reasons discussed throughout this book, including the 'invisibility' of social work skills, the limitations of its research base and the privileging of individually focused interventions to address social problems, social work needs to hold on to its unique contribution to responding to service users' needs. From a 'talking/responding' and 'listening' skill perspective, MI and social work are a good match. However, part of the social work value system also requires that we retain the knowledge, values and skills to engage with social critique so that social workers also acknowledge the social, economic and indeed political structures that may be contributing to problems being experienced by service users and their families. Additional skills such as advocacy, and championing social justice form part of the social work value system and these should not be sacrificed for the sake of adopting an exclusively evidence-based approach to practice. BASW confirm there is an ethical responsibility on social workers to demonstrate 'Respect for human rights and a commitment to promoting social justice'. This reflects the emphasis on social justice, social change and collective responsibility in the global definition of social work (BASW, 2014).

Social work involves understanding and responding to complex situations. Remaining true to the ethical standards of the profession involves possessing the skills to engage service users in a collaborative and complex relationship. They must respond to both individuals in terms of eliciting intrinsic motivation to change, supporting service users' autonomy and building self-efficacy, while also addressing the broader social factors that may impinge of the individual's ability, access to resources or opportunities to resolve their problems effectively.

MI and social work practice should be a great fit. However, despite moves to develop 'motivational social work' as a recognised approach within social work practice (Wilkins & Whittaker 2017) there are concerns that social work education may not be equipping social workers to demonstrate these basic skills. Worryingly, in a UK study, Forrester et al. (2008) found that during simulated interviews, child welfare social workers:

- Spoke the majority of the time
- Asked closed-ended rather than open-ended questions
- Minimised reflections
- Offered few affirmations

Research on adherence to MI is very advanced. This includes established criteria against which adherence to MI standards of practice can be measured. Applying these measures to social work practice as with the Forrester (2008) study has provided some indications that social workers, at least in some settings, are not applying or are applying only in a limited fashion the required core counselling skills such as asking open questions, using reflective responses, conveying empathy or engaging effectively. He further comments that although MI is a good fit with social work in terms of skills and values, 'social workers can often tell parents what to do or try to persuade them to do things that have been identified as important. This can lead to conversations becoming unhelpful and sometimes counterproductive, an indication of an overreliance on using closed questions and advice giving' (Forrester 2016). This is particularly concerning since the HCPC (2017) standards of proficiency for social workers in England specify requirements around effective communication which indicate that the communication skills involved in OARS are part of basic social work competencies.

Unfortunately, research to date does not capture sufficient information about factors that are mitigating against employing these skills. As we know from other social work research (Loughran et al. 2010), factors such as role adequacy, role legitimacy and role support are important variables in influencing social work practice. A sense of role adequacy is achieved when there is confidence in ability, and role legitimacy refers to an acknowledgement that the activities/skills are appropriate to the work. Role support is necessary to provide opportunities to develop skills, but also in ensuring a work environment where the employment of these skills is feasible and valued. Research has shown that training in MI alone is not enough; ongoing coaching is crucial in order to transfer learned MI skills into practice. Findings showed that MI can be implemented successfully within the child welfare system, and that caseworkers believed MI, supported by ongoing coaching, to be a valuable tool in engaging families in the assessment process (Snyder et al. 2012, p. 9). In fact Schwalbe et al. (2014, p. 1292) have shown that 'the level of post-training expert supervision needed to sustain MI skills is somewhat modest – approximately three to four contacts totalling at least 5 hours of contact time over a 6-month period was sufficient for the average study to sustain training effects over a 6-month window'.

Like many other ways of working with service users MI may appear at first to be a pretty intuitive method. It may even appear to be simple to implement. Miller and Rollnick (2009, p. 135) suggest that 'MI is simple but not easy'. Often when discussing the basic ideas of MI people will recognise some of what they already think about or do in conversation with service users. This may be a reflection of the influences of the well-established theories suggested in Figure 10.1. That is a great start, of course, because it indicates that there is already a willingness to accept the core principles required to work in this way: the spirit of MI. However, as with any other method, once you begin to practise applying your skills in the particular way MI employs them then it becomes a bit more challenging. Add to this the fact that one of MI's strengths is its well-evidenced research base and then you realise that there is more to being MI-adherent than agreeing with the underlying spirit and principles of the method.

In addition, the skills required for MI are a good fit with social work counselling skills. MI can be taught early in the social work curriculum once the students have covered basic counselling skills. It is helpful for students to begin to make connections between what seems like simple conversation skills (listening, reflecting, questioning and affirming) and an evidence-based method of employing these skills that is compatible with the social work role and value system. Notwithstanding there is reason for concern about the education and training of social workers, especially from research conducted by Forrester et al. (2008).

Final comment

Writing about people who want to know if you can do MI in five minutes, Miller and Rollnick (2009, p. 136) clarify that 'to us that is like asking can you play the piano for five minutes? Of course you can'. It reminded me of a famous comedy sketch by two UK comedians, Morecombe and Wise, in the 1970s. It involves Morecombe undertaking to play the piano in an orchestra under the baton of André Previn. When Morecombe plays what are basically random notes instead of Grieg's Piano Concerto, Previn as conductor challenges him that he is not playing the right notes. Morecombe replies 'I'm playing all the right notes but not necessarily in the right order' (Braben, 1971). In a very simple way this explains what is happening when applying counselling skills in MI, or any other method for that matter. First you have to know the right notes, i.e. the core counselling skills, but unless you also know the theory and method which inform when and how you need to apply the skills (musical score) you will probably not deliver them in the right order, that is, an order that is likely to be effective. Also, it takes practise to build up your level of skill and your ability to keep a satisfactory level of fidelity to the method. Unlike a musician our audience generally cannot decide to leave because they don't think we are 'playing' well so that puts the onus on the professional to ensure that they are indeed accountable for their performance.

Exercise 21 Practising open questions and reflections to engage the service user and elicit change talk

(Informed by Miller and Rollnick 2013 and Motivational Interviewing Network of Trainers (MINT 2014) Motivational Interviewing Training New Trainers Manual, pp. 165–166. (With thanks to Mike Clarke.) https://motivationalinterviewing.org/sites/default/files/tnt_manual_2014_d10_20150205.pdf

To do this exercise you need to work in a group so that there is an audience and you can generate feedback. You need one person to play a service user and at least one person role-playing the social worker. This exercise can also work with a number of people taking turns or working as a team to interact with the 'service user'.

Preparation: Place five seats in a row (1 to 5) as in Figure 10.3, with one or more chairs opposite. Have the social worker sit opposite the row of seats.

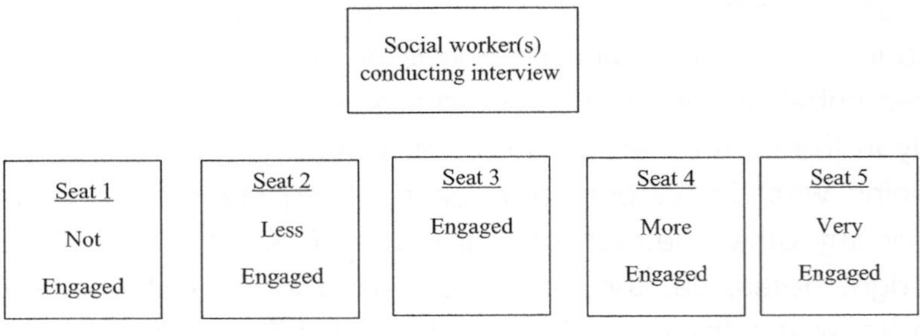

Figure 10.3 Engaging service users

Purpose: The service user either stays in the same seat to indicate that they have not become and more or any less engaged, or moves to a lower numbered seat (e.g. 2 or 1) – this indicates that the conversation has resulted in them feeling less engaged. Alternatively, they can move to a higher numbered seat (e.g. 4 or 5) to indicate they are becoming more engaged. The movement from seat to seat, without comment, but in line with their sense of engagement provides a visual cue to the social worker about the impact they are having on the service user's level of engagement.

To start the exercise, the service user role player can sit in the middle seat 3 (this gives the social worker a bit of a head start; realistically, the service user may start in seat 1).

It is useful after the exercise to consider how realistic it would be for the service user to take up that middle seat. This allows for discussion on what the service user might be feeling in meeting you (the social worker). Would they be open to the relationship, sceptical, concerned, even intimidated? It might depend on their previous experiences with your other social workers, the issues to be discussed and the level of anxiety or fear they have regarding the involvement of social work in their lives.

Pick any topic you like for the role play, but it should be something about a need to change that the person is undecided about. Decide on what social work setting you are in and why you are seeing this service user. You can do this with a number of people sharing the social work role, but you need one person to be the service user.

If you want to start with a non-social work option you can ask for a volunteer who will just talk about their own experience. Make sure if you are doing this that the topic they pick is appropriate and does not bring up more difficult issues that cannot be supported or managed in the role play. I sometimes take the service user role and get the student to try to work with me about my exercise habits. Or you can use the following example.

Start with the role player (Ali) sitting in seat 3. It is a healthcare setting. The issue being discussed is Ali has been identified as needing help changing behaviour around exercise, as she has developed some serious health problems. You are going to use MI based on the understanding that working with Ali to enhance motivation to engage in behaviour change will be helpful. However, Ali is clearly not totally convinced that change is needed and is somewhat annoyed that so much attention is being given to this issue. Start by practising OARS.

SW: You ask some open questions, e.g. tell me about what led you to seeing me today *or* I know that Dr Jones asked you to come and see me today; it would be helpful if you filled me in on what has been going on.

Ali: in the role you just answer the question however you think fits.

If Ali feels the initial question makes him/her more engaged then s/he moves to seat 4, if less engaged moved to seat 2; if it has had no particular impact just stay in seat 3. As the conversation moves on Ali just responds to the social worker as the role player as appropriate and silently moves seats to indicate more or less engagement.

There are a number of points that you can consider as the exercise goes on. Suppose Ali is in seat 3 and then moves to seat 4. When you ask a more difficult question or provide a complex reflection, e.g. 'Ali as we have been talking I can hear that you given this a lot of thought. You seem to be caught between finding it difficult to stick with an exercise plan and yet knowing that you need to deal with this soon, where does that leave you?', Ali then moves to seat 2. What might that indicate? It should not always be seen as a failing in engagement; it may indicate good timing of a complex reflection. By raising this point only when Ali is at least in seat 3 (engaged) it may be a good time to make a more strategic move towards checking out commitment to change. You have Ali in a more engaged position (seat 3) before handling a complex or challenging point highlighting Ali's ambivalence and then when Ali moves to seat 2 you still can retrieve the situation because Ali is still engaged to some point. The ability to respond to shifts away to less engaged is critical for the social worker. This fits with the focus on engagement and helps to judge when the appropriate opportunity arises to elicit change talk. After conducting the role play in this way for up to 5 minutes you can then stop the role play. Ali and the social worker(s) reflect on what worked and what was less helpful. Give Ali the chance to talk you through why s/he did or didn't move, what s/he felt engaged by and what s/he reacted against against. It is a wonderful chance to get direct feedback on using open questions and reflective responding as your skills of engagement. Be sure to de-role after the exercise.

11 Applying counselling social work skills in group work

- Consider social communication skills in the context of groups.
- Group work will be contextualised as one of the three traditional social work methods of intervention: one to one (case work), group work and community work.
- Look at group work and working in groups and consider the tasks or content of the group and group process.
- Explore the application of the core social work counselling skills to group work: Thinking, listening and talking/responding.

Introduction

In this chapter, we will look at social work counselling skills as they are used in group work. We will first look at our level of social skills in communication in group settings. Perhaps one of the most interesting things about counselling skills, as used in group work, is that practitioners often find it difficult to explain the skills that they are using to facilitate groups. When training people in group work, I find myself having to remind them that they should draw on the same communication/counselling skills that they would use in other settings but just in a different way and with a different purpose in mind. We will look at this later in the chapter.

Social communication in a group context

So, let's look at our social communication skills associated with being in groups. For me, there is a sort of paradox about counselling skills in group work. The paradox is that unlike solution-focused counselling or motivational interviewing, communicating in groups is something with which we are all very familiar. By this, I don't mean that you are familiar with the skills required to facilitate group work in a professional context, but rather that humans are by their nature social creatures. They are involved in groups and need to be involved in groups in various ways. So in some ways, being involved in groups is very familiar. On the other hand, as we look at how counselling skills are applied in working in the professional group work context, it becomes clear that the level of skills and confidence required is probably even more complex and at a more advanced level than some of the other counselling skills approaches. A good place to start is usually to think about your own experience of being involved in groups.

Exercise 22 First step: your groups

Make a list of the various groups you are involved with.

As you make this list, notice whether the groups are ones that you are part of without making a choice (naturally formed) or ones that you have chosen to be involved with (formed). Typically people are members of naturally formed groups such as families and members of groups that they have been formed for a particular purpose. For example, they may be a member of a group of students while they are studying, later a group of work colleagues. They may be part of a team; a sports team or charity group or other hobby or interest group. The range of groups you belong to can be quite extensive. Once you make that list of all the different kinds of groups that you are involved with and distinguish between formed and naturally formed groups, the next thing to observe is to think about your part in these groups.

Exercise 23 Second step: role and commitment

Rank-order the groups in terms of '1' being most important to you and so on. Select a couple of those groups and identify your role or the part you play in the group. One of the most interesting things to think about is whether you act the same in each of the groups.

Just take a look at a few examples of your behaviour. Pick out one of the groups that you are very committed to. Look at what that means in terms of your behaviour, your engagement in the group, how you behave towards that group, the sort of communication style that you employ when you are involved in that group. Compare this now to a group that may be further down your list and see, first of all, the difference it makes for you, whether you are very committed to the group and to the activities of that group, or whether it is something that perhaps you are less committed to or that you have lost interest in. There may be groups you were more involved in sometime back or maybe even a group that you were involved in only because you had to be involved. As you do this kind of comparison you will begin to notice that although you have a certain level of social communication skills, you may not employ them all in the same way in different groups. Part of this concerns the fact that your level of commitment to the activities of the group may to some extent dictate how you communicate and behave within that group.

Exercise 24 Third step: communication in groups

Try to capture a sense of your communication skills in groups.

Begin to pay more attention to how you talk and communicate in one of your groups. Look at how conversations happen in that group, what you/others tend to contribute to the conversation. You might notice that in some social groups that you are involved with the conversation flows very readily, that people self-disclose and offer information in a discussion in a very easy way. There may be very little necessity for anyone to ask questions or draw people into the conversation. Also look at whether the group you are considering is one that you see as providing a lot of support, emotional or otherwise; is it an easy and a safe place to express yourself? How does that work? What impact does that have on you and your involvement with the group? Compare this to a group you are less committed to or to a group that you don't want to be part of. This can happen in a work situation where you have been put on a project team that you don't want to be on. Is it different if you have been asked to do certain tasks that other members are reluctant to take on?

What's interesting is that as you make observations and reflect on your own experience of being a group member, you will notice that in contrast with other applications of counselling skills you have a lot of experience managing yourself in group settings. In some ways, being in groups can feel so familiar that you forget how much skill is required to facilitate a group in a social work context. In our introductory chapter, we looked at the risk that social work counselling skills go unacknowledged as they seem to be just part of social interaction. Likewise, group work requires a level of professional competence to enable you to apply social work counselling skills in the complex and often challenging context of group dynamics.

Group work as a social work method

Social work in the past was traditionally considered to incorporate three core components, often classified as case work, group work and community work. Ward (2002) noted that this classification has all but disappeared. The focus has become more and more on individual and family work, which is often focused on legal and assessment processes. Ward (2002, p. 151) says that 'social workers' confidence in themselves has been profoundly shaken. It is not surprising that they have come to feel safer operating within instrumental but more clear and defensible frameworks, reflected in buzzwords such as competencies, risk assessment and case management'. This discussion about side-lining group work as a social work activity is mirrored in Preston-Shoot's work (2007). He notes that 'group work continues to occupy a variable position within social work, sometimes central, sometimes peripheral and increasingly invisible' (2007, p. 5). What both Ward (2002) and Preston-Shoot (2007) identify is that group work as a way of utilising and employing social work counselling skills is highly compatible with our social work value base. Group work speaks to values around enhancing and supporting equality and addressing issues of social injustice and social exclusion. We will return to these very important aspects of group work later in the chapter. Figure 11.1 provides a guide to some of the main theories, methods and skills for group work.

Working in groups or group work

Ward (2002, p. 152) notes that 'there is a good deal of evidence of a continuing interest in groups'. For now, one of the things that we need to consider is looking at the difference between working in groups and group work. It may be easy to use the terms group work and working in groups interchangeably and in many ways that is understandable. However, when it comes to looking at the specific skills involved in group work, it is very clear that there is a difference in orientation and in the skills employed for working in groups as distinct from group work. So just for clarification purposes, we will defer to Ward (2002) in terms of making the distinction between these two aspects of groups. Indeed, he notes that there is a considerable amount of work taking place *in* groups. However, it is not recognisable as group work. It does not pay substantial attention either to the knowledge base of group dynamics or to the practice

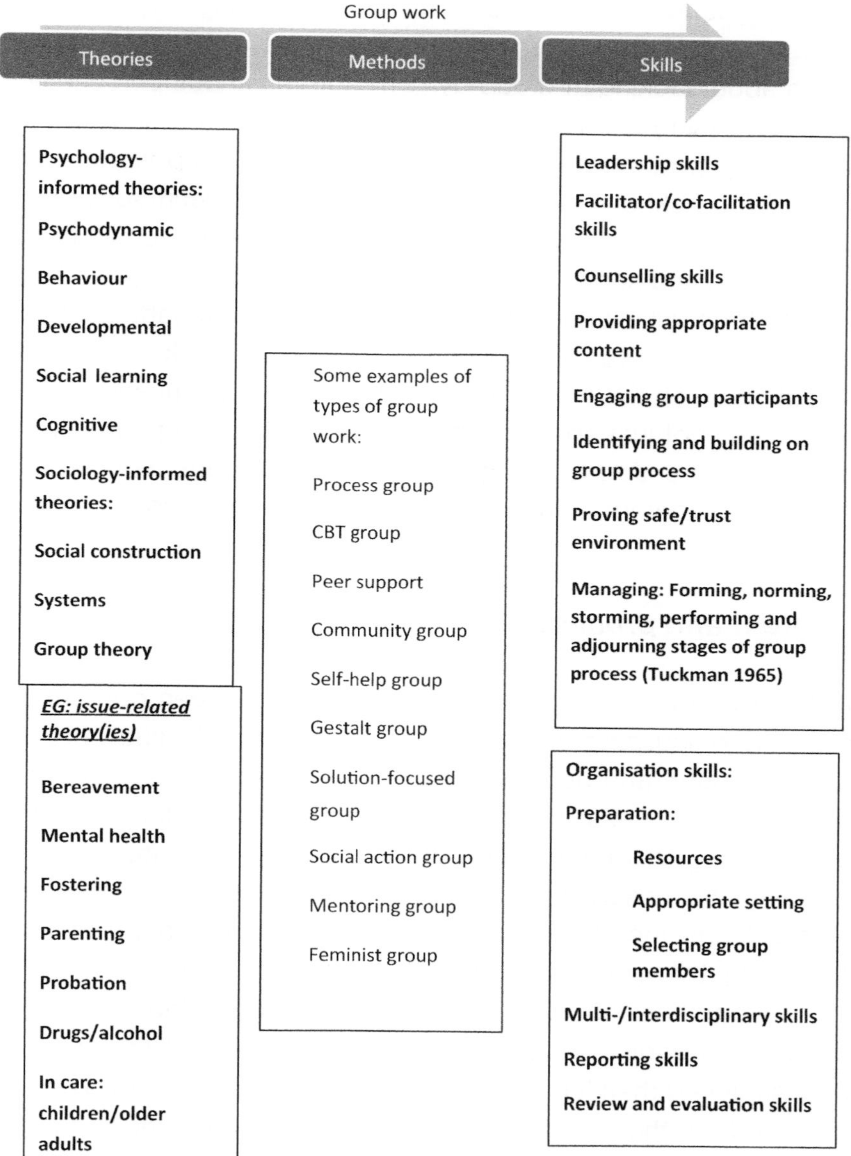

Figure 11.1 Brief overview of group work

base of group work methods and skills. Nor does it incorporate the democratic and collective values that are, as we will see, at the core of group work. It may be somewhat confusing, as not all of those who have written extensively about group work make this distinction. For example, in his work on groups, Tyson (1998) refers to working in groups, but the content of his work is very much about looking at group dynamics from various perspectives and addressing a very important issue of capturing and working with group processes that is associated with group work. Tyson (1998) also acknowledges the compatibility between social work values and group work, both of which espouse to address issues of inclusion and social injustice while at the same time providing a service for service users within a range of different settings. In the current context, we will be talking about group work which does, in fact, draw on the competencies of social work counselling skills to address not just specific issues with specific groups but which also pays attention to the group itself. This means working with both group content or tasks as well as attending to group process.

Content and process

It is important to recognise the difference between content the group is discussing and process which supports such discussion. Johnson and Johnson (1991, p. 48) explain the difference as: 'group process involves such things as leadership, decision making, communication and controversy. Content is what is being discussed; process is how the group is functioning'. Content can include inputs or materials designed to facilitate achieving the goals and aims of the group. Vernelle's (1994, p. 47) emphasises that the group needs to find a balance between attending to task/content and process. If this balance isn't achieved then it is unlikely that the goals of the group can be achieved, as the purpose of employing a group work method is in fact to harness group process to address group goals. Social work skills are used to engage and develop the group itself as part of helping the change process. When we look in particular at the core skill of thinking, you will see how this works more clearly. In fact, the same basic formula of talking, listening and thinking are applied to group work. This is true whether you are working with individuals, working in groups, or engaged in group work. The core skills we have looked at in the first part of this text all have a place in delivering support and help in any group work setting. What might be different would be the purpose of the group, the theoretical and therapeutic approach that informs the type of group, knowledge of group process and dynamics. It also requires knowledge about the context within which the group is happening. However, most importantly, 'it requires that the social worker apply their skills so that they can both participate in group content while at the same time observing the group process' (Johnson & Johnson 1991, p. 48). The skill of the social worker is to attend to process issues as and when they assist or detract from the success of the group.

As I mentioned earlier, although these counselling skills are utilised in facilitating groups, it will become clear that the level at which these skills are employed requires a high level of both confidence and competence on the part of the social worker. While your personal experience of being a member of a group may shape some of your views about groups and how important they are, it may even shape your ideas about whether groups are good things to be involved in. You will probably notice that some of the characteristics and communication styles that you employ in those groups you are very committed to will also be of use in facilitating groups. However, as we consider the three core components of groups as talking, listening and thinking, you will begin to see a picture of the challenges involved in group work. It is, in my view, a challenge worth meeting. If social work is to hold on to its place in providing group work for its service users it is a challenge that social workers must meet and that agencies and providers of social work services need to support and encourage.

Counselling skills and group work

When beginning to develop group work skills people often make the mistake of thinking they are a completely different set of skills to those employed in counselling. In fact, the same basic formula of talking, listening and thinking can be applied to working in groups. This is true whether you are working with individuals but in a group setting (working in groups) or whether you are facilitating a therapeutic group, facilitating group work. In fact, you will see that the skills we have looked at in Part I all have a place in delivering support and help in any group work setting. What might be different would be the purpose of the group, the theoretical and therapeutic approach that informs the type of group and of course the context within which the group is being held.

Applying the core skills of talking, listening and thinking in group work practice

In this book we have categorised social work counselling skills in three main categories: talking, listening and thinking. In each of these categories a number of subcategories or specific application of skills has also been discussed. While the main text has reviewed these in the order of talking, listening and thinking, hopefully the discussion has made it clear that the skill of thinking is a critical and central element to developing professional proficiency in counselling skills. Both to emphasise this and to reflect the reality of applying social work counselling skills to group work practice, this chapter presents the skills in the order of thinking, listening and talking.

The skill of thinking

While thinking and planning should be core aspects of all social work interventions, this is particularly clear when looking at group work. Most textbooks dealing with group work emphasise the importance of preparation in setting up and managing groups, for example, Doel (2006). Preston-Shoot (2007) and Shulman (2009). This emphasis on the preparatory stage of group work is an example of good practice. This is supported by recognition that in order for a group work intervention to work, group facilitators need to be clear and in agreement on how the group will operate, what the purpose of the group is, and have the support of their organisation/agency to facilitate running the group.

Earlier there was some discussion about different ways of considering the skill of thinking. We looked at thinking, processing and reflecting as important elements of the skill of thinking. These different terms are helpful in distinguishing the various stages of the application of thinking in group work practice. For simplification, Figure 11.2 shows thinking as three different stages; in practice, these inform each other. Even the stage of planning can be revisited during the group sessions if facilitators observe that the plan isn't working.

Start with the preparation and planning stages of group work and the need to think through a number of issues before even starting group. Once the plan is in place and there is an agreed agenda and focus for the group intervention, get started. In practice, you hear social workers who are running groups comment that while planning is critical, you also need to have an element of flexibility as there are times when the plan doesn't quite work out and you need to be able to think through and manage what actually unfolds in the group. For the purposes of distinguishing this aspect of thinking skills, we will refer to them here as processing skills. This means

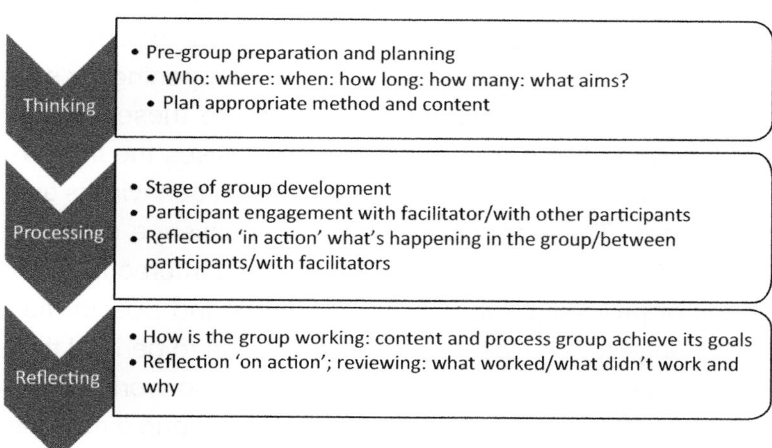

Figure 11.2 The skill of thinking in group work

that, with the plan – which encompasses a theoretical framework, appropriate methodology, group theory and knowledge about the particular issue/issues to be addressed in the group – there is also the need to take cognisance of the response of the individual participants within the group. Tracking group dynamic as the group moves through various developmental stages helps to identify this important aspect of the skill of thinking.

Distinguishing the thinking skills involved in planning and managing group process from those required to learn and build on the experience of group work intervention provides a helpful reminder that reflection in and on action form another part of thinking skills. This aspect of thinking is not the preserve of the post group review, but rather it is the application of reflecting on each group session as it happens and utilising new understandings or information to amend and adapt the group work intervention. Hence, these three aspects of applying our thinking skill in social work group work can provide a template for building and developing expertise in the planning and delivery of group work interventions.

Stage one: thinking through preparation and planning

As we mentioned before, thinking involves really understanding and being able to apply the filters of multiple theoretical explanations for human behaviour and understanding what's happening for service users in any particular context. In addition to these general theories of human behaviour, group work emphasises the importance of having a theoretical understanding of social behaviours and social interactions. These theories underlie the essence of group work, which is to harness and utilise such social interactions for the purposes of providing support, new insights and possibilities to facilitate change for service users. So in addition to general theories, the social worker has to take account of group work theory. Group work theory typically highlights the nature of group dynamics (Doel 2006; Preston-Shoot 2007), and the developmental stages of group process which can be expected in particular as this applies to groups set up for the purposes of helping/therapeutic goals.

Group work theory also highlights the role of the group facilitator in terms of understanding issues such as leadership styles and co-facilitating in groups. It is also important, as it is with more individually focused interventions, to consider not just the interaction with service users as individuals and then as a group but also the social worker's own experiences and responses to being part of the group process.

In addition to general human behaviour and social interaction theory there is also a need to have an in-depth appreciation and knowledge of the particular issues relevant to the service users for whom the group intervention is designed. For example, if a group is set up for parents whose children are in care, then it will be important to have knowledge and understanding of what that experience is like for parents and also to have a clear picture of what is likely to be helpful in working with this group of service users. Clarity about realistic outcomes and the place of ongoing social work intervention in their lives is critical.

In the same way, if the group is set up to support people who are caring for a family member, to work with service users experiencing domestic violence or children who have experienced bereavement, it is important that the plan and implementation of the group employs best practice in relation to the needs of that specific issue.

Apart from all of these theoretical aspects of group work there are in addition issues concerning the context and setting within which the group work is to be established. This means that the social worker as a group worker has to think about their organisational responsibilities, their professional values and ethics in establishing and running a group. This may involve both legal and health-related aspects associated with particular service user's issues. However, it also involves pragmatic issues such as the availability of resources to run groups, to provide a suitable venue and to have support and follow-up available if and when required. The counselling skill of thinking in relation to groups is complex and needs to be addressed comprehensively.

Stage two: processing

When all decisions about planning the group have been finalised and the first group meeting happens, then the distinction between group content (which includes the theoretical framework, method to be employed, skill base of the social worker, the materials to be used, and relevant information about the particular service user group involved) and group process (which includes the stages of group development and group dynamics, including interaction between group members themselves, interaction between facilitators and group members and interaction between facilitators themselves) begins to take on a life of its own influenced by but also in some ways independent of the plan that has put in place. At this stage the skill of thinking involves being able to observe and understand the interaction between the group plan and group performance. In other words, while keeping track of the goals, expectations and methods being employed, the group worker must also now take into account how the service users in the group are reacting to and experiencing group interaction. This information comes through observation, discussion and feedback within the group. This new level of information along with pre-group knowledge and information provides a really good example of what is meant by the aspect of processing that is part of the skill of thinking. This stage may also be viewed as reflection 'in action'. Because of the complex layers of interaction referred to as group process, it is advisable to work with a co-facilitator. One facilitator can take the lead allowing the other to take time to reflect and observe group interaction. It also allows time to consider how the group is reacting when one facilitator has more of an observer role. This provides a unique opportunity to address group interaction as it unfolds and to harness the group's self-help resources.

Taking account of the stage of group development is also important. Groups take time to reach a point where members feel safe to talk about more personal and troubling issues. While such discussion may be desirable it is important for facilitators to recognise what type of disclosure is appropriate for the stage of group. Theories of group development provide some guidance about what to expect of group members over time in terms of group cohesion, commitment to group goals, trust among members, confidence in the facilitators, willingness to self-disclose and willingness to give honest feedback to each other. The notion of the stages of development is helpful in establishing and running groups as it provide a baseline from which to measure group interactions. One of the best-known version of this is Tuckman (1965), who proposed that groups go through a number of stages which he called forming, storming, norming, performing, mourning or adjourning. This tracks groups from the early and more guarded interactions to building trust through testing out the group and the facilitator and then establishing norms or acceptable behaviours so that the group can then work together to achieve agreed goals. Towards the end, group members will usually begin to think about endings and what that means in preparing to finish the group.

Stage three: reflection on action

The final part of thinking as a skill in group work that we will look at is that of learning from practise. Having done all the appropriate preparation and planning and taken on board the new information that emerges through the group process, the final aspect of applying thinking is reflecting on actions and assessing whether the plan fitted with the needs of the service users and whether the plan worked as it was designed. If the plan or specific aspects of the plan did not meet the needs of service users or presented particular problems as the group progressed, then these must be identified and attempts made to understand what happened to contribute to the difficulties.

Opportunities and challenges of co-facilitation

It is worth spending time on co-facilitation at all three stages of thinking. In the preparation stage it is important that co-facilitators have an agreed or at least compatible view of theoretical influences, an agreed agenda, a shared sense of responsibilities and that they have negotiated a style of working together that will enhance group tasks and support a positive development of group process. As you can imagine, if the facilitators do not work well together it won't take the group long to figure that out. If there is unresolved tension between facilitators it will undermine the development of trust and openness in the group. This is inevitable because it will become obvious when the leaders are not modelling openness and trust with each other.

Once the co-facilitators have paid attention to their working relationship in group they can successfully bring diverse perspectives and experiences, even different disciplinary backgrounds, to enrich the group experience.

Reflection 'in action' is probably easier in group work than in any other method of social work intervention, but only where you have a good working relationship with your co-facilitator. Once you pay attention to working together it becomes possible to read each other in group and take the lead from each other with regard to speaking out or sitting back and observing. Good co-facilitation brings with it a sense of having a safety net, where you can have confidence that between you the important points regarding content and process will be picked up and managed.

When working as co-facilitators the process of reflecting on action can also be enhanced through routinely reflecting on each group session in an open and supportive way. This reflection can also be further enhanced by support of supervision from a more experienced or perhaps objective group facilitator. One important aspect of this reflection on action is that such a reflection should result in adapting and modifying group work practice by learning from the service users and from the experience of running each group session.

In all stages of thinking it is particularly helpful if the group intervention is designed to seek ongoing feedback from the service users. Their input and reflections on how the group is working or not for them allows the social worker to respond to previously unidentified needs and issues as appropriate.

The skill of listening

Considering reflection in and on action provides a related and important link to developing and utilising the skill of listening in the group setting. Reflection implies means listening to yourself as well as to the service user and your colleagues, but let's focus primarily on the skill of listening to service users in a group context. As mentioned earlier, we are looking predominantly at group work settings rather than working with people in groups. This distinction is particularly relevant when thinking about the skill of listening. This is because if the purpose of the group is to deliver information and content then while listening to participants in the group is important it is not the primary purpose of the group. In group work, listening to group members is one of the most important aspects of practice.

Group work by its definition involves getting together a number of service users, typically somewhere between six and ten participants. While these participants usually share some common concerns, it is not necessary, and probably not even possible, for the group to be homogeneous. Some shared similarities, whether they be the particular experience of concern, age, stage of lifecycle, gender or some other variables that participants in group share, are usually a necessary component of providing an environment in which participants can feel a sense of group cohesion developing. Heterogeneous groups, while there may be more variation in terms of membership characteristics, usually share at least some common experience or aspect of the experience for which the group has been established.

So what does this mean for the skill of listening? It means that you have typically eight participants in a group with ideally two facilitators. They may share some commonality, but they also have very different stories. Usually group work is time-limited both in terms of the number of sessions and the length of each session. This means that you have between eight and twelve people who have maybe an hour or an hour and a half to build relationships, develop group cohesion, and actually get some benefit from the group. If you take out the two facilitators then you have six to ten people trying to tell their story and doing their best to listen to other people as well. This is very challenging for group participants, particularly in the early stages when often their main desire is to tell their own story and see if this is going to be a safe place for them to find support and help. If the group is working and group facilitators have been able to provide this environment, then as you can imagine there's a lot of talking going on. If you are new to group work, the amount of information and discussion may seem overwhelming. When listening to one person on a one-to-one basis you not only track what they are saying, but also focus on the non-verbals with little distraction. In a group setting, you are not only trying to listen to each group member as they speak, you are also trying to listen to what group members are saying to each other, both verbally and non-verbally.

In addition, you are trying to observe what's going on in the group while at the same time paying active attention to the individual in the group who is speaking at any one time. It really is a test of your listening skills and it requires time and experience to develop your listening skills to this level of competence. Perhaps that is why there is a concern about group work within social work practice. For social workers to develop both the level of competence and confidence for group work they need to have opportunity and support from colleagues with more experience and from organisations and employers. Enhancing and developing these listening skills will of course be beneficial not only in group work settings, but in all interactions with service users, whether that be one-to-one, in a family setting or even in a community setting. The ability to listen to the verbal and non-verbal communication of more than one person at a time is invaluable. Optimising your active listening and non-verbal communication skills becomes critical in group work, especially in light of some of the challenges we will consider in terms of talking in groups. It is important to remember to use observation skills, to notice who is talking and who is not talking, who is listening and who is distracted, who does not appear to be engaged and who is overinvolved.

You need also to track communication patterns between participants: do some members take over, speak for others, do some seem marginalised or even excluded by one or more members? Are some members aligning themselves with you or against you? Watch out for stages of development: challenges to leaders, challenges for leadership between participants, a member who wants to be seen as expert. Also notice how members are managing themselves in group, especially when they feel challenged by other members: a member who demonstrates a lot of emotion (for example crying) throughout the group. When asked for feedback how do members manage this, do they follow the lead of one member, do they take risks, are they supportive or critical, are members adhering to group rules and norms, are they respectful to each other, do they listen or interrupt? Whatever you are noticing you need to process (think about/reflect 'in action') and then you need to decide on a response. The response can be talking, of course, which we will deal with next, but you can also use non-verbal communication such as eye contact, nod your head, use a hand gesture to indicate inclusion or wait or to make space for the person to speak. Employing a range of response options is important as it helps with managing the limited and valuable resource of talk-time in the group.

The skill of talking/responding

As you might imagine there is a direct link between practising the skill of thinking, listening and the skill of talking, and this is nowhere more evident than in group work practice. While you as a social worker/group worker are talking then group participants are not talking and they may or may not be listening, depending on their level of engagement with the group at any one time. While we have discussed some of the limitations of emphasising the counselling skill of talking, you can see that in group work employing the skill of talking must be done in a very economical and purposeful way if it is not to get in the way of providing time and space for the service users to talk. The place of talking on the part of the group facilitator depends on the method being employed in the group and the stage of group development. Tuckman's (1965) theoretical understanding of group development alongside the particular orientation of the group worker indicates the level of content, talking that is appropriate for the group leader at different stages in the group. For example, in the early stages of the group while the group is testing out how trustworthy the group facilitators are, it may be important for the facilitators to speak more and provide evidence of their competence and commitment to the group. It may also be helpful for the group facilitators to model appropriate levels of disclosure and discussion, especially at the early stages of group. However, if the purpose of the group is to facilitate group members finding their own voice in supporting and giving feedback to one another, then it will be important to fully utilise your counselling skills to find the right balance between talking and providing space for service users to talk. It is important to recognise that talking is not the most important aspect of group facilitation; the skills of listening and thinking are critical. As always, it is the quality of the listening and thinking skills that will inform the effective use of talking skills. It is also important to remember that in group work the talking skills you use are the core counselling skills already discussed in earlier chapters: open questions, closed questions, summaries, linking summaries, affirmations and reflections both complex and simple.

Finding your voice in group work

While this chapter has emphasised the importance of the skill of thinking, both in terms of planning and delivery of a group work service, it is useful to look at the experience of finding your voice as a group facilitator when you first start to develop your counselling social work skills in this context. With all that's going on in the group and with all the theoretical knowledge you are trying to keep in mind, group work can seem a bit overwhelming at first. However, once you get into it the satisfaction of seeing participants grow and work together to help one another makes it very rewarding.

Personal reflection

When I started working in a group work setting it was very challenging. I was lucky enough to work with a very experienced colleague who in fact came from a different professional background and had a very different set of theoretical frameworks influencing their ideas. My colleague was a psychologist who described themselves as a behavioural psychologist. I, on the other hand, as a social worker had been trained at that time in a theoretical framework influenced by systemic thinking. I was more familiar with getting to know service users in the context of their family life, and indeed having the opportunity to visit them in their home and see for myself more about their lifestyle and experiences. This combination of systemic thinker and a behaviourist should ideally have offered a much broader and creative perspective within which to provide a group work experience for the service users. However, the difficulty was that my colleague was a very experienced group worker while I had very limited experience of facilitating groups. I remember thinking that although I saw the world through a very different lens that my colleague's lens was more appropriate or perhaps it was delivered with more conviction than I at that time could command. It took quite some time to realise that combining and comparing these different perspectives only added to what we could offer as facilitators in the group.

However, I'm jumping ahead. Before this could happen I had to find my voice. In other words, I had to move from being able to think and process information I was gathering from the group discussion to formulating an output that I felt confident would be of some value. In other words, I had to say something! I was sitting back allowing my colleague to do all the talking and directing and facilitating while I contemplated on what an amazing job my colleague was doing and wondering if I would ever have the confidence to take part of that facilitation process. So even though I had a very good knowledge of group theory, stages of group development, theories of human behaviour, theories about change, and a lot of experience in terms of counselling social work, somehow finding my voice in the group was a challenge. I realised later that the challenge was in the skill of processing what is going on in the group.

If you think listening is a demanding and challenging skill to develop, to me it is nothing compared to what you have to develop in order to keep up with what's going on in a group. Think about it. While you might be familiar with listening to one or perhaps even two or three people in the context of an individual meeting with the service user or some members of the family, in a group context, you're probably listening to somewhere in the region of six to possibly ten people. You are listening to each of their stories and you are observing (listening for) the information that you can gather from their interactions with each other. You are also trying to track their interactions with you and with your co-facilitator. There's a lot going on. If for whatever reason you have not been given the opportunity to become more confident in your counselling social work skills, then it's possible that group work and applying those skills in the group work setting will be even more challenging. In terms of thinking, there is a lot going on as well. So finding my voice was less about not understanding the theory of group work and the skill of thinking and processing. It was more about finding a voice that allowed me to deliver an output that I had confidence in. I keep this experience in mind when teaching group work because for me, social workers have the skills required to be group workers. The issue is more to do with their confidence to engage those same counselling social work skills in a group work context.

To finish my story, once I found my voice, I realised that while I might not have been as quick on the uptake as my colleague, what I had to offer was usually perceived as helpful by my colleague and it seemed to be experienced as helpful to most of the group members. I realised that what I needed was to develop the skill of co-facilitating. I needed to learn to work with somebody so that we could work together with service users. Perhaps one of the most useful things I learned from this experience was that not only could I rely on my colleague to provide support and direction for me in my early experiences of developing my group work skills, but in fact I could also rely on the service users who participated in those groups. While at the beginning stages of any group work experience the service users may have different levels of commitment to participating in the group, inevitably at least a number of the participants will become engaged and committed to the successful outcome of the group. After all, the whole purpose of the group is to try and assist service users to find their voice. So it makes sense that those service users were helpful to me in finding my voice. This is a lesson that I have never forgotten.

Final comments

Group work has been established as part of social work. It draws on the same core counselling social work skills that provide the foundation of social workers' professionally competent communication skills. Group work is informed by additional theoretical ideas about group activity, group process and how groups can help themselves. However, the skill of harnessing your thinking, listening and talking to formulate meaningful, purposeful responses to service users' needs is fundamentally the same. Taking on board all the action that is happening in groups can be challenging. It requires the ability to think through or process a range of sources of information from theoretical knowledge base to multiple service users' disclosures, from observation of group interaction to tuning in to your own reactions. You are doing all this while establishing a safe place for strangers to share life experiences, be challenged, take power and feel supported. You need to have confidence that your skill in applying the core counselling skills will provide you with the tools to operationalise ideas and therapeutic interventions in a group work setting. You will need time to reflect and learn from your experiences, your co-facilitators, your supervisors and most importantly from the service users who make the group work.

Case example: Bereavement group in a medical social work setting

Here is a brief case example which will highlight how formulating even one response can offer a myriad of possibilities/ challenges.

Setting: Hospital social work department

Context: Voluntary participant in group for those bereaved in the previous 12–18 months

Eligibility: Death of friend/family member in this hospital, experiencing either complicated or uncomplicated grief, over 18 years of age, not currently engaged with treatment in mental health services. Group work is informed by the following:

- Theoretical orientation of group: adopting a perspective informed by systems theory, social construction and cognitive behavioural theories
- Theoretical perspective on grief, bereavement and loss: Kübler-Ross and Kessler (2005) and Stroebe and Schut (1999). Also cognisant of crisis theory (Loughran 2010)
- Group work theories including Yalom and Leszcz (2005) and Tuckman (1965)
- Standards and guidelines for practice in bereavement and in medial hospital setting with this group of service users. Legal and professional regulations
- Social work values and ethical standard for practice

In addition, in preparation for running the group the social workers/ facilitators should:

- Review any specific needs of the identified group participants
- Through supervision, reflect on their own experience, professional and personal, as they impact their participant in the group
- Consult with their co-facilitator about the roles and process of group facilitation and how they will work together
- Familiarise themselves with any materials or manualised programme information to be employed

Thinking in action will involve processing the interactions within the group in the context of all the about theoretical and methodical factors. Clearly the counselling skill of listening is essential to successfully gather and observe this live interaction in the group and to monitor both participants' contributions and the social workers' reactions and decision-making. Ultimately all these will provide a rationale and direction to what is said by the social worker in the group.

The group

You have decided to have six participants in the group, because the participation is by invitation and anyone eligible can be included, often resulting in a diverse group membership. The purpose of the group is to provide a safe place for people to talk about their experiences of bereavement, to encourage the normal grieving process and to facilitate the development of peer support.

Group participants

Anne's 26-year-old son died by suicide 15 months ago
John's 17-year-old son died by suicide a year ago
Ola's mother died 18 months ago aged 85; she had Alzheimer's for 10 years
Cathy's estranged husband died following a road traffic accident 12 months ago
Omar's husband of 1 year died after a brief illness 14 months ago
Erik's partner died 16 months ago following 3 years fighting cancer

Considerations

- age, gender
- diversity in religious, cultural and/or ethnic perspectives on death
- length of time since bereavement
- cause and circumstances of death
- relationship to the person who died; not just the formal label of the relationship but the quality of the relationship as perceived the bereaved
- stage of grief/how person is coping or not with the loss
- stage in group process

An example of employing counselling skill of responding/talking to make intervention in the group

The group are now in their second of four weeks of meeting as a group. As it's week two of four you might expect the group to have already moved into the storming and norming phases. Some level of trust has already been established as there has been a lot of disclosure among the group members about their sadness and also some expressions of anger. So far the group have been accepting and supportive of each other while at the same time each seem to need time to talk about their own loss and so it was difficult for them to give time to each other and to listen. (SW thinking: they are beginning to trust and develop some sense of group togetherness/cohesion but struggling to be available to each other emotionally/altruism.)

Midway through the second session there is an exchange between Cathy and Omar.

> Cathy: I feel so angry about Luke dying. I really hoped we would sort out things and that we could have a good life together. I just don't get how Omar can't appreciate that Phil loved him and wouldn't have abandoned him if he had a choice. Omar was lucky.

To formulate a response to the exchange, it is important to think about group process as well as the actual content of the exchange. Address in the content may look as follows:

> SW: You feel angry with Luke and that is making this more difficult for you.

(A simple feelings reflection response focused on Cathy.)

Things to think about: you have chosen to focus on Cathy's anger toward her husband. This implies an acceptance of what she has said and offers an invitation for her to continue. This would be useful in terms of process if Cathy has said very little and is at risk of being isolated in the group. It is a response that might help her engage. However, not addressing that she was directing her frustration/anger at Omar may impact the group process; for example:

- It undermines the group sense of acceptance, trust and safety
- It gives a tacit acceptance to a group member's sense that her grief is worse/more important than Omar's
- It may contribute to members' seeing some loss valued more than another
- It ignores any underlying factors that might trigger Cathy's anger toward Omar, for example connected to a perception about sexual orientation or religious/ethnic background. If so, this can damage group cohesion and in particular Omar's sense of belonging
- Cathy may be unaware that she is expressing anger toward Omar because she can't express it to her husband
- It makes Omar feel more isolated

Think of a possible response to Cathy that draws on group process and provides a link or connection between Cathy and Omar rather than emphasising their differences:

> SW: Cathy you seem angry with Luke because you have lost the hope of a life together, a sense of loss that Omar probably shares with you and with others in the group.

(A complex reflection connecting anger with lost hope and drawing in Omar's experience.)
Thinking: This is an attempt to remind the group of their shared rather than their different experiences of loss. It still doesn't speak to Cathy about not being more sensitive to Omar's grief, but does attempt to help her reflect on their similar sense of lost hopes for the future.

Or:

> SW: Sounds like it is really hard for you to listen to Omar's sadness because you feel he knew that Phil still loved him.

(A complex reflection connecting her anger with seeing others in love which highlights her lost love.)
Thinking: You are being supportive to Cathy yet reframing the anger towards Omar to indicate that he too has a right to be sad. Drawing group attention to ways in which we can express our feelings in

ways that hurt others, even unconsciously. This gives a message to the group that the social worker sees this and will make sure it is noticed and addressed. This response keeps the focus on Cathy and her interaction with Omar. It does not draw on the power of the group to help both of the members understand their feelings and reactions.

You might add a group-focused piece to your response such as:

> SW: Sounds like it is really hard for you to listen to Omar's sadness because you feel he knew that Phil still loved him, this is something others in the group might understand too.

(A complex reflection supporting her feeling of anger yet connecting it to Omar's sadness and to the sadness of the group members.)
Thinking: This attempt to work on a group level to acknowledge Cathy's upset, Omar's sadness and the wisdom of the group that they all understand the struggle it is to manage these emotions.

Or:

> SW: What do you think about Cathy's point?

(An open question inviting the group to respond to Cathy.)
Thinking: If you are satisfied that the group has progressed to a working stage of development you might simply ask the group to respond to Cathy. If the group has developed an acceptance and concern for each other, one of the group members may well be in a better position to help Cathy reflect on her emotions.

Group member responds:

> Anne: I know that you are hurting Cathy, you are mad at Luke for dying but even madder at him for leaving you. Maybe that's why it's hard for you to hear how much Phil and Omar still loved each other but you know we are all here because we are hurting too.

(Group member's supportive yet honest feedback which is inclusive of Cathy as a group member and demonstrates concern for her as well as concern for Omar. The feedback also offers an

opportunity to Cathy to reflect on her comments and how they might affect other group members.)
Thinking: The group members have insight and mutual experiences to draw on to support and give honest feedback to each other.

NB: There is no one right response. Your response is a starting point for what will be a sequence of interactions between Cathy, the facilitator and the group. You might decide to prioritise facilitating Cathy's opening up about her anger and come back to supporting Omar later in the session. Ideally, if the group process is already 'performing' someone else will pick up on this anyway. The options are provided to give a sense of the factors you might want to consider in formulating your response.

Appendix 2.1 The social work toolkit

Listening: Verbal and non-verbal communication gathered through all available devices/all the senses. Ears, eyes, nose.
Thinking: Processing all the information gathered from listening through the multiple filters of information in your brain including:

- Awareness of self and own experiences, values, attitudes, beliefs that influence your thinking
- Interpretation and understanding of the context in relation to: your responsibilities as social worker, your agency requirements, statutory/policy guidelines, the particular circumstances of the service user and the problems or concerns that are being explored
- Your professional experience, values, skills and knowledge of:
  - Theories of human development and behaviour
  - specific factors/information associated with particular issues or concerns
  - Intervention methods
  - Related research

Talking: Communication of intervention informed by listening and thinking.

- Question, reflect, affirm, focus, advise, motivate, etc.

Appendix 4.1 Listening, thinking to inform your response

Case example: Al is 18 years old. When he was 16 he was out binge-drinking with a group of his friends when a fight broke out. The fighting escalated and resulted in Al knocking out his friend who suffered very serious head injuries. He was sentenced to detention in Young Offenders secure accommodation having been found guilty of assault.

You are discussing his future as he is preparing for his release. You are attempting to gain an understanding of his perception about what happened and in particular assessing if he has benefitted from the services he received, what if anything he has learned about his behaviour. In the course of the conversation you are talking about his future and he says:

> Al: I just want to hang out with my pals, have a good time, and enjoy a few drinks, y' know?

Instruction

Here are a number of response options. Each option is informed by different theoretical interpretations about human behaviour, and each theoretical influence then suggests a related social work method. Listening and thinking are the skills that inform what you say next. Read the options and consider what theories and methods may have influenced your thinking and listening to formulate that response.

1. Sounds like your friends are very important to you.
2. Yes, I can see that would be nice for you, spending time with pals is important for us all.
3. You say you enjoy having a few drinks with the lads. What other pastimes do you enjoy?

4. You mentioned earlier that your pals were very upset that you ended up in trouble. Have any of them been in this kind of trouble themselves?
5. Do you really think those guys are your friends? They stood by and let you nearly kill your pal.
6. You see drinking as having a good time.
7. So one of the nice things about drinking for you is that you get to spend time with the lads, what other things do you like about drinking?
8. You don't really get how much trouble drinking has caused you, do you?
9. Your drinking caused you to seriously injure someone, that means you can't go drinking again.
10. You are talking about having a few drinks. Does that mean that you want to be able to enjoy yourself so you know you need to make sure that it doesn't get out of hand?
11. What do you think needs to change so that you can go drinking without getting into trouble again?
12. Al, it's great to hear you looking forward to the future. This whole thing has been a bit of a crisis in your life, what do you think you have learned from the experience?

Soundings: The theory and method that might influence that response. Consider the nature and base for the response:

1. Directive reflection: client-centred, solution-/strengths-based response. Demonstrate empathy with service user. Draw on a positive aspect of the statement and without posing a question invite the service user to consider the possibility that friendship is a resource for him.
2. Empathise with the desire to spend time with friends, normalise this for him. This is behaviour reinforcement, a solution-focused and client-centred way of connecting with him.
3. Reflect content accepting the enjoyment aspect of drinking for Al, then redirect to identify if he has ideas about alternative/ additional sources of enjoyment. Elicit his perspective on what might be positives. This is consistent with a MI or a solution-focused perspective.

4. Drawing on previous discussion to cushion introducing a challenging comment which is directing his attention to the quality of the friends he is referring to. Cognitive and developmental base. Checking out his ability to be discerning about friends and what level of maturity his peer group may have attained. Sociological or social learning base which would be concerned with: checking out peer and/or cultural context; is getting into trouble expected, accepted, even valued among his peers?
5. Interrogative question, followed by confrontation of reality. Traditional confrontational base, informed by ideas of defence mechanisms including denial and minimising informs this challenge of his view of what friendship is about.
6. Selective reflection: client-centred base, simple reflection to encourage engagement and demonstrate empathy.
7. Reflective statement followed by redirection. Motivation base: acceptance of his enjoyment of drinking, reflect that one reason for this enjoyment is that he gets to spend time with friends, then broaden the discussion to access other possible areas for enjoyment that might be a resource to Al. (Note: MI has moved away from this as it is now thought that it may promote talk that supports staying the same rather than changing).
8. Confrontation: traditional confrontational base/psychoanalytic: challenge his denial and minimise the trouble with his drinking and also possible resistance to change.
9. Confrontation followed by prescriptive goal of abstinence. Traditional base; the history of his drinking and seriousness of the consequences, combined with his denial are seen as indicative of addiction for which the only answer is total abstinence.
10. Directive reflection, followed by question to support change. Behaviour and motivational base. Draw attention to behaviour change in alcohol consumption. Could follow up with more specific discussion about acceptable/managing drinking levels.
11. Open question directed towards emphasising the need to change, reinforcing goals of social drinking and staying out of trouble as positive and attainable goals. Looking at a better future which includes drink but without trouble, accessing service user's own understanding of what he needs to do to

address these goals. Behaviour reinforcement, enhancing motivation and being solution-focused.

12. Reflection of feeling to engage Al and demonstrate a positive connection. Informed by crisis theory you are looking to see if he has learned from the crisis and if so how that has changed him. Because you are focusing on potentially very upsetting feelings you start with underplaying the language so as to encourage him to open up. Hence using 'this whole thing' rather than assaulting your friend or this experience instead of 'being detained'.

Appendix 4.2 Reflection on two axes

Individual versus society and strengths/resources versus deficits.

<table>
<tr><td rowspan="4">INDIVIDUAL</td><td colspan="2">STRENGTHS/RESOURCES</td><td rowspan="4">SOCIAL</td></tr>
<tr><td>Box 1:
Possible view:
When I think about problems I look at the individual and think about how they can use their strengths to bring about change</td><td>Box 3:
Possible view:
When I think about problems I look at society and think about how society can use its strengths/ resources to change</td></tr>
<tr><td>Box 2:
Possible view:
When I think about problems I think about the individual's deficits that block change</td><td>Box 4:
Possible view:
When I think about problems I look at society and think about societal deficits that block change</td></tr>
<tr><td colspan="2">DEFICITS</td></tr>
</table>

Ask yourself some questions to see where you fit in the four boxes. Is it always the same place, what factors contribute to you moving from one box to another or how are the boxes connected for you?

Are problems caused by individual deficits or societal deficits?

Should change be the responsibility of the individual or society?

If society is responsible for the problem, where does that leave me if I'm working with an individual or family?

Do I think more about what's missing (deficits) or what's there (strengths)?

Reflection

When listening to a problem description, focusing on individual strengths and resilience makes sense (Box1), but then thinking about what has contributed to the problem(s) in the first place suggests that society has failed/societal deficits (Box 4). As a social worker how do you understand these two positions, because they seem to be opposites? If you see a service user's strengths then should they not be responsible for change, but does that let society off the hook? Does placing responsibility for problems and change on the individual fit with social work values of human rights and social justice?

Appendix 4.3 Reflection exercise using two-axis tool to explore your thinking about 'Childhood Obesity'

Think about your position with regard to Childhood Obesity using two axes: Individual–Social and Responsibility–Deficits.

INDIVIDUAL	**Responsibility**		**SOCIAL**
	Box 1: Parents should be held responsible for resolving the problem	Box 3: The State should be held responsible AND/OR Other systems outside the individual/family are responsible	
	Parenting deficits/individual deficits (genetic/ personality/ motivation/ life choices/ knowledge/ management abilities, etc.) cause obesity	Box 4: Failure of the State to regulate food-related industries cause obesity Failure of the state and/or others to provide necessary information/ resources cause obesity	
	DEFICITS		

References to additional resources to inform your thinking:

Jones, D., Gonzalez, M., Ward, D., Vaughn, A., Emunah, J., Miller, L., & Anton, M. (2013). Should Child Obesity be an Issue for Child Protective Services? A Call for More Research on this Critical Public Health Issue. https://doi-org.ucd.idm.oclc.org/10.1177/1524838013511544

Jones et al. (2013, p. 113): 'Advocates ... support the involvement of child protective services (CPS) in mandating family-focused lifestyle changes aimed at reducing child overweight and, in the most extreme cases, the removal of the obese child from the home'.

Jones et al. (2013, p. 114): See obesity as meeting child risk criteria for example obesity stems from (a) a caregiver's neglect of proper nutritional needs of a child (i.e. similar to the inclusion of undernourishment and/or failure to thrive included in current definitions of neglect).

Murtagh, L., & Ludwig, D.S. (2011). State intervention in life-threatening childhood obesity. *The Journal of the American Medical Association*, 306, 206–207. doi:10.1001/jama.2011.903

Murtagh et al. (2011, p. 207): State intervention may serve the best interests of many children with life-threatening obesity, comprising the only realistic way to control harmful behaviors. Child protective services typically provide intermediate options such as in-home social supports, parenting training, counseling, and financial assistance, that may address underlying problems without resorting to removal.

Hanson, M., Mullins, E., & Modi, N. (2017). Time for the UK to commit to tackling child obesity. *British Medical Journal*, 356:j762. doi: https://doi.org/10.1136/bmj.j762

House of Commons Health Committee (2017). Childhood obesity: Time for action, Eighth Report of Session 2017–19 Report, together with formal minutes relating to the report.

House of Commons Health Committee (2017). Childhood obesity is also a leading cause of health inequality. The burden is falling disproportionately on children from low-income backgrounds. Obesity rates are highest for children from the most deprived areas and the inequality gap has widened every year since formal recording began as part of the child measurement programme.

Childhood Obesity; A plan for action (2016). HM Government.

https://assets.publishing.service.gov.uk/government/uploads/system/uploads/attachment_data/file/546588/Childhood_obesity_2016__2__acc.pdf

HM Government (2016, p. 3). The burden is falling hardest on those children from low-income backgrounds. Obesity rates are highest for children from the most deprived areas and this is getting worse (p. 9). Children aged 5 and from the poorest income groups are twice as likely to be obese compared to their most well off counterparts and by age 11 they are three times as likely (p. 10).

The Guardian (2018). Leading the fight against child obesity. Letters, Wednesday 25 July 2018, 17.53 BST.

www.theguardian.com/society/2018/jul/25/leading-the-fight-against-child-obesity

Appendix 4.4 Thinking filters as a framework for reflection: before, in and on action

Consider this:	Your thoughts on these filters
Social work context: Responsibilities, legal and agency/policies/guidelines and regulations Expectations of agency/service user in this context.	
Knowledge base: Grand theory perspective Preferred theoretical framework Subtheories that may apply Key concepts that might be/were useful Knowledge about the particular issue(s), cultural competence	
Service user's needs and concerns: SU expectations, fears, status, power social and economic disadvantage, diversity	
Systems factors: The social context, the political context, the economic context (are they relevant and how?) Issues to do with: power, resources, social justice, human rights	
Social worker's values: Social justice, human rights, respect, respect for diversity, etc.	

Consider this:	Your thoughts on these filters
Service user's values: What is important for SU, personal values, family values, ethnic, cultural, religious values, sexual identity, etc.	
Social work method: Preferred method(s) Appropriate or most helpful method(s), ability to deliver a method	
Social worker's self-knowledge: Self-awareness, personal emotions, values potential impact on the work	
Service user's: Experiences, strengths, resilience, resources, risks	
Resources and priorities: Limitations and possibilities associated with availability of resources Where does this service user/ the issue sit in terms of priorities/ waiting lists/service provision and what are the implications?	

Appendix 5.1 Checking out open questions, closed questions and reflective responses

Which of the following is an open question, closed question or reflections? (No question marks included in case that gives it away)

	Open	Closed	Reflection	**Mother concerned about her son not attending school**
A				What are the things that concern you the most about his behaviour
B				What age is Sola
C				And Sola is
D				How many days has he missed school
E				His father has spoken to him about what's going on
F				What about his friends, what's happening with them
G				It sounds like you are really angry with him
H				You can't understand Sola because you had no problems with the older children
I				Did you bring Sola to the doctor for a check up
J				You seem to have managed the other children very well
K				What did you find were the most helpful ways of coping with the other children

	Open	Closed	Reflection	Mother concerned about her son not attending school
L				What are your worst fears about this situation
M				Sola was very well behaved until you moved here so you think maybe this is the reason he's acting out
N				This is obviously very upsetting for you

Formulate your own two **open** questions:

Formulate your own two **closed** questions:

Formulate your own two **reflections**:

To get the most from this exercise you should have a discussion about these suggestions

	Open	Closed	Reflection	Mother concerned about her son not attending school
A	x			What are the things that concern you the most about his behaviour? (Inviting disclosure of concerns)
B		x		What age is Sola? (Looking for a factual reply)
C		x		And Sola is (There is a question implied)

	Open	Closed	Reflection	**Mother concerned about her son not attending school**
D				How many days has he missed school? (Fact)
E			x	His father has spoken to him about what's going on. (As reflection voice inflect is down so there is no implied question)
F	x			What about his friends, what's happening with them? (Invitation to say more about his peers)
G			x	It sounds like you are really angry with him. (Reflection of feeling)
H			x	You can't understand Sola because you had no problems with the older children. (Reflection of content)
I		x		Did you bring Sola to the doctor for a check-up? (Fact)
J			x	This is more difficult for you because you never had anything like this problem with the other children. (More complex because she mentioned this was all new to her so you are taking a guess and amplifying that she had no problems before)
K	x			What did you find were the most helpful ways of coping with the other children? (Invitation to be open about coping skills)

	Open	**Closed**	**Reflection**	**Mother concerned about her son not attending school**
L	x			What are your worst fears about this situation? (Invitation to talk about her fears)
M			x	Sola was very well behaved until you moved here so you think maybe this is the reason he's acting out. (Reflective summary of what you have so far understood)
N			x	This is obviously very upsetting for you. (Reflection of feeling)

Appendix 7.1 Empathetic observation

Let's look at a simple situation where you are meeting a friend for coffee. When your friend arrives you both sit down and immediately your friend says 'I'm really fed up with work'. You are probably going to respond pretty quickly to this comment and maybe not even think too much about where your response comes from. So let's take a look at unpacking a little bit where that response might come from or what might influence that response.

The first thing to look at would be context. You would need to think about questions such as how long you have known this friend, what kind of relationship you have with this friend, what you know about their current situation. So let's look at this for an example. This friend is somebody you have known for 15 years, you were at school together, you don't work with them but you do have a very close relationship and you share a lot of information about your personal lives. You know that work hasn't been going well with this person, or perhaps you thought that everything was going OK with them at work. The context would make a difference to your response.

Let's look at one possibility. Your friend arrives for coffee, you sit down immediately and the first thing they say is 'I'm fed up with work'. In a certain set of circumstances it might be very appropriate for you to say 'Oh, I know I feel the same a lot of the time, let's plan a holiday'. This might be exactly the right response, a very empathetic response if the certain situations are in place. So if this is just a pretty routine thing that is said every now and then that is thrown into a conversation and if you know that your friend is just a bit tired and fed up with work and that there is nothing particularly unusual about the situation, it is very like something you have shared and talked about before, then your response is empathetic. However, a clue might be if it is normal for this to be the headline topic of conversation, or perhaps your friend made a special arrangement to meet you for coffee. Is this something that is a little bit out of the usual, in which case organising an additional meeting for coffee or perhaps organising to meet for coffee instead of going for a drink so that you could meet in a quiet place and then opening with this headline may indicate that there is something more going on. These are all things that you may not even be aware of thinking through when the situation arises, but the object of this exercise is to try and figure out a little bit more about all of the information you have about your friend, about their tone of voice, about how they handle meetings with you, about the kinds of things they talk about with you and about what you know about their workplace; all inform the potential response that you might make.

So, let's look at another possibility. Your friend has made this arrangement, you realise it's a bit different. She wants to meet for coffee, she starts off quite distressed, her tone of voice is not her usual chatty tone of voice. When she says she's really fed up at work, you know there is something else going on. Supposing that you know that she has been involved in a relationship with one of her colleagues at work and it hasn't been going well, that might influence what you think is happening and what feelings your friend is experiencing at that point in time. Another scenario might be that things at work have become very pressurised and maybe even that there has been talk of redundancies, in which case that would add a different understanding to what is going on.

While your ability to be empathetic to a close friend with whom you have shared a lot of information is probably going to be pretty accurate, it might still be possible to misjudge the situation if you are not open to hearing some other difference in how this particular 'fed up' has been presented. In reality, if you respond in some way which doesn't fit the bill and doesn't really express empathy, your friend will probably be able to let you know that pretty quickly by saying something as simple as 'Oh, no you've got the wrong end of the stick' or 'No, that's not what it's about today, this is something different'. Once that is said, it may be important to have more of an exploration of what is going on so that you can understand more accurately what is happening. So, in that kind of a situation, starting off with 'Oh, I feel the same and maybe we should just go on holiday' would not be a very empathetic response. In fact, in the wrong context, that kind of response may end up making your friend feel misunderstood and that you have in some way underestimated the upset that they have been expressing. As you can see, this kind of assumed understanding about what is going on for your friend can have the same kind of negative consequences as in a professional context if you jump to the conclusion that you understand and that you are able to empathise with somebody without really checking it out; it can have the effect of making the person feel misunderstood and that somehow you have diminished their upset or their distress. Yet in the context of a friend, you have so much help in terms of your chances of being able to empathise. You have a solid relationship built over time, you have lots of examples of understanding one another, you have lots of examples of having long conversations in which your friend has expressed feelings and so you know not only how they think, how they feel but also how they tend to express themselves. So, you have a lot of information available to you to help you to come up with an empathetic understanding of what is happening. You even have a sound relationship which will allow you to make mistakes and misinterpret what is happening and at the same time be able to rectify that and redeem the situation with relative ease.

In the context of a friendship, then, empathy is probably more likely going to be influenced by your knowledge of each other, your personalities, your history together, the context of what you know is going on and, in some ways, an established way or rapport that you have between you. Most of these insights are not going to be available to you to assist when you are dealing with somebody in a professional context.

Appendix 9.1 Case example: Jack

Jack is a 22-year-old single man living at home with his parents. He has an ex-girlfriend, Amy, with whom he has a daughter Ivy (1-year-old). Amy and Jack never lived together as they were not able to get the money to get a flat for themselves even though Jack was earning good money at the time. They were interested in having a good time and Jack's mother was fed up with them because she thought they were both very irresponsible and immature. This was made worse when Amy got pregnant and Jack and Amy didn't go to the hospital until a few weeks before the baby was due. They only went then because Amy was feeling sick and got worried. She decided to get herself 'checked out'. Everything went OK but shortly after Ivy was born they split up. They had a row about taking care of Ivy. Jack thought that Amy needed to stay home more and cut back on her partying. He accused her of leaving Ivy with her parents all the time so she could hang out with her pals.

Jack was working as a plumber and was getting jobs through one of his pals even when things were a bit tight. He was good at the job and until last year had been very reliable. Since Amy and Jack split up, Jack became increasingly unreliable at work. He missed work, showed up hungover and in the past few months he had come to work clearly strung out. He has always been a drinker but had no interest in other drugs. Before they were expecting Ivy he got in with a crowd who were smoking cannabis and he got into that, mostly at weekends. In the past couple of months he seems to be partying more and his pal has told him he can forget getting jobs from him because he has turned into such a waster. Jack is still in contact with Amy and Ivy and he takes Ivy to his mother's house on a Saturday to give Amy a break. He hopes that they will get back together if Amy could get her act together. Amy would like to be with Jack too, but now that he isn't earning any money she sees no hope for sorting out their mess. She is mad at Jack for wasting money on drugs but sees no problem with drink.

Appendix 9.2 Edited version of case example: Jack

In this edited version:

- The problem-saturated perspective is highlighted in *italics*
- The solution-focused perspective is in **bold**

Where some aspect of their story can be interpreted from either perspective (sometimes by use of reframing) it appears in ***bold italics.***

Jack is a *22-year-old single man* ***living at home with his parents***. He has an *ex-girlfriend*, Amy, with whom ***he has a daughter*** Ivy (one year old). Amy and Jack *never lived together* as they were *not able to get the money* to get a flat for themselves even though **Jack was earning good money** at the time. They were interested in having a good time and Jack's mother was fed up with them because she thought they were *both very irresponsible and immature*. This was made worse when Amy got pregnant and Jack and Amy *didn't go to the hospital until a few weeks before the baby was due.* They only **went then because *Amy was feeling sick and got worried*. She decided to get herself 'checked out'**. **Everything went OK** but *shortly after Ivy was born they split up. They had a row about taking care of Ivy*. Jack thought that Amy needed to stay home more and ***cut back on her partying***. He *accused her of leaving Ivy with her parents all the time* so she could hang out with her pals.

Jack was working as a plumber and was **getting jobs through one of his pals** even when things were a bit tight. **He was good at the job** and until last year **had been very reliable**. Since Amy and Jack split up, Jack *became increasingly unreliable at work*. He missed work, *showed up hungover* and in the past few months he had *come to work clearly strung out*. He has always been a drinker but **had no interest in other drugs**. Before they were expecting Ivy *he got in with a crowd who were smoking cannabis* and he got into that, **mostly at weekends**. In the past couple of months *he seems to be partying more* and his pal has told him he can *forget getting jobs from him because he has turned into such a waster*. **Jack is still in contact with Amy and Ivy** and **he takes Ivy to his mother's house on a Saturday to give Amy a break. He hopes that they will get back together** if Amy could get her act together. **Amy would like to be with Jack too,** but now that *he isn't earning any money she sees no hope for sorting out their mess*. **She is mad at Jack for *wasting money on drugs*** but *sees no problem with drink*.

Appendix 10.1 Stages in wheel of change (TTM)

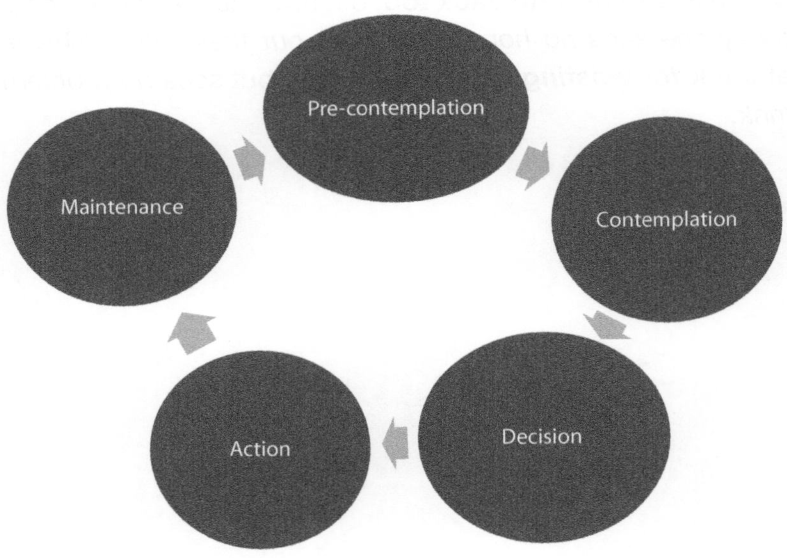

Adapted from Prochaska and DiClemente (1983).

References

Asay, T. & Lambert, M. (1999) The empirical case for the common factors in therapy: Quantitative findings, in Hubble, M., Duncan, B., & Miller, S. (eds.), *The heart and soul of change: What works in therapy*, Washington, DC, American Psychological Association: 33–55.

BASW. The Policy, Ethics and Human Rights Committee (2014). *The code of ethics for social work: Statement of principles,* BASW.

Beresford, P., Croft, S. & Adshead, L. (2008) We don't see her as a social worker: A service user case study of the importance of the social worker's relationship and humanity, *British Journal of Social Work,* 38:1338–1407.

Berg, I.K. (1994) *Family based services: A solution focused approach*, New York, Norton.

Berg, I.K. & Miller, S. (1992) *Working with the problem drinker: A solution-focused approach*, New York, Norton & Co.

Biehal, N. (2005) *Working with adolescents: Supporting families, preventing breakdown*, London, BAAF.

Biestek, F.P. (1957) *The casework relationship*, Chicago, Loyola University Press.

Black, P. & Feld, A. (2006) Process recording revisited, *Journal of Teaching in Social Work*, 26(3–4):137–153.

Bland, R., Laragy, C., Giles, R. & Scott. V. (2006) Asking the customer: Exploring consumers' views in the generation of social work practice standards, *Australian Social Work*, 59:35–46.

Bohart, A. & Tallman, K. (2010) Clients: The neglected common factor in psychotherapy, in B. Duncan, S. Miller, B. Wampold & M. Hubble (Eds.), *The heart and soul of change: Delivering what works* (2nd ed.). Washington, DC, American Psychological Association:83–112: 2009-10638-003 10.1037/12075-003

Braben, E. (1971) Morecambe and Wise Christmas Show 1971. www.brainyquote.com/quotes/eric_morecambe_370203

Brandon, M., Bailey, S., Belderson, P., Gardner, R., Sidebotham, P., Dodsworth, J., Warren, C. & Black, J. (2009) Understanding serious case reviews and their impact: A biennial analysis of serious case reviews 2005–07. *Research Report DCSF-RR129*. University of East Anglia.

Brandon, M., Belderson, P., Warren, C., Howe, D., Gardner, R., Dodsworth, J. & Black, J. (2008) Analysing child deaths and serious injury through abuse and neglect: What can we learn? A biennial analysis of serious case reviews 2003–2005. *Research Report DCSF-RR023.* University of East Anglia.

Cameron, H. (2008) *The counselling interview: A guide for the helping profession*, Basingstoke, Palgrave Macmillan.

Carkhuff, R. (1969) *Helping and human relations*, New York, Holt, Rinehart and Winston.

Children's Workforce Development Council. (2009) *The common assessment framework for children and young people: A practitioner's guide*, London, CWDC.

Cooper, M. (2011) *Essential research findings in counselling and psychotherapy: The facts are friendly*, London, Sage.

Clark, A. (2010) Empathy: An integral model in the counseling process, *Journal of Counseling and Development,* 88:348–356.

Compton, B., & Galaway, B. (1999) *Social work processes* (6th ed.), Pacific Grove, Brooks-Cole.

Cottrell, S. (2011) *Critical thinking skills: Developing effective analysis and argument*, (2nd ed.), London, Palgrave MacMillan.

Coulshed, V. & Orme, J. (2006) *Social work practice: An introduction* (4th ed.), BACP. Basingstoke, Palgrave.

Dalai Lama XIV; Retrieved 19/02/2018. www.goodreads.com/quotes/7062036-when-you-talk-you-are-only-repeating-what-you-already

Davis, K. & Jones, R. (2015) *Skills for social work practice*, London, Palgrave.

Department of Education (2009) *Early identification, assessment of needs and intervention, Common Framework for Assessment for Children and Young People: A practitioners guide*, London, CWCD. http://webarchive.nationalarchives.gov.uk/20130102192341/https://www.education.gov.uk/publications/eOrderingDownload/CAF-Practitioner-Guide.pdfD)

de Jong, P. & Berg. I.K. (2002) *Interviewing for solutions*, Pacific Grove, Brooks/Cole.

deShazer, S. (1988) *Clues: Investigating solutions in brief therapy*, New York, Norton.

deShazer, S. (1991) *Putting differences to work*, New York, Norton.

Devine, L. (2015) Considering social work assessment of families, *Journal of Social Welfare and Family Law*, 37(1):70–83. DOI: 10.1080/09649069.2015.998005

Doel, M. (2006) *Using groupwork*, Routledge, London.

Duncan, B., Miller, S., Wampold, B. & Hubble, M. (eds.) (2010) *The heart and soul of change: Delivering what works in therapy* (2nd ed.), Washington, American Psychological Association.

Fahim, M. & Masouleh, N.S. (2012) Critical thinking in higher education: A pedagogical look, *Theory and Practice in Language Studies*, 2(7):1370–1375. DOI: 10.4304/tpls.2.7.1370-1375

Farmer, E., Sturgess, W. & O'Neill, T. (2008) The reunification of looked after children with their parents: Patterns interventions and outcomes. *Report to the Department for Children, Schools and Families*, School for Policy Studies, University of Bristol.

Ferguson, H. (2018) How social workers reflect in action and when and why they don't: The possibilities and limits to reflective practice in social work, *Social Work Education*, 37(4):415–427.

Forrester, D. (2016) *The Guardian, Social Care Network*. www.theguardian.com/social-care-network/2016/mar/08/motivational-interviewing-quick-guide-social-work

Forrester, D., Kershaw, S., Moss, H. & Hughes, L. (2008) Communication skills in child protection: How do social workers talk to parents? *Child & Family Social Work*, 13:41–51.

Forrester, D., Westlake, D. & Glynn, G. (2012) Parental resistance and social worker skills: Towards a theory of motivational social work', *Child and Family Social Work*, 17(2):118–129.

Galvani, S. & Forrester, D. (2011) How well prepared are newly qualified social workers for working with substance use issues? Findings from a national survey in England, *Social Work Education*, 30(4):422–439. DOI: 10.1080/02615479.2010.504981

Gavin, C. & Seabury, B. (1984) *Interpersonal practice in social work: Processes and procedures*, Englewood Cliffs, Prentice-Hall.

Gelles, R. (1996) *The book of David: How preserving families can cost children's lives*, New York, Basic Books.

George, E., Iverson, C. & Ratner, H. (1999) *Problems to solutions: Brief therapy with individuals and families*, London, Brief Therapy Practice.

Gerdes, K. & Segal, E. (2011) Importance of empathy for social work practice: Integrating new science, *Social Work*, 56(2):141–148.

Gibbons, J. & Gray, M. (2004) Critical thinking as integral to social work practice, *Journal of Teaching in Social Work*, 24(1–2):19–38. DOI: 10.1300/J067v24n01_02

Goh, E. (2012) Integrating mindfulness and reflection in the teaching and learning of listening skills for undergraduate social work students, *Social Work Education*, 31(5):587–604.

Gordon, T. (1970) *P.E.T.: Parent effectiveness training*, New York, Wyden.

Greeno, E., Ting, L., Pecukonis, E., Hodorowicz, M. & Wade, K. (2017) The role of empathy in training social work students in motivational interviewing, *Social Work Education*, 36(7):794–808.

Hanson, J. (2005) Should your lips be zipped? How therapist self-disclosure and non-disclosure affects clients, *Counselling & Psychotherapy Research*, 5(2):96–104.

HCPC: Health and Care Professional Council (2017) *Standards of proficiencies: Social workers in England.* www.hpc-uk.org/ assets/ documents/10003B08Standardsofproficiency-Socialworkersin England.pdf

Healy, K. (2014) *Social work theories in context: Creating frameworks for practice* (2nd ed.), Basingstoke, Palgrave McMillan.

Hohman, M. (2012) *Motivational interviewing in social work practice*, New York, Guilford Press.

Homonoff, E. (2014) Gimme that old fashioned refection: Process recording, *Field Instructor*, 4(1):1–6.

Hood, R. (2016) Assessment for social work, in Davis, K. & Jones, R. (eds), *Skills for social work practice*, London, Palgrave: 82–104.

Inskipp, F. (1996) *Skills training for counselling*, London, Sage.

Islington Social Workers. *Doing what counts and measuring what matters: One minute guide to Motivational Social Work (MSW).* University of Bedfordshire/Islington. Retrieved 13/02/2017.

www.proceduresonline.com/islington/childcare/user_controlled_lcms_area/uploaded_files/One%20Minute%20Guide%20-%20Motivational%20Social%20Work%20%28MSW%29.pdf

Ivey, A. (1994) *Intentional interviewing and counseling: Facilitating client development in a multicultural society* (3rd ed.), Pacific Grove, Brooks/Cole.

Johnson, D. & Johnson, F. (1991) *Joining together: Group theory and group skills,* Englewood Cliffs, Prentice-Hall.

Jordan, M., Lanham, H., Crabtree, B., Nutting, P., Stange, K. & McDaniel, R. (2009) The role of conversation in health care interventions: Enabling sensemaking and learning, *Implementation Science*, 4:15. https://doi.org/10.1186/1748-5908-4-15

Keen, S., Parker, J., Brown, K. & Galpin, D. (2009) *Newly qualified social workers: A practice guide to the assessed and supported year in employment*, London, Sage.

Kelly, N. & Milner, J. (1996) Child protection decision-making, *Child Abuse Review*, 5:91–102.

Knight, C. (2012) Social workers' attitudes towards and engagement in self-disclosure, *Clinical Social Work Journal*, 40(3):297–306. DOI: https://doi-org.ucd.idm.oclc.org/10.1007/s10615-012-0408-z

Knox, S. & Hill, C. (2003) Therapist self-disclosure: Research-based suggestions for practitioners, *Journal of Clinical Psychology*, 59:529–539.

Koprowska, J. (2010) *Communication and interpersonal skills in social work* (3rd ed.), Exeter, Learning Matters.

Kübler-Ross, E. & Kessler, D. (2005) *On grief and grieving: Finding the meaning of grief through the five stages of loss*, London, Simon and Schuster.

Kuntze, J., van der Molen, H. & Born, M. (2009) Increase in counselling communication skills after basic and advanced micro skills training, *British Journal of Educational Psychology*, 79:175–188.

Lambert, M. & Barley, D. (2002) Research summary on the therapeutic relationship and psychotherapy outcome, in Norcross, J. (ed.) *Psychotherapy relationships that work: Therapists contributions and responsiveness to patients*, New York, Oxford University Press, pp. 17–36.

Lipchik, E. (1988) *Interviewing with a constructive ear*, Dulwich Center Newsletter:3–7.

Lipchik, E. (2002) *Beyond technique in solution focused therapy: Working with emotions and the therapeutic relationship*, New York, Guilford Press.

Loughran, H. (2003) Teaching evidence-based addiction practice: Project MATCH comes to the classroom, *Journal of Teaching in the Addictions*, 2(1):1–15.

Loughran, H. (2010) *Understanding crisis therapies: An integrative approach to crisis intervention and post-traumatic stress*, London, JKP.

Loughran, H. & Broderick, G. (2017) From service-user to social work examiner: Not a bridge too far, *Social Work Education*, 36(2):188–202, DOI: 10.1080/02615479.2016.1268592

Loughran, H., Hohman, M., & Finnegan. D. (2010) Predictors of role legitimacy and role adequacy of social workers working with substance-using clients, *British Journal of Social Work*, 40(1):239–256.

McLeod, J. & McLeod, J. (2011) *Counseling skills: A practical guide for counsellors and helping professions* (2nd ed.), Maidenhead, Open University Press.

Miller, W. (1983) Motivational interviewing with problem drinkers, *Behavioural Psychotherapy*, 1:147–172.

Miller, W. (2018) *Listening well. The art of empathetic understanding*, Oregon, WIPF and Stock.

Miller, W. & Rollnick, S. (1991) *Motivational interviewing: Helping people change* (1st ed.), New York, Guilford Press.

Miller, W. & Rollnick, S. (1995) What is Motivational Interviewing, *Behavioural and Cognitive Psychotherapy*, 23(4):325–334.

Miller, W. & Rollnick, S. (2013) *Motivational interviewing: Helping people change* (3rd ed.), New York, Guilford Press.

Milner, J. & O'Byrne, P. (2009) *Assessment in social work* (3rd ed.), Basingstoke, Palgrave MacMillan.

Morrison, T. (2007) Emotional intelligence, emotion and social work: Contexts, characteristics, complications and contribution, *British Journal of Social Work*, 37:245–263.

Moyers, T. (2014) The relationship in motivational interviewing, *Psychotherapy Theory Research Practice Training*, 51(3):358–363. DOI: 10.1037/a0036910

Moyers, T. & Miller, W. (2013) Is low therapist empathy toxic? *Psychology of Addictive Behavior*, 27(3):878–884.

Munro, E. (1998) Improving social workers' knowledge base in child protection, *British Journal of Social Work*, 28:89–105.

Myers, S. (2000) Empathic listening: Reports on the experience of being heard, *Journal of Humanistic Psychology,* 40(2):148–173.

Nelson-Jones, R. (2011) *Basic counseling skills: A helper's manual* (3rd ed.), London, Sage.

Neukrug, E. (2010) *Counselling theory and practice*, Belmont, Brookes/Cole.

Neukrug, E., Bayne, H., Dean-Nganga, L. & Pusateri, C. (2013) Creative and novel approaches to empathy: A neo-Rogerian perspective, *Journal of Mental Health Counseling*, 35(1):29–42.

Norcross, J. (2010) The therapeutic relationship, in Duncan, B., Miller, S., Wampold, B. & Hubble, M. (eds.) *The heart and soul of change: Delivering what works in therapy* (2nd ed.), Washington, American Psychological Association:113–142.

Orford, J. (2008) Asking the right questions in the right way: The need for a shift in research on psychological treatments for addiction, *Addiction*, 103(6):875–85.

Orlinsky, D., Ronnested, M. & Willutzki, U. (2004) Fifty years of psychotherapy process-outcome research: Continuity and change, in Lambert, M.(ed.), *Bergin and Garfield's handbook of psychotherapy and behavior change* (5th ed.), Chicago, Wiley:307–389.

Papell, C. (2015) Process recording revisited: An essay on an educational artifact as a cognitive exercise, *Social Work with Groups*, 38(3–4):345–357. DOI: 10.1080/01609513.2014.951821

Plutchik, R. (2001) The nature of emotions: Human emotions have deep evolutionary roots, a fact that may explain their complexity and provide tools for clinical practice, *American Scientist,* 89(4):344–350.

Preston-Shoot, M. (2007) *Effective groupwork* (2nd ed.), Basingstoke, Palgrave Macmillan.

Prochaska, J. & DiClemente, C. (1982) Theoretical therapy: Towards a more integrative model of change, *Psychotherapy, Theory, Research and Practice*, 19:276–288.

Prochaska, J. & DiClemente, C. (1983) Stages and processes of self-change of smoking: Toward an integrative model of change, *Journal of Consulting and Clinical Psychology*, 51(3):390–395.

Ratner, H., Evens, G. & Iveson, C. (2012) *Solution focused brief therapy: 100 key points and techniques,* London, Routledge.

Redmond, B. (2006) *Reflection in action*, Farnham, Ashgate.

Richmond, M.L. (1917) *Social diagnosis*, New York, Russell Sage Foundation.

Robinson, W. (1974) Conscious competency, the mark of a competent instructor, *Personnel Journal*, 53:538–539.

Rogers, C. (1957) The necessary and sufficient conditions of therapeutic personality change, *Journal of Consulting Psychology*, 21(2):95–103.

Rogers, C. (1965) *Client-centred therapy*, New York, Houghton Mifflin.

Rogers, C. (1986) Carl Rogers on the development of the person-centered approach, *Person-Centered Review*, 1(3): 257–259.

Rollnick, S. (n.d.) *Excerpts: The method of Motivational Interviewing*, CMI, Premier Publishing and Media, accessed 15/05/2018. www.pesi.com. www.youtube.com/watch?v=I_76po-CiK8

Rollnick, S., Butler, C., Kinnersley, P., Gregory, J. & Masham, B. (2010) Motivational interviewing, *British Medical Journal*, 340. DOI: https://doi-org.ucd.idm.oclc.org/10.1136/bmj.c1900

Schon, D. (1983) *The reflective practitioner: How professionals think in action*, New York, Basic Books.

Schwalbe, C., Oh, H. & Zweben, A. (2014) Sustaining motivational interviewing: A meta-analysis of training studies, *Addiction*, 109:1287–1294.

Scott, D. (1998) A qualitative study of social work assessment in cases of alleged child abuse, *British Journal of Social Work*, 28:73–88.

Sevel, J., Cummins, L. & Madrigal, C. (1999) *Student guide and workbook for social work skills demonstrated. Beginning direct practice CD-ROM*, Boston, Allyn & Bacon.

Sharry, J. (2004) *Counselling children, adolescents and families: A strengths-based approach*, London, Sage.

Shebib, B. (2003) *Choices: Counseling skills for social workers and other professionals*, Boston, Allyn & Bacon.

Sheldon, B. (1995) *Cognitive-behavioural therapy, research, practice and philosophy*, London, Routledge.

Sheppard, M. (2009) High thresholds and prevention in children's services – the impact of mothers' coping strategies on outcome of child and parenting problems: A six-month follow-up, *British Journal of Social Work*, 39(1):46–63.

Shulman, L. (2009) *The skills of helping individuals, families, groups and communities*, Belmont, Wadsworth.

Skinner, N., Roche, A.M., Freeman, T. & Addy, D. (2005) Responding to alcohol and other drug issues: The effect of role adequacy and role legitimacy on motivation and satisfaction, *Drugs: Education, Prevention, and Policy,* 12(6):449–63.

Snyder, E., Lawrence, C., Weatherholt, T. & Nagy, P. (2012) The benefits of Motivational Interviewing and Coaching for improving the practice of comprehensive family assessments in child welfare, *Child Welfare*, 91(5):9–36.

Stroebe, M. & Schut, H. (1999) The dual process model of coping with bereavement: Rationale and description, *Death Studies*, 23:197–224.

Taylor, B. & Devine, T. (1993) *Assessing needs and planning care in social work*, London, Arena.

Teater, B. (2014) *An introduction to applying social work theories and methods* (2nd ed.), Maidenhead, Open University Press.

Thompson, N. (2009) *Understanding social work* (3rd ed.), Basingstoke, Palgrave MacMilllan.

Thompson, N. (2011) *Effective communication: A guide for the people professions*, (2nd ed.), London, Palgrave McMillan.

Thompson, N. & Stephney, P. (2018) *Social work theory and methods: The essentials*, London, Routledge.

Tomm, K. (1988) Interventive interviewing: Part III. intending to ask linear, circular, strategic, or reflexive questions, *Family Process*, 26:167–183.

Tuckman, B. (1965) Developmental sequence in small groups, *Psychological Bulletin,* 63.

Turney, D., Platt, D., Selwyn, J. & Farmer, E. (2011) Social work assessment of children in need: What do we know? Messages from research, www.gov.uk/government/uploads/system/uploads/attachment_data/file/182302/DFE-RBX-10-08.pdf;

Turney, D., Platt, D., Selwyn, J. & Farmer, E. (2012) *Improving child and family assessments: Turning research into practice*, London, Jessica Kingsley.

Tyson, T. (1998) *Working with groups* (2nd ed.), South Yarra, Macmillan Education Australia.

Vernelle, B. (1994) *Understanding and using groups*, London, Whiting & Birch.

Vicary, S., Young, A. & Hicks, S. (2017) A reflective journal as learning process and contribution to quality and validity in interpretative phenomenological analysis, *Qualitative Social Work,* 16(4):550–565.

Wahab, S. (2010) Motivational interviewing and social work practice, in van Wormer, K. & Thyer, B. (eds.), *Evidence-based practice in the field of substance abuse*, Thousand Oaks, Sage:197–210.

Walker, S. & Beckettt, C. (2011) *Social work assessment and intervention*, London, Russell House Publications.

Walsh, J. (2006) *Theories for direct social work practice*, Belmont, Thomson Brookes/Cole.

Walsh, J. (2013) *Theories for direct social work practice* (3rd ed.), Stamford, Cengage Learning.

Walsh, T. (2002) Structured process recording: A comprehensive model that incorporates the strengths perspective, *Social Work Education*, 21(1):23–34.

Walsh, T. (2010) *The solution focused helper: Ethics and practice in health and social care*, Maidenhead, Open University Press.

Wampold, B. (2010) The research evidence for common factors models: A historically situated perspective, in Duncan, B., Miller, S., Wampold, B. & Hubble, M. (eds.) *The heart and soul of change: Delivering what works in therapy* (2nd ed.), Washington, American Psychological Association:49–82.

Ward, D. (2002) Groupwork, in Adams, R., Dominelli, L. & Payne, M. (eds.) *Social work: Themes, issues and critical debate* (2nd ed.), Basingstoke, Palgrave:149–158.

Ward, H., Brown, R., Westlake, D. & Munro, E. (2010) Infants suffering, or likely to suffer, significant harm: A Prospective Longitudinal Study. Research Brief DFE-RB053. London, Department for Education.

Westert, G. & Groenewegen, P. (1999) Medical practice variations: Changes in the theoretical approach, *Scandinavian Journal of Public Health*, 21:173–180.

Witkin, B. & Trochim, W. (1997) Towards a synthesis of listening constructs: A concept map analysis, *International Journal of Listening*, 11(1):69–87.

Wilkins, D. & Whittaker, C. (2017) Doing child protection social work with parents: What are the barriers in practice? *British Journal of Social Work*, 1–17. https://doi.org/10.1093/bjsw/bcx139

Woodcock Ross, J. (2011) *Specialist communication skills for social workers: Focusing on service users' needs*, London, Palgrave McMillan.

Yalom, I. & Leszcz, M. (2005) *The theory and practice of group psychotherapy*, New York, Basic Books.

Index

Note: Page numbers in *italics* and **bold** denote figures and tables, respectively.